G000291604

The Book of
CHITTLEHAMHOLT
with WARKLEIGH & SATTERLEIGH

The Book of
CHITTLEHAMHOLT
with WARKLEIGH & SATTERLEIGH

A Photographic History

RICHARD LETHBRIDGE MBE

HALSGROVE

First published in Great Britain in 2002

This book is dedicated to the residents of Chittlehamholt, Warkleigh & Satterleigh.

Frontispiece photograph: *Chittlehamholt Flower Show, c.1945.*

British Library Cataloguing-in-Publication Data
A CIP record for this title is available from the British Library

ISBN 1 84114 144 5

HALSGROVE

Halsgrove House
Lower Moor Way
Tiverton, Devon EX16 6SS
Tel: 01884 243242
Fax: 01884 243325
email: sales@halsgrove.com
website: www.halsgrove.com

Printed and bound by
Bookcraft Ltd, Midsomer Norton

CONTENTS

The Chittlehamholt, Warkleigh and Satterleigh Parish Council, 2002. Left to right: Rosalyn Wright, Alex Hill, Ann Hamilton Clarke, David Buckle, Bill Congram, Christopher Thorne, John Robinson.

The Parish Council in 1994. Left to right, back row: Jim Page, Wilson Holland, David Bearne, Bill Congram, Frank Jones; front: Margaret Hammett, Rosalyn Wright, Franky Sheath (Chairman), Rosemary Williams.

INTRODUCTION

In 2000 I wrote a book about the Tiverton Staghounds, and when I had finished, people started to ask what I was going to write next. I had been thinking about writing something about the parishes of Chittlehamholt, Warkleigh and Satterleigh, and when Halsgrove of Tiverton learned of my idea, they were keen for me to produce something for their Community History Series. As in their other publications, the subjects of war, schools, families, farming, etc. have all been tackled. I believe that it is very important to record people's memories – especially those who were born in the early part of the last century – and I hope that by writing this book, I've gone some way to capturing these memories through interviews with local people, and photographs both old and new. I hope that you have fun reading it.

Richard Lethbridge MBE

Chittlehamholt schoolchildren outside the old schoolhouse, now known as Searles.
The children's names are unknown but one of the teachers is thought to be Mrs Burgess, late 1800s.

View of Chittlehamholt Chapel and the Exeter Inn, early 1900s.

Thomas Heard, Miss Etherington and Mary Courtney (standing) with Mrs Tickle the dog sitting on John Fry the pony. They are pictured in front of the cottages which were pulled down many years ago. Silver Birch Bungalow now stands on this site.

ACKNOWLEDGEMENTS

I would like to thank everyone who has helped by providing their memories and by lending photographs and documents for this book — Heather Petherick, Ivor and George Slee, Maurice Thorne, Maureen Woolacott, Marilyn and Alan Bowen, Dorothy Ayre, Norman Hancock, Mr and Mrs Ken Stenner, Walter Heard, Mr and Mrs Cyril Morgan and David, Peter Nicholls, Jimmy Porter, Mr and Mrs Raymond Turner, Jan Sharp, Ken Guard, Martin Neil, Elizabeth Gibson, John Lawdey, Ken Snow, Christine Stuckey, Bill Congram, Mr and Mrs Wilson Holland, Novello Gregory, Mr and Mrs Harold Snow and David, Kathleen Ford, Muriel Moore, Vera Geatches, Terry Sedwell, Ian Tucker, the late Bill Bowden, Edwin Fewings, Diana Lethbridge, Margaret Bolt, David Ryall, Ruby Kingdon, Raymond Squire, Harold Beer, William Beer, David Glenister, Mr and Mrs Arthur Tucker, Revd John Bell, Stafford Constable, David Elworthy, Rosalind Reed, Janet Judd, Pauline German, John Harris, Carol Snell, Brian Barrow's War Collection, Roger Bickley, John Streetly, The Devonshire Association, The *North Devon Journal*, Rosalyn and Sam Wright, Jim Moore, Harold Congram, Raymond Congram, Steve Knight (the RLK Knight Collection), Beattie Newcombe, Joan Baker, Raymond Ayre, Alex Hill, Roger Grimley (extracts from his *Tom Wills* book), Marion Sanders, Mrs M. Pope. Apologies to anyone whom I have omitted.

Looking up through Chittlehamholt village with September Cottage and Fir Cottage on the left, early 1900s.

*The late Sir Laurence Olivier alongside Mrs Pam Neil and her daughter Collette Potter.
Sir Laurence is seen here opening the Stumbles lace and linen shop in South Molton
in October 1981.* Courtesy of North Devon Journal.

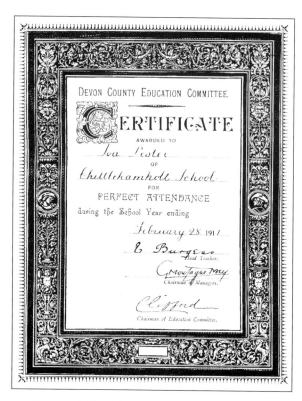

*Iva Pester of Chittlehamholt School received a perfect
attendance certificate, 28 February 1911.*

*Sgt Maj. Eddy Cox during the First World War.
This is the only known picture of him as a young
man – most people simply knew him as Mr Cox.
He lived in the village until he was in his eighties.*

Chapter 1

AN OVERVIEW OF THE PARISHES

The parishes of Chittlehamholt, Warkleigh and Satterleigh are situated on a high ridge in close proximity to each other. They rise up from the Taw, Bray and Mole valleys, with their rivers running close by. The Barnstaple to Exeter railway line, with its 39 miles of track, also reveals itself within the fabric of the landscape nearby. Situated between Exeter and Barnstaple, with the towns of South Molton and Chulmleigh close by, they offer lovely views of Dartmoor and Exmoor. This is *real* Devon, with gentle pastures and sunken lanes with high hedgerows, offering tantalising glimpses of beautiful views. Each of the parishes offers its own particular history and charm.

Aerial view of Chittlehamholt village, 1993.

Elizabethan times, those who came to gather wood in the holt (Old English, meaning wood) decided to settle there once the area had been cleared. The holt's state of decay was even noted in the middle of the sixteenth century, when a contemporary description noted that there was hardly a tree to be found and much firewood was rotting on the ground.

The original name for Chittlehamholt was Chittlehamptonholt, which indicates its close links with its neighbour. Nowadays it is linked with Satterleigh and Warkleigh. The name of Chittlehamholt can confuse some people who get it mixed up with Chittlehampton – even local people and the local papers sometimes get it wrong – but although the two are inextricably linked, there is no doubt that Chittlehamholt is firmly and proudly a separate entity.

The village centre of Chittlehamholt is strangely bisected at its northern end by the boundary with Warkleigh – The Old Gate House and Hills House Farm being the dividing line. Both occupiers have fun in telling people that their front door is in Warkleigh and their back one is in Chittlehamholt, and that they can walk from Chittlehamholt to Warkleigh within a few feet.

Chittlehamholt became a separate parish in 1885. *Kelly's Directory* of 1890 describes Chittlehamholt:

Chittlehamholt's Early History in the Forest

It is well known that Chittlehamholt was formerly part of Chittlehampton. Chittlehampton was divided into quarters, and Chittlehamholt was known as the South Quarter. It was originally a clearing in the wood and became a logging station to which the people of Chittlehampton came to cut timber, and it eventually grew into a separate hamlet.

Throughout the Middle Ages and up to the reign of Henry VIII, Chittlehamholt was a park belonging to the Earls of Devon. It does not appear to have been turned into farmland until the seventeenth century, but there were always people living on the riverside at Slew, Presbury, Lower and Higher Ditchaton Water on the Taw, and at Head and Snydles on the Mole. An early-fourteenth-century reference describes the area as an enclosed wood of about 800 acres containing wild game. Gradually, during

... an ecclesiastical parish formed July 28th 1863 but constituted a civil parish on March 25th 1885 and is about 3 miles northeast of Portsmouth Arms station on the North Devon branch of the Southern (late London and South Western) railway and 7 miles South West from South Molton station on the Somerset and Devon branch of the Great Western Railway. It is in the South Molton division, union, County Court district and rural deanery of South Molton, archdeaconry of

11

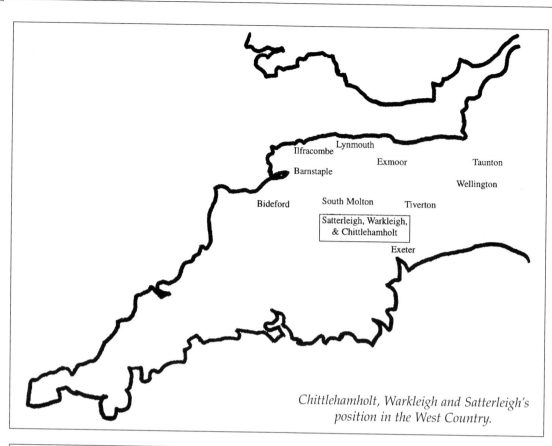

Chittlehamholt, Warkleigh and Satterleigh's position in the West Country.

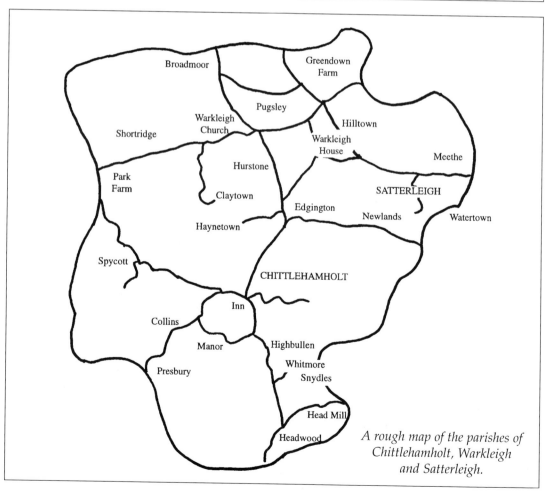

A rough map of the parishes of Chittlehamholt, Warkleigh and Satterleigh.

Barnstaple and diocese of Exeter. The area is 1,959 acres of land and 40 of water and the population of 310 is engaged in agriculture, the rateable value of £1,745.

In more recent times, cannon balls have been discovered in the village, including the ones found by Sid Harrison at Cobblestone Court, suggesting that Chittlehamholt was the scene of a skirmish during the Civil War. Some write it off as fanciful romanticism, but with the magnificent views over the Taw Valley, it is tempting to believe that this vantage point attracted the two warring factions. Further evidence of a possible battle is recalled by Maurice Thorne who was told by his father of a big channel (a gully) in Shortridge Wood, thought to be connected with a battle fought there. If you look in the right place you can still see a depression.

Heather Petherick's Thoughts on Chittlehamholt Village

My husband Steve and myself moved to Chittlehamholt in 1971, soon after getting married. Having no money to buy a house, we did what everyone in those days did and applied for a council-house. I filled in 12 forms, one for each village, and when a letter arrived telling us we'd been given a home in Chittlehamholt, we had to get a map out to see where it was. We found it 'in the sticks', up a hill (and down) and up more hills until we came to a spot with the most magnificent views and just the occasional wind – heavy-duty clothes pegs are essential up here. No matter which house you visit in Chittlehamholt the view is spectacular and all are slightly different and appealing. We're lucky – we look down the Taw Valley past woods and fields, catching a glimpse of deer if we're lucky, and can see the river, occasionally flooded or clouded in fog-like cotton wool while glorious sun shines above. We often see the train snaking its way along the valley bottom to hide and emerge between the trees. We can view surrounding villages, Codden Hill, and even Saunton on a clear day, but it varies according to the weather.

Chittlehamholt is my idea of heaven, with great neighbours and a fantastic view. On a summer evening nothing can beat it. After a day teaching at school at the 'chalk face', nothing could be better than to sit at the bottom of the garden and watch the wildlife and amazing sunsets, hear the chattering swallows on the telephone lines above and watch the shrieking swifts overhead.

We are a close village and our children have grown up together. With new people moving in, the numbers of children in the village is still growing. When the children recently decided to walk seven miles to South Molton School to raise funds I was delighted to be asked to join them. It made a very pleasant change

from the normal ten-minute car drive and we all enjoyed the experience.

Chittlehamholt has always been a friendly place – take a walk around the village and you always meet someone off to post a letter, exercise the dog, or just out for a pleasant stroll. I remember Mr Dicker (Richard's grandfather) – he was a dear, white-haired man with a corgi dog and a twinkle in his eye. He was always cheerful and had time to stop for a chat. Another character was Fred Scrivener who lived three doors from me with his brother Bernard and sister Dora. When they all lived in Lincolnshire, Fred ploughed the land with a team of horses. He always had a tale to tell and was wonderful with the children, bringing them gifts of books when he found out what their interests were. He sadly died one Christmas Day after going down into the woods. It was quite fitting for a countryman such as he.

George and Ivor Slee next door are wonderful neighbours. They've lived in Chittlehamholt all their lives and at 5 Taw View since it was built. George was a farm worker for the Congrams at Wards before moving on to the Mays' farm at Farrs. He spent 44 years here and received a long-service award. Ivor worked on the roads for the council. I will always remember the leather gaiters he wore. They both cycled to work and tried to teach me how to garden effectively like them. I'm still always weeks behind George's planting. George has an amazing vegetable patch at the back, and his front garden is a riot of colour. I try to emulate him but fail miserably.

Mrs Webber lived alone at No. 2 and on her 70th birthday the children and I decided to give her a special tea and invite the neighbours. She was delighted and later confided in me that she had never had a birthday cake in her life; she never even had a cake on her wedding day as it was during wartime.

Another character of the village was Mr Cox, who lived in a run-down house with cobwebs at the windows and part of a tree growing in his porch. He always wore a bobble hat and a hessian sack over his shoulders on wet days. On Sundays he would visit George and Ivor Slee, who always provided him with a Sunday lunch which he took home to eat. I remember one Sunday when our family was having Sunday lunch with George and Ivor; we later played a game of Connect 4 (which my son John – then aged eight – had mastered quite well and he could usually beat us all) when Mr Cox came to collect his dinner. He stayed for a chat and challenged John to a game. John was soundly beaten, even though Mr Cox had never played before. Mr Cox kept sheep at Russons and Highbullen and would be seen walking through the village daily with a sackful of food over his shoulders for them.

Maurice Thorne, who knew Mr Cox well, gives his thoughts on this remarkable character:

I spent hours with Mr Cox, he used to come over to

Holtgate, especially in the winter, and would be there every night except Sundays. We always put a meal aside for him and he enjoyed every bit. After watching the television he would say, 'turn off that piffle Maurice and get out your quiz book, something more interesting and educational.' He was very well-educated and every much a part of Chittlehamholt. He had been a Sgt Major in the First World War and had seen the harshness of life and death and was a very interesting man to talk to. He was also an agent for Spillers Food and kept geese and ducks. Sometimes he would bring one over in a bag and get mother and father to hold it while he gave it a tablet. Another time Mr Cox had a goose sitting on some eggs over at Highbullen and father let out the dog and frightened it and the goose took off and landed down at Lenton.

Warkleigh – A Potted History
by Jan Sharp

The parish of Warkleigh covers 2,451 acres. A population survey in 1851 gave the number of people resident in the parish as 337. Exactly 100 years later, in 1951, the figure was 127. Now, 50 years on, it has probably not changed very much.

Warkleigh House was built in 1844 on land originally belonging to Higher Beers Farm, as the rectory for Revd William Thorold. The house stayed with his family after his death in 1888, when it became known as Warkleigh House. The house was sold for the first time in 1937 and was run as a guest-house, although apparently not a very successful one. It later became the home of the Pepper family and from the 1960s until the turn of the century the Featherstonehaughs lived there.

Preston, at Warkleigh Cross, became the rectory and was occupied by Revd Gentlemen from 1832. It was once named Mansion House. Many additions have been made to the Old Rectory and most of the original building was demolished in 1952.

The Old Parsonage dates back many hundreds of years. It is known that Revd Richard Bowden lived in the house for 46 years until 1841, after which it is recorded to have been in a very dilapidated state. It was taken over by Revd Thorold, who spent some money on restoration before moving to the new rectory, Warkleigh House, which he privately owned. The old cottage part of the house was divided from the main part of the house to provide living accommodation for Revd Thorold's coachman. This part of the house was later Warkleigh Post Office, before once more becoming an integral part of the Old Parsonage.

The Old School is next to the Old Parsonage. In 1846 the school was built on some glebe land. Money was found in parish charities to pay a school-mistress £2 for teaching eight poor children to read. The rector and the churchwardens were trustees and by 1857 the number of children at the school had risen to 20. It was known as a National School and fees had to be paid.

Not everyone was a faithful follower of the Church of England. At exactly the same time another school was started at Deasons. This was a free school and was supported entirely by Mr Stevens, the farmer at Deasons. Most of the children who attended the Deasons school were from the families of Chapel folk and the school was a meeting-place on Sundays for the Bible Christians. It is not known how long this Chapel school existed, but the National School acquired more funds and the new school was built in 1876. The school was used by children from Warkleigh and Chittlehamholt until 1948. It then became derelict and was eventually bought by Warkleigh parishioners and used as a social centre. It was later sold to be converted into a house and the proceeds invested to help with the upkeep of the Village Hall in Chittlehamholt.

Like Satterleigh, Warkleigh at one time had a manor and similarly very little remains as a clue to its existence, but it stood in what was once the Town Place, beside Warkleigh Barton. Town Place, measuring about 80 yards by 50 yards and larger than Chittlehampton's Town Place, indicates the historical importance of the area.

Warkleigh Barton was probably built between 1870 and 1880 and is very much in the style of other up-market dwellings constructed at that time in the area. A rough drive through the farmyard leads to Church Cottage, one of the old parish poorhouses. This became a pair of cottages for farm workers and now it is just one cottage.

Found among some miscellaneous parish papers was a document dated 7 January 1785 and signed by P. Beavis. It reads:

Mary Rooke is with me and complaining of Hardships she labours under in the Poor House at Warkley. I think she ought at least to have a Bed to lie upon, in the first Place, and that an allowance of two Shillings a Week, is by no means too much for herself and Child at this inclement Season, to be paid her every Week.

Satterleigh – A Potted History
by Jan Sharp

The tiny parish of Satterleigh, just 510 acres, is bounded on the east side by the Rivers Bray and Mole. The rivers form a natural boundary between Satterleigh, South Molton and King's Nympton. To the west and south the boundary is with Warkleigh and to the north is the parish of Chittlehampton. In all probability, Satterleigh is a Saxon parish; the reasoning being that at the time of the Domesday Book in 1086 it was a manor, and some time after that it was given as a free holding to Warkleigh. It is likely that Satterleigh became a parish when it was still an independent manor. The fact that the church in

Satterleigh stands close to the Barton, where the manor once stood, adds weight to this theory. Traditionally, in Saxon times, the church was close to the manor as the lord of the manor was also the founder of the church. Satterleigh and Warkleigh were united as one civil parish in 1894. The Barton was, for many hundreds of years, the home of moderately affluent gentry. Now ponds and garden walls remain the only relics of past connections with the manor. By 1839 the Barton had become a farmhouse.

Kings House, a close neighbour, was once the home of Mr W. Hancock, who made his much-acclaimed cider there. Kings was bought by Mr M.A. Elworthy of Satterleigh Barton in 1957.

In 1839 the Glebe consisted of three parcels of land amounting to 31 acres. Opposite Pearce and Dyers, at Satterleigh Cross, stood the Old Parsonage. A rural dean making a Visitation in 1877 reported that it was 'a very poor old cottage, worthless to the benefice and, in his opinion, should be demolished.' The tiny garden then became part of the Parsonage Meadow and the main piece of garden, across the road, became the site for 1 and 2 The Villas, built as council-houses in 1929. Some of a wall belonging to the Old Parsonage remains as part of a field boundary.

Little Satterleigh, sometimes known as West Satterleigh, is an old farmstead, possibly dating back some 500 years. Higher Beer, although just over the parish border in Warkleigh, once belonged to the rector of Satterleigh, probably to add additional income to what was a very poor living.

The 'leighs', in Satterleigh and Warkleigh, mean 'clearings in woodland'. In the case of Satterleigh, this was probably a clearing used by robbers. But that was a long time ago.

A Story About Satterleigh
Claimed to be true and handed down through the generations.

About the middle of the eighteenth century, a Captain Charles Byne of Newcastle died leaving two young orphans, a boy and a girl. The children were left in the care of an uncle who sent them to a remote and run-down farmhouse in the Cheviot Hills to be looked after while he took charge of the property their father had left them. The children were neglected, uneducated and left to run barefoot over the hills.

When the boy was old enough, he was sent away to earn his living as a coal heaver. He was a tall and strong lad and after a while he decided to enlist. The Army moved him to different locations and he eventually came to Taunton. Whilst in Taunton he fell in love with a Miss Mary Anne Wade, the sister of Col Wade of Bineton House, Somerset, to whom, oddly, the wicked uncle was at that very time paying a visit. The young lady had gleaned a lot of information from the uncle about his family and affairs and

further enquiries led to the truth of Mr Byne's parentage. The relationship was brought to light and a portion of his property recovered. Mr Byne became an officer and married the young lady.

When the regiment moved to Devonshire they had quarters in South Molton and Mr Byne sent for his sister, who was still living in the Cheviot Hills. Whilst living in South Molton they became acquainted with Mr Cummings, who was the tenant of a fine old house in Satterleigh. He was very taken with Miss Byne and sent her to school in Bath, with the intention of marrying her when her education was complete. However, when Miss Byne returned after two or three years, a well-educated young lady, she married Revd Richard Bowden, the rector of Warkleigh and Satterleigh.

Mr Cummings was furious and tried to recover the fees for Miss Byne's schooling. It is not known if he was successful, but it was thought that Miss Byne did well in not marrying him as it was said locally that he was an atheist!

Captain Byne's wife died, leaving him with four children. But he was very handsome and as he was riding with his regiment through the High Street of Exeter, a Miss Prockter Thomas saw him through the window and exclaimed at once that he was the man she would marry. An introduction was arranged. Miss Prockter Thomas was an heiress and just 20 years old so, not surprisingly, her parents objected to her marrying a man with four children. But she was a determined young lady and on her 21st birthday she announced to her parents that she would be marrying Captain Byne the following day. And so she did. She was the niece of Admiral Melhuish, the owner of Satterleigh Barton. This estate was left to Mrs Byne and her brother, Mr Prockter Thomas, but the siblings quarrelled, resulting in a long lawsuit with great financial loss to all concerned. The house at Satterleigh went to rack and ruin and was eventually demolished.

An Article on Satterleigh
by Jan Sharp

I have been asked to write about life in Satterleigh. We are relative newcomers, having moved to the parish from Wiltshire in 1996, soon after my husband retired. We have been very happy here.

To say that Satterleigh is quiet would be an understatement. Many people in South Molton do not know of its existence. We cannot see our nearest neighbours and it is quite possible to stand in the garden in the evening and hear no sound at all. The nearest road, the B3226, is half a mile away in the valley and the traffic cannot be heard. When the wind is in the south, we can sometimes just hear a train on the Tarka Line, and, on a very still evening, faint sounds of gunfire from the Okehampton ranges, many miles away. On moonless nights it is dark and there is no intrusive lighting to spoil the night sky.

Satterleigh is too small for a village and because a hamlet is usually considered to be a small group of houses without a church, it is hardly that either. It consists of just eight houses, well scattered over a tiny parish of 510 acres, with a population of 19. The oldest inhabitant is over 90 and the youngest is about 80 years younger. The range in ages is as different as the people themselves and a peaceful neighbourliness exists. No public transport reaches Satterleigh, there is no telephone box, nor even a postbox.

When we first moved to Satterleigh a mobile shop came around once a week selling most things. It was a great help to elderly folk. Sadly, the man who ran the business moved on and there has been no shop for several years. The milkman has also disappeared. We get a postal delivery once a day, before lunch, and we are very fortunate to have daily papers delivered by the shop in Chittlehamholt. These are left for collection in a variety of places, including boxes, pipes in hedges and even in a hollow tree. The school bus does not reach Satterleigh. Children have to be taken by car, way beyond the parish boundary, to meet up with the bus several miles away.

Most of Satterleigh is of course agricultural, with mixed crops, sheep and cattle. Tractors and milk tankers trundle the roads occasionally. There are few passing places and everyone in Satterleigh has to get used to reversing. At harvest time, circular routes are planned by the farmers, using a one-way system to avoid meeting another working vehicle. Anyone wanting to go out at this time has to go in the same direction as the tractors and join in their game. Difficulties only arise when an unsuspecting milk tanker is confronted with a tractor and trailer. Fortunately, most of the tanker drivers are very good-natured about reversing.

When we arrived in Satterleigh, our garden was just a large area of grass and few birds visited us. We planted hedges and shrubs, and encouraged the birds to the garden with food and housing. We put up a bird table and a number of nesting boxes. Now, as well as the usual garden birds and a fine sparrow gang, we have pheasant and partridge. Two years ago we were visited for the first time by a merlin, which swooped in to take unsuspecting blue tits feeding on peanuts. We have had occasional visits from a merlin since, in the winter and early spring.

Deer sometimes come into the garden, but are more usually seen in the field beyond. Moles and young rabbits are brought in alive by our two cats in the spring. It is always a relief when the young rabbits become too large to be pushed through the cat flap. Foxes and badgers are not uncommon and Satterleigh is even the home of wild boar, although these are farmed and not running free. Sheep have a habit of finding their way out of their fields and, as we tend to leave our gate open, they are prone to coming in and mowing our grass. Being situated between two dairy farms, we have had urgent telephone calls asking us to get into the lane in order to foil the escape of runaway cows. Sometimes it has been necessary to round up sheep and cows wearing gum boots and pyjamas.

Satterleigh is high, about 500 feet, so the views are a delight. Both Exmoor and Dartmoor can be seen easily on a clear day. Being high and with relatively few trees, wind is quite a feature and horizontal rain is something often experienced. A few years ago, in exceptionally high winds, we lost some lead from our roof and some of our slates were displaced. We have had to retrieve the roof from our new shed which blew into the next field. At one time we had frequent power cuts, but recently the electricity company has made improvements and power failure is now rare.

The lanes get wet and mucky in the winter and in icy conditions Satterleigh Hill, being so steep, can be impossible for an ordinary car. Long green ribbons of grass decorate the middle of the lanes and the banks on either side have become steep over the years, as agricultural vehicles get ever larger and push the lanes further into the hedgerows. In the lanes, soon after Christmas, snowdrops appear in the hedgerows, followed quickly by wild daffodils and primroses. Later, red campion, bluebells, the dog rose, meadowsweet and foxgloves turn them into a carpet of colour.

I could not write about Satterleigh without mentioning the church. St Peter's is a tiny church hidden behind Satterleigh Barton. Surrounded by an old stone wall with a lych-gate, it stands in a churchyard kept tidy by grazing sheep. It is the epitome of rural charm. St Peter's Church is now in the care of the Churches Conservation Trust and its maintenance is their responsibility. The church is featured in a publication about the work of the Trust. The parish is permitted to hold six services a year and the novelty of worship in this lovely little church makes these services very popular. A congregation of 40 just about fills all the pews and it is not unusual to have 30 or more at a service. The Team Clergy also seem to enjoy conducting services here, although one recently admitted to having a little worry about spiders in the sounding board above the pulpit! The services held in St Peter's are always traditional, usually Matins, but Holy Communion, carols and patronal festivals are also held on occasions. Collections from these services go to the Churches Conservation Trust, to be used for the continuing upkeep of St Peter's. It is hard to imagine a more delightful place to worship.

Satterleigh has changed in the six years we have been here. Three of the eight houses have had a change of occupancy. Two farmhouses have been sold with their land bought separately by neighbouring farmers. The current trend for small farms to disappear is apparent, even in Satterleigh.

Chapter 2

ROADS, FOOTPATHS, BRIDLE-WAYS & TRANSPORT

Today we pay for our roads through taxes, although some new bridges, such as the Severn Bridge and the Forth Road Bridge, are partly paid for by tolls charged on all who cross. From the beginning of the eighteenth century, many of our main roads and some minor ones were similarly maintained with tolls being paid by almost everyone who travelled along them. Roads so maintained were called turnpike roads. The name turnpike itself originally referred to the spiked gates which were erected to stop sudden horse-borne attacks. Later it came to mean the turnstile erected at the side of the gate to admit foot travellers and hence turnpike gates and turnpike roads came into common usage both as terms and as features of the landscape. One person may buy several toll-roads and pay someone else to collect the tolls and live in the house. Chittlehamholt and Warkleigh toll-roads were mentioned in the *North Devon Journal* from 1829 and here are just a few interesting extracts:

It's not the miles you travel but the PACE that kills at this place.

Barnstaple Turnpike Trust

4th June 1829

Notice is hereby given that a special meeting of the Trustees of the said roads will be held in the Guildhall of the town of Barnstaple on Friday the 12th day of June next, at 1 o'clock, for the purpose of directing a toll-gate to be erected on the road near the cottage belonging to Thomas Burgess, on the north side of Chittlehamholt village, in the parish of Chittlehampton.

27th August 1830

Barnstaple Turnpike Trustee Meeting

It was resolved on the motion of John Marshall esq., seconded by John Gribble esq., 'that the Chittlehamholt Gate be continued one year longer, and that previous to that time a meeting be convened to determine on its after continuance or removal; as it is stated that this toll is very oppressive to persons going to Southmolton market.'

It was moved by J. Gribble esq., 'That the renters of the gate be allowed ten days rent as a compensation for the impediment to travelling by the severe weather last winter.' An adjourned auction was then held for letting for one year from 8 September next the remainder of the gates belonging to the Trust, when the following were taken:

Pilton Bridge Gate by R. Rowden for 551s.0d.
Two Potts Gate by Peter Camp for 193s.0d.
Chittlehamholt Gate by W. Hanford for 34s.0d.
Chappletown Gate by R. Pristacott for 275s.0d.
Puddlepool Gate by S. Drew for 86s.0d.
At the Wick Cross, Abbot's Marsh and Lee Cross Gates, toll-collectors are to be appointed by the Trust.

27th July 1831

Barnstaple Turnpike Trustee Meeting

John Brown esq. represented the hardship of taxing persons going to South Molton with a toll at Chittlehamholt, who travel not more than three quarters of a mile over the roads of the Trust. The subject was debated and produced a motion from John Gribble esq. that the gate at Chittlehamholt remain where it is for one year from the 8th of September next, previous to which time the expedience of removing it shall be considered. John Brown esq. moved an amendment that the gate at Chittlehamholt be removed from its present position to the south side of the village.

2nd August 1832

Barnstaple Turnpike Trust

At a General Meeting held this day in the Guildhall, JOHN GRIBBLE Esq., in the Chair, the following gates were taken by the persons and at the sums hereunder mentioned:

	New Rent	Old
Newport Gate, by Petherick	£1,070	£999
Sticklepath Gate, by Williams	£531	£530
Chappletown Gate, by Petherick	£311	£310

Right: *A much-valued Chittlehamholt AA sign.*

Below: *An old milestone for Barum, the old name for Barnstaple. Three of these stones can be seen in the parishes. Chittlehamholt, Warkleigh and Satterleigh were once on the Barnstaple–Exeter main road.*

Right: *A photograph showing what is known locally as the old fisherman's bridge across the Taw close to Simmons Farm in 1943. Standing on bridge are, left to right: Vera, Muriel, Olive and Kathleen Wright.*

Kingford Bridge under construction in 1908.

Wickross & Abbots Marsh, by Woolacott

	£206	£187
Chittlehamholt Gate, by Marshall	£26	£21
Lee Cross Gate, by Williams	£102	£75
Ilfracombe Local Toll, by Parker	£215	£188

12th September 1833

Barnstaple Turnpike Trust

An adjourned survey was next held for letting several of the gates for which no bidders appeared at the auction on the 7th ultimo. The Chappletown Gate (which let last year at £311) was first put up in £280, and after a spirited bidding was taken by John Marshall for £334. The Wickcross and Abbottsmarsh Gates (let last year for £206) were put up in £190 and taken by William Woolacott, at £190. The Puddlepool Gate (last year's rent, £61) was put up in £50, and taken by Robert Pristacott for £78. The Chittlehamholt Gate (let last year at £26) was put up at £20 and was taken by J. Hooper for £26.

Barnstaple, March 17th 1843

Notice is hereby given that a special meeting will be held on Friday the 7th day of April next, at one o'clock in the afternoon, in order to consult about Erecting a Toll Gate or Bar across the said Turnpike Road, at or near the north side of Newland Lane, in the Parish of Warkleigh, about half a mile from the Chittlehamholt Toll Gate, and that Tolls be collected there for the benefit of the Lessee of the said Chittlehamholt Gate.

Barnstaple Turnpike Trust

At the usual monthly meeting of the Trustees held in the Guildhall on Thursday last, Revd James Arthur in the chair. It was unanimously resolved on the motion of Revd John Pyke, seconded by Mr John Bremridge, that the Toll Bar at Newland Lane near Chittlehamholt, be forthwith removed. This is one of the Bars which the South Molton Trust had complained of as grievous and vexatious.

Dated April 11th, 1844

According to the *Journal*, there was a toll-house at Broadmoor, over which there was a dispute in 1854:

July 13th 1854, Barnstaple Turnpike Trust meeting at the council room of the Guildhall, the Revd James Arthur in the chair. [The topic of agenda was the Broadmoor Corner Toll House.]

A letter was put in and read by Revd A. Loveband, which had been addressed, through him, to that meeting by Mr Braginton, steward to the Trustees of the late Lord Rolle, complaining that the Barnstaple Turnpike Trust had caused a toll-house to be erected at Broadmoor Corner, in the parish of Warkleigh, on land belonging to the aforesaid Trust without the consent of the owners, and also injuring thereby the roots of three oak trees. The chairman said the house was a very small one and the ground on which it was erected was wasteland. The Turnpike Act only spoke of 'enclosed' and 'unenclosed' land and they had, by law, a right to erect a house on, or take materials for repairing their roads from, any waste, that is to say, any unenclosed land, without giving notice or making compensation, or having any regard to the trees that might happen to be growing on it. The Trust was empowered to widen roads to any extent within 30 feet of the centre if the lands bordering them were unenclosed. It was held that, if enclosed, the road could be claimed by the Trust if it gave legal notice of its intentions and provided compensation. Revd A. Loveband said the house had been erected four years ago and the party complaining had been in the constant habit of passing that way. He thought it rather strange that they had not complained until now. Mr Bremridge said that Broadmoor Corner had always been wasteland. The clerk was instructed to write to Mr Braginton and tell him that the Trustees considered the ground on which the house was built to be wasteland, and that they had acted in accordance with the law.

Vital clues to the road system of yesterday can be found in some of the names around the parish. The house in Chittlehamholt Square, known as The Old Gate House, reminds us that tolls would have been handed over here, as well as just outside the village, at the house known as Holt Gate, and further on at Swingate Cross and then Broadmoor Cross, where we know there was a toll-house. Further clues are found on three old milestones: one in the hedgerow between Whitmore and Highbullen; one between Holt Gate and Haynetown; and the last one near Swingate Cross. The name 'Barum' is imprinted into these stones – this being the old name for Barnstaple – along with its distance in miles. The main route between Exeter and Barnstaple was once through Chittlehamholt, long before the new road along the River Taw was constructed.

The Lengthman

In the 1920s, Bob Medland was the local lengthman for the parishes. He was responsible for clearing the ditches beside the road. Hanson Hammett recalls Bob letting the farmers know in good time when he was coming so they could repair their hedges and he could clear the gutters afterwards to let the water flow freely. Bob Medland was also the local stone-cracker, known as Stonecracker Bob. The roads, before tarmac was used, were made of stone and chunks of rock were hauled to the roadside depots by horse and cart from places such as Head Quarry. Newspaper reports tell us there was a quarry at Hawkins in the early 1900s and Raymond Ayre remembers going to Drakes Quarry for .22 rifle-shooting practise whilst in the Home Guard. This quarry is covered in now. Bob, wearing gauze glasses, would crack the rock using a hammer and chisel to cut them down into tiny stones

Ian Black, 2001.

Alan Smith.

Jean Fraser (left) and Georgina Bowman in 2001.

Michelle May with her daughter Miriam in 2001.

Charlotte Moseley on Bugsy (left) and Sophie Zeidan on Midas, 2001.

Vicky Featherstonehaugh in 2001.

Marion (left) and Carol Sanders in 2001.

Sally Oatley (left) and Emma Lazarus in 2001.

the size of eggs. The stone-crackers were paid according to how many stones they cracked. Earth was taken out of ditches, spread on the stones and watered in. They used the clay to bind the road surface and a steamroller was used to compact them both together.

The first cars seen in the parish were few and far between and only owned by the gentry – people such as the Pollards from Whitmore, the Bryants from Highbullen, the Carters from The Manor and the Beaumonts from Edgington. Beattie Newcombe (née Lugg) lived at Head Post Cottages in 1918 and when a car went past she would go rushing out to the gate to see who it was – generally it was the Bryants from Highbullen. She thought it was marvellous to see someone with a car in those days, but she thinks that there are too many cars around today.

Harold Congram is now in his eighties. His parents told him of the first mechanically propelled vehicle to come through Chittlehamholt village – a motor bike ridden by Sir Harry Bater of The Manor. The whole village came out to witness the event.

Kingford Bridge
Before the bridge was built at Kingford there was a ford across the river – hence the name. On the Chittlehamholt side, the entrance to the ford was further upstream than the present road, nearer the Portsmouth Arms. The ford came up opposite the road to Cowlas by Taw Cottage. On the Chittlehamholt side, the remains of the lane leading down to the ford can still be seen. To mark the site and direction of the ford there was a thick wire stretched across the river between two trees, very useful when the water was high, or to 'furriners' (foreigners) fording the river. The bridge, built by the Barnstaple firm of Woolaways and mainly financed by local public subscription, was opened in 1908 and the day when it will reach its centenary is looming. A large crowd of local people were present at the official opening ceremony. I wonder if such a crowd will turn out for the centenary – only time will tell. Imagine what a difference the building of the bridge made to communications between Burrington, High Bickington and Chittlehamholt – young men who did not own a horse could go courting without getting their feet wet!

Head Bridge
On the other side of the valley, with the bridge crossing the River Mole and close to Head Mill, stands Head Bridge. Ken Guard talks of how, when standing on this bridge, you can be standing in three parishes at once – King's Nympton, Chulmleigh and Chittlehamholt.

Talking with Alex Hill
Footpaths and Bridle-ways Co-ordinator for Warkleigh, Satterleigh and Chittlehamholt.

Opening up the original footpaths and bridle-paths started off as a Government initiative to get all the public rights of way in good condition by the year 2000. The Government gave money to the Countryside Commission, who then made it available to County Councils. Devon was one of the first to become involved and had a pilot scheme to see how well it would work. The County Council then offered the money to any interested parishes who would get on with the work of upgrading the footpaths and bridle-ways in their parish. They were given a yearly budget – originally for three years, then extended to four. We were one of the original parishes in Devon to become involved in the scheme. When we started it was called the Parish Paths Partnership Scheme, or P3 for short, obviously because it was a partnership between the County Council and the Parish Council. It wasn't only Parish Councils though. In some parishes where the councils were not interested, like Bratton Fleming, a voluntary group was formed to work on the paths.

The original scheme started in Devon in April 1992 and we started in January 1993. We did a survey of all the paths in the three parishes of Warkleigh, Satterleigh and Chittlehamholt, to see what sort of condition they were in, and we identified that Mucksey Lane, the bridle-way between Highbullen and Whitmore, was the worst in the area, so that's where we started work. If it's a large job, you can get outside contractors and pay them, but we contacted the British Trust for Conservation Volunteers who work on general conservation projects. They have groups of volunteers who come for a daily charge, and so they came for two days to help clear the undergrowth from Mucksey Lane. A lot of the local villagers came as well when we advertised for help. After we cleared all the undergrowth and trimmed back the hedges on either side, it was largely a matter of trying to improve the surface of the bridle-way because there had been a lot of erosion on the steep section beyond the Highbullen golf course. We then bought some sleepers from Mole Valley Farmers and put those in to stop the water eroding the surface any more. We then worked on other paths, making certain they were open and clearly waymarked.

The County Council will provide some things for free; stiles, kissing-gates and hunting gates, etc., and you can put them where you think necessary, where the old ones have rotted, or where you cannot get over fences. Once a month a few of us get together as a working party, and we decided it would be a good idea to purchase tools for use in the parish. We bought some hand tools, a strimmer, a hedge trimmer and a drill so we could do some woodwork. You can go on training courses to use strimmers, etc., and get the necessary certificates to be able to use them in public places. On the Little Shortridge footpath we put in a gate and a stile. On the footpath from Chittlehamholt village across to the church, passing the golf course, we put in a stile and Mr Geoff Derbyshire helped us a

Fred Clarke with his pony and jingle outside Cobblestone Court, c.1930.

Below: A train, seen here in the Taw Valley, on the Barnstaple–Exeter railway line. On the left of the photograph is Presbury Farm, Chittlehamholt.

Above, left: For many years Terraneaus Tours of South Molton picked up the children in the parishes. They are no longer trading. Their Mercedes coach is seen here at Buckfast Abbey in 1992.

Left: Portsmouth Arms Station in its heyday, not far from Chittlehamholt village, c.1930.
From the RLK Knight Collection © Steve Knight.

great deal on this project by constructing a dog gate at the side. As the entrance on to the road close to the church was not very good, the Council provided a kissing-gate which the owner installed.

One of the other bridle-ways we worked on runs from Satterleigh Barton down Cotley Lane, coming out on to the B3226, and then passes through the Bowens' fields at the bottom. The last field was overgrown with trees, so we employed a contractor to cut some of them back.

In 1996 the Tarka Trail became interested in making a circular walk from Umberleigh so you could walk around and back to the railway station, which comes up through the parish into the village and proceeds back down through Shortridge Wood and across to Broadmoor. There is a footpath that goes opposite Shortridge, up across to Broadmoor where there is a little stream which was in very bad condition, and the Tarka Trail interest group paid for the stile that went over the stream there.

We put a sleeper bridge in Pool Lane, and in 1997 we built a bridge across the stream on the footpath which runs from Claytown into Shortridge Wood, coming out on the bridle-way going towards Spiecott. The County Council did a lot of work there, and we built some steps and various approaches either side so people could cross over the stream.

Opposite Shortridge Farm there is a footpath which runs past the derelict buildings of Little Shortridge. We put in a stile there and a contractor installed a bigger gate for the adjoining landowner so people could join the proper route. We were involved in 1998 when the floods swept away the Mole footbridge that crosses from Woodleigh Cottage into the parish of King's Nympton. I think a big tree was coming downriver and managed to lodge against the bridge and remove it. It seemed a substantial bridge, but perhaps there had been a bit of erosion on one of the piers. At first the County Council said it would be terribly expensive to replace and was doubtful if it could bear the cost of such a big wooden bridge going right across the river. However, I think that as we were members of the P3 scheme there was more pressure on the Council and 18 months later it announced that it had raised enough money to replace the bridge.

Taxis & Bus Services

Around 80 years before the time of writing Fred Clarke from Chittlehamholt provided a taxi service for the village with his pony and jingle. At the same time Tom Martin, from the Exeter Inn, ran horse-drawn carriages as taxis. In April 1921 Tom bought a Model T Ford charabanc, fitted with a 14-seater body and painted grey and black. It is not known whether Tom used it to provide a regular taxi service or just for outings. The 'Tin Lizzie', as it was known, had a short life in the village and was sold to Moors' Garage in South Molton at the end of November in the same

year, being replaced by a smaller Ford vehicle which served as the village taxi. Tom Martin, who also farmed, died in an accident in 1936 when the cattle lorry in which he was riding was hit by a train in the Teign Valley.

The Devon Motor Taxation Records of 1920–22 show Thomas Robert Henry Martin, of the Exeter Inn, Chittlehamholt, owning the following vehicles:

1920 – 2 horse-drawn carriages
1921 – 1 horse-drawn carriage
1922 – No horse-drawn carriages.
Motor Vehicles:
1921 – TA977 Hackney coach Ford. Colour: Grey and
*   black; 14 seats.*
1922 – T7808 Hackney Ford. Colour: Blue and black;
*   6 seats.*

The register of first owners shows that the vehicle TA977 – a 22.4hp Ford (Model T) – was first registered on 9 April 1921 and was new to Thomas Martin. It was then sold to Moor and Son, South Molton, on 29 November 1921. The taxation card also shows that this vehicle was last licensed to Charles Ingle of Haldon Gardens, Kenn, Exeter, on 31 December 1929.

The word 'Hackney' tells us that the vehicles were available for hire. The 14-seater charabanc was used during the 1921 season and was then changed for a car which was used as a taxi from 1922. There is no mention of the lorry or lorries, which we know Tom Martin used in later years until his death in 1936. I was lucky to obtain all the information on Tom Martin from Roger Grimley, a transport enthusiast.

In 1920 a bus service owned by T. Heard & Son ran twice daily from Chittlehampton and passed through Chittlehamholt village.

Competition between services continued until the Road Traffic Act of 1930 came into force and a new national system of licensing for bus services was introduced. This led to considerable change and the effect in North Devon was immediate. First, William Parker decided that his future lay in goods haulage so he sold his bus service and coach-hire business to Albert Turner of Chulmleigh. At about the same time, T. Heard & Son withdrew their Chittlehampton service and concentrated on their Exmoor enterprises. This left Chittlehamholt without a service until Lionel Hammett of Rose Cottage – now known as The Old Gate House – was asked by people who had been passengers on Heard's bus if he would carry them to and from Barnstaple in his taxi car. A charge of three shillings return per head was agreed and, from the spring of 1931 until the summer of 1932, this was a regular run.

The business was started by Lionel's brother Donald, but he died young – at only 26 – and Lionel took over. Lionel built the garage that goes with the cottage today and it was here that he sold petrol in 2-gallon cans. Lionel's son, Hanson, tells me he has still got some of those cans with sprats written on them. After getting married Lionel moved to Kinnings Farm. He gave up the taxi service because he could not cope with both the taxi and the farming, and didn't get another car for private use until 1948. When Chittlehamholt and Warkleigh schools were closed in 1948, Fred Spear from Chittlehampton would taxi the children from Chittlehamholt to Chittlehampton. Fred Spear's driver, Stan Neil, was driving Maurice Thorne back from Chittlehampton school one day and, approaching Furze Barn, the back door flung open and Maurice fell out into the hedge. He rolled a few times, but luckily escaped with only a few scratches. After Fred Spear gave up, Bill Skinner of the Exeter Inn took over the taxi service. When he gave up, Lionel Hammett took over once again, winning the school contract which was extended from Chittlehamholt to Umberleigh. Hanson Hammett drove the car a lot at that time as well.

In 1932, Tom Wills Coaches of Atherington ran a bus service from Chittlehamholt every Friday. I remember travelling on his familiar blue-and-cream coaches on Sunday-school outings until the firm was disbanded in 1975.

Motor Bus Service between Chittlehamholt and Barnstaple, Fridays only.

Chittlehamholt depart 9.00a.m. – Barnstaple arrive 10.05a.m.

Barnstaple depart 4.00p.m. – Chittlehamholt arrive 5.05p.m.

Fares to Barnstaple:

From	Single	Return
Chittlehamholt	1s.9d.	3s.0d.
Warkleigh	1s.6d.	2s.6d.
Chittlehampton	1s.3d.	2s.3d.
Cobbaton	1s.3d.	2s.0d.

Fridays were the busiest days on the bus services, being the principal market day in Barnstaple. It became the custom for Mrs Cissie Wills to act as conductress as her husband Tom, the driver, did not like handling money, so she would ride with him and take the fares. The two buses, one from Barnstaple and one from Chittlehamholt, covered the same road from Fishleigh Rock into Barnstaple, so Mrs Wills would start on the Burrington service, take the money, then get out at Fishleigh Rock or Chapeltown and take the fares from the Chittlehamholt people.

When I was growing up in the 1960s and '70s, Terraneaus Tours of South Molton would pick up the children in Chittlehamholt village and take us to Chittlehampton school. Then, when we were old enough, the journey would continue on into South Molton comprehensive school. Milk from South Molton was carried in the boot of the bus and dropped off at Chittlehampton school. I remember one of their coaches had a cab for the driver which used to leak when it rained and many a time he would put up an umbrella. Another time, on the return journey from South Molton comprehensive via Chittlehampton, one of the pupils, whilst getting

Watertown House, early 1900s. The photograph is thought to show the Owen family.

off the bus at Chittlehampton, turned off the petrol tap. We nearly got as far as Hudscott before the inevitable happened and the bus stopped. We then had to wait for a replacement. The humpback bridge at Bray Mill caused some excitement to the children in the back of the coach if the driver decided to put his foot down. The drivers and buses varied from week to week. The different drivers who drove us over the years included Frank Smallridge (Smiler), Ian Nuttal, Bill Thomas, Ray Kingdon, Ron Darch, Noel Clements, Dave Willis, Steve Moore, David Prestcott and Tony Bradford. The style and comfort of the buses has changed dramatically since the 1970s and the ones I remember from back then would be classed as antiques today. I remember a couple of registration plates of the Terraneaus coaches being ENT and PYB. Sadly, in 1999, Terraneaus Tours gave up after many years of trading since the early 1900s. Now, T.W. Coaches, who took over from Terraneaus, take the pupils from Chittlehamholt into South Molton and Hales bus service from Filleigh takes the juniors into Chittlehampton. On Fridays Turners Tours of Chulmleigh provide a bus service for the people of Chittlehamholt, taking them into Barnstaple. This company also picks up pupils from the village and takes them to North Devon College.

5 December 1969
Notice to residents in Chittlehamholt and District
A Fortnightly BUS SERVICE to BARNSTAPLE will commence on Friday, 12 December, leaving:
CHITTLEHAMHOLT   *9.55a.m.*
WARKLEIGH   *10.00a.m.*
UMBERLEIGH   *10.20a.m.*
Returning from Barnstaple   2.15p.m.
TURNERS TOURS
Phone CHULMLEIGH 242

The Railway

The Barnstaple to Exeter railway was opened in 1854 and, like the river, spans the boundaries of Chittlehamholt and Warkleigh for some five miles. After pulling out of King's Nympton Station, the train follows the parishes from Headwood and then leaves at Park Farm before heading for Umberleigh. The whole stretch of line from Barnstaple to Exeter takes in some lovely scenery. At Snape Farm, High Bickington, you are looking right down on the railway as it makes a big twist, with Presbury Farm, Chittlehamholt, on the other side of the valley, just a gun shot away from the line. From this position it is like looking down on a Hornby train set, with Portsmouth Arms Station just around the corner. When the wind is in the right direction, you can hear the train quite distinctly in Chittlehamholt village.

At first, King's Nympton Station was called South Molton Road Station. This was soon changed because people were getting off the train thinking they had arrived at South Molton. An argument then ensued as to whether to call it Chulmleigh or King's Nympton.

The coming of the railway changed rural life, with towns and villages becoming more accessible. People were able to travel, giving rise to a thriving souvenir industry selling items such as pieces of china with 'A Present From ...' engraved on them. We are lucky enough to have a teapot with 'A Present From Chittlehamholt' on it. Farmers could now move their animals to and from the markets via the trains, which was much quicker than walking them miles to the nearest market. At this time most stations had regular markets held nearby with auction pens. The Portsmouth Arms was in the quarry where the sawmill is at the time of writing. These markets heralded the beginning of the end for the village fairs and markets which had existed for centuries. In 1854 the parishes had easy access to a nearby station at Portsmouth Arms, Umberleigh and King's Nympton. Milk, mail and newspapers were also transported with freight trains carrying heavy goods such as coal and timber.

In 1854, the Exeter to Barnstaple railway was called the North Devon Line, but today is known as the Tarka Line, which traces the journey of Tarka the Otter in Henry Williamson's classic novel. In all, the line covers 39 miles of track.

Christine Stuckey (née Congram), who was born at Wards Farm, Chittlehamholt, remembers walking to Portsmouth Arms Station with her mother and brothers as a child before the Second World War, because it was cheaper to do this than to go to Barnstaple on the bus. They used to go in the October half term to get fitted out for winter clothes. Later on, when Christine was courting George Stuckey, she used to cycle to Portsmouth Arms and catch the half-past-three train, leaving her bicycle at the station. George would get on at Umberleigh, where he lived, and they would travel on to Barnstaple to do a bit of shopping. They would go to a café on the strand and have a cup of tea and a box of Turkish delights. On the return journey, George would get off at Umberleigh and then cycle to Portsmouth Arms, meeting Christine again to see her home.

The youngsters at the time did not know any different than cycling everywhere because it was the only form of transport they had. Not every parent owned a car to take their children to and fro like they do today. Raymond Ayre can remember cycling regularly with Claude Eastmond down to South Molton to the cinema to see the second house. One evening they went to the half-past-six showing and as they didn't fancy the trailer, they decided to cycle down to Barnstaple to go to the cinema there. By the time they had seen the film and had cycled home it was nearly 2 o'clock.

Right: *The dedications of the Warkleigh and Satterleigh procession cross at Warkleigh Church in 1967. Left to right: Marion Congram (candle bearer), Marion Tucker (crucifer), Susan Lethbridge (candle bearer).*

Above: *The Revd Robbie Bowen performs a short service at Russons, Chittlehamholt, to bury Fred Scrivener's ashes, c.1991. Looking on are Fred's brother and sister, Bernard and Dora.*

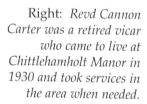

Right: *Revd Cannon Carter was a retired vicar who came to live at Chittlehamholt Manor in 1930 and took services in the area when needed.*

Below: *Revd George Dampier-Bennett presenting John (Jack) Congram with a silver sauce boat and a cheque on his retirement in 1973 after 45 years as church treasurer. Alongside Jack is his wife Florence.*

Below: *Aerial view of Chittlehamholt Church, 1993.*

Below: *Chittlehamholt Church. Note that the trees are no longer there.*

Chapter 3

RELIGIOUS AFFAIRS

Revd Robbie Bowen

Robbie Bowen was a childhood friend of mine. Everybody assumed that when he grew up he would work with trains as he had always been very keen on them; almost every Saturday he would cycle down to King's Nympton Station to help Mr Bird in the signal-box, and when it was sold, Robbie's mother and father bought him all the signal equipment for his birthday. However, Robbie didn't work with trains, he became a Methodist minister.

At school, everyone was given a Gideon Bible and Robbie would read a few verses every night. After leaving school he got a degree in physics and started studying to be a lay preacher. He felt that, instead of going straight into the ministry, he should get some experience of other work first, and began working at GEC in Manchester, developing railway signalling equipment. He stayed for seven years before applying to join the ministry. He was turned down but, when lay preaching at South Molton, he told the congregation that the ministry hadn't seen the last of him! Robbie then spent a year at a lay college – Cliff College in the Lake District – before going to Belfast and working as a lay pastor. He then applied to join the ministry again and this time was accepted.

He trained at Queen's College, Birmingham, and was then sent to Sierra Leone for four years. But not long after he arrived, civil war broke out. During a service one morning, shooting was heard nearby. Robbie, along with some others, picked up what food and money he could and left as quickly as possible. They walked for five days, with very little to eat, before they got some transport down to Freetown. When it was safe, Robbie returned to Sierra Leone for a further two years, after which he came home. Robbie loved the people of Sierra Leone so much that he was ordained there.

The ministry would not let Robbie go back to Sierra Leone as the troubles had started again, so instead he was sent to the Gambia. There he met Ruth, a lay preacher, and the two were married in 2001 in Shropshire. When they returned to the Gambia and their missionary work, the people held a marriage thanksgiving service for them. The church in Brikama was decorated for the occasion and the ceremony included choirs and African drums.

Chairs were carried down from the church to the Methodist compound where speeches were made and gifts presented. The feast had started the day before with a sheep and a bullock arriving on foot to provide meat for the occasion. Both animals were gifts from villages in the locality. The other food, which included 4cwt of rice and piles of vegetables, was cooked in huge cauldrons over open fires to feed the 800 guests. Celebrations continued until six o'clock the next morning.

When Robbie comes home he often preaches in the church at Warkleigh.

A Warkleigh and Satterleigh Project, 16 January 1967

Barbed wire and disused farm machinery were among parts used to make a new cross for the churches of Warkleigh and Satterleigh. The project for the cross was initiated by the rector, Revd A.H. Jones. He wanted it made from materials which would symbolise the life and history of the parishes. The cross was dedicated by the Archdeacon of Barnstaple. It was made by Mr H. Kingdom from the spokes of an old cartwheel, provided by Mr M.A. Elworthy of Satterleigh Barton. The boss in the centre, carved by Mr Graham Taylor of Tawstock, has a wheatsheaf motif on one side and a bunch of grapes on the other, representing bread and wine. It was made from a piece of oak taken from an ancient beam in some local stables. The oak was cut out by Mr W. Langley of Warkleigh Cottages whose search among old machinery also produced an old binder for the radials. The cross mounting was turned from an old gatepost found on Mr C. Shapland's farm at Great Shortridge. The cross of thorns was made from barbed wire taken from Mr J. Pincombe's farm at Pugsley. The staff is made from oak given by Mr F. Brend and taken from a barn pillar at Parsonage Farm, an ancient building which was the rectory for several centuries. The joints are made from old copper piping salvaged from a scrap heap by Mr Alan Bowen of Snapdown. Silver plating of all metal parts was carried out, as a gift to the parish, at Messrs E. Gale & Son of Barnstaple, by Mr Pocklington, a craftsman from Chittlehamholt, and the turning and assembling of the staff and mounting were done voluntarily by Mr G. Peters of St John's Cottage, Barnstaple.

The following kindly made donations to defray the cost of the carving, faculty fees, etc.: Miss H. Fletcher, Miss Jessie Harding (whose sister was for many years headmistress of Warkleigh School), Mrs O. Radcliff, Major Owen, Capt. Whitty, Miss Thorold and Mr Frank Pepper. The Warkleigh and Satterleigh processional cross was dedicated at a service in Warkleigh church with Marion Tucker, the crucifer, having the honour of carrying the cross, accompanied by Marion Congram and Susan Lethbridge as candle bearers *(see photograph page 24).*

There follows an article, written by Revd John H. Bell, the rural dean of the churches of St John the Baptist, Chittlehamholt; St John the Evangelist, Warkleigh with Satterleigh; and St Peter, Satterleigh. It was written in 2001, before he left Chittlehamholt, Warkleigh and Satterleigh churches after 15 years of ministry to go on to be the vicar of the United Benefice of Blackawton, with Stoke Fleming and Strete.

On 4th September 1986, at 10.00p.m., I pulled up the handbrake of our old Austin Allegro and got out of the car. The roof-rack was bulging, the boot was jam-packed with essentials, and duvets and pillows were stuffed around the children as they slept, huddled in the back seat. Hazel (my wife), Andrew (aged 9), Katie (aged 8) and I (aged 36) had arrived at King's Nympton Rectory. Our world was magical: a place of dark leafiness, squishy slugs, hooting owls, low-flying bats, and mice rustling in last Autumn's leaves. A new set of parishes, a new kind of life. What were we going to make of the Devonian folk with their lovely accents? And what would they make of us? This was going to be very different from Southampton where I worked in a large eclectic university church and very different from my first job as an art and biology teacher in Secondary Modern Schools in the City of Leicester.

September 2001, and we are packing ready for another move – still in Devon (hurrah!) but this time to the South Hams, to Stoke Fleming, near Dartmouth. In October 2001 I became Vicar of the United Benefice of Blackawton with Stoke Fleming and Strete. But that's another story. What about the 15 years when Chittlehamholt, Warkleigh, Satterleigh, George Nympton, Romansleigh and King's Nympton were the parishes for which I had special responsibility as Team Vicar within the South Molton Team? During those years the people I grew older with did not seem to get any older. It was only the young who seemed to change; hormones and all that! Many are the weddings I conducted, later to baptise the children of those couples. It was hard to credit that some-one who married at, say, 21, was only 6 when I first came to North Devon. One thing that puzzled me about the middle-aged to older male farmers was how their heads always seemed to support an amazing growth of hair compared to mine. Was it the fertiliser floating around in the agricultural air that had nourished their roots?

Garden Safaris and Open Gardens with Cream Teas, Sales of Produce and Draws, Coffee Mornings,

Bell-ringing Festivals, Concerts of various kinds, Christmas Bazaars, Jumble Sales and Sales to raise funds for worthy causes, Flower Festivals – all these and lots more are the stuff of village life. Where would we be without them? They help to reinforce a community's identity. Then there are the more churchy events: the January Plough Service, the Family Pet Service (held before the 'Vicar of Dibley' made them famous!), the Arts and Crafts Service, the Harvest Festivals with their wonderful suppers (some held in barns – come to Devon to see how they should be done!), the Christingle Service (which supports the Children's Society) and the special Christmas events: the joint ecumenical Carols by Candlelight in the village hall, the late Christmas Eve Holy Communion and the Christmas Day morning Family Service swelled by visitors from Highbullen Hotel. And let me not forget the six (usually) services we are permitted at Satterleigh Church, now so well attended since this little gem of a building became the responsibility of the Churches Conservation Trust. Many memories of wonderful times of worship as well as fun and fellowship.

Someone has suggested that I speak of 'characters' I have known in the three parishes. If I use their names I will have to suffer the consequences of, 'Why didn't you mention so-and-so!' Perhaps it's safest – though I doubt it – to make brief mention of a tiny selection of those past and present and leave you to establish their identity.

Chittlehamholt goes first. One member of a family of four, now all deceased, each of them unmarried and who came from 'up north', sticks in my memory. I would visit him at home often to find him peeling the spuds (not teddies) with his flat cap turned back-to-front. During the weeks in South Molton Community Hospital before he died, he recorded in a notebook the names of everyone who had come to visit him. As his terminal illness progressed, his writing deteriorated into squiggles. I still have that little book somewhere; it is very special. Another man – also no longer with us – had a captivating smile. He loved his bell-ringing. A short time before his unexpected death he offered to help me carry my heavy case out of the church to my car. I had forgotten to fasten it properly so, when he kindly picked it up, all my papers and books went flying. Together, we tried to do the re-packing. And what about the ladies? When first I saw her across a crowded church, I thought the light from a stained-glass window (there are no such windows in Chittlehamholt Church!) was playing on her hair, but no, it was a purple rinse. One Christmas, down at The Manor, she and I danced the night away – well, actually, it lasted for a couple of minutes. And what about the juggling, the dog-breeding, and the tombstone phobia? Can you guess who that is?

Warkleigh goes next. Like love and marriage, it's impossible to have one without the other. This couple's attendance at church, in foul weather and fine, was as regular as clockwork during my time there. The wife had a pet church spider called Fred. Fred had always lived in his hole by one of the pews but I think the present one must be the thirty-somethingth or so descendant of the one I first knew (how long do spiders live anyway?). There was the dark, softly-spoken gentleman with the kind of hair I spoke of, enviously, above. And then there were my two 'aunties'. Where would I have been without them? Another lady of senior years used to turn up to church in an old open-topped tractor. Am I making it up or did she sometimes wear a yellow sou'wester on her head and a protective layer of body sacking tied on with farmer's friend (bailer cord) to keep out the rain? Warkleigh is the windiest of all my churches and it really knows how to chuck it down up there! In the post-tractor years, our hero would sometimes walk home after church, refusing lifts from younger folk. Sadly, the yellow hat has disappeared.

Finally, Satterleigh. You should not find it hard to work out who's who in this tiny parish! Actually, one member has already had a mention – she's one of my 'aunties'. Another parishioner has the distinction of putting what he thought was delicious Devon cream on his mince pie at some 'do' or other near Christmas, only to discover on biting the thing that it was salad cream!

However, every parishioner had his or her own distinctiveness, his or her own gift or gifts to bring to church or community life. And I include the younger folk who, amongst other things, helped to run the family services and keep me young, well, just a little bit! Once, in a family service, I was talking about the poor in foreign lands and asking the congregation to imagine what it was like living in a slum. One little girl put up her hand and said, 'My Mum says we live in a slum!'

Well, that's a few of the people, now for the buildings. Chittlehamholt Church was built in 1838 as a Chapel of Ease, literally to make it easier for the people of the village to worship there without having to go elsewhere. Its simple design was enhanced in 2000 with a new heating system and in 2001 with new lighting and reordering and refurbishment of the west end. The whole interior was redecorated and two beautiful hangings were suspended from either side of the chancel arch. The Church Councils and a supportive community worked hard to get the church building into a state of which we are all proud.

Warkleigh Church is a medieval (first mentioned in 1276) listed and protected building, which was restored in 1869 and 1888. The church has retained its fifteenth-century roof with carved bosses and has a tall western tower that houses a peal of six bells, which are rung regularly by a dedicated team. Its claim to fame is the restored Warkleigh Pyx, a unique Elizabethan wooden box, anciently used for carrying the reserved Sacrament

The Warkleigh Tabernacle, a small wooden box which remained unnoticed in the parish chest until discovered by Revd S. Baring-Gould in 1888. It is thought to have been designed to house the pyx or ciborium used to carry the Blessed Sacrament to the sick, made and decorated in the third quarter of the fifteenth century.

to the sick. Sadly, the box has now been removed for reasons of security, but pictures of it are on display in the church.

Satterleigh Church has the rare distinction of standing on an elevated position yet being invisible from the road; the building is approached through Satterleigh Barton farmyard. There has probably been a church here since Saxon times though it was first mentioned in 1288. The earliest recorded rector is Sir Simon de Ralegh in 1318. A 'new' church was built on the site in 1439. Built in the perpendicular style it has an unusual windowless north wall. Responsibility for the building now rests with the Churches Conservation Trust. The building was completely restored by the Trust, inside and out, during 1995/6. Because St Peter's is no longer, properly speaking, a parish church, St John's Warkleigh is now referred to as the Parish Church of Warkleigh with Satterleigh. The Trust limits the number of services that may be held there to six a year.

Each of these three churches, together with the Chapel across from the Exeter Inn at Chittlehamholt, are important places where we can meet together to celebrate our Christian faith and where we can hold funerals, weddings and other large events. Places where the wonderful Gospel may be heard and the purpose and meaning of life affirmed as God is worshiped in a variety of ways. These churches offer a wide range of services to suit most tastes. For a very long time, Chittlehamholt services have dovetailed with the Warkleigh and Satterleigh service pattern. In 2001 various new ventures were started, two examples being a Drop-In Lunch on the first Wednesday of each month in Chittlehamholt Village Hall, and Young Church during Warkleigh Church Services.

So-called Collaborative Ministry, clergy and lay people working together, has worked its way into the warp and woof of our church life. Today it is usual for folk to read from the Bible and lead the prayers at public worship. It is also possible for occasional lay-led services to be held without a clergyperson being present. This is the pattern and shape of the future as over-stretched rural clergy, with the ever-increasing workload of present-day ministry, share their role with others. The vicar will always have a specialised part to play in rural ministry but there is much more that lay folk can do (and are doing) – a pattern that is much nearer to what I believe our good Lord intended.

I have looked back over 15 years of ministry, from 1986 to 2001, in just three of my parishes. These small churches have been going for a long time – two of them for a very, very long time! Isn't it amazing how God calls both church people and the community at large to *support His Church down the ages? In years to come, when another book is written, what will the vicar of the day say then?*

John H. Bell
September 2001

The Church of St John the Baptist, Chittlehamholt

Chittlehamholt's population in 1838 was 400. Something had to be done to save the inhabitants the long Sunday walk to Warkleigh or Chittlehampton church, and so it was decided to build a local place of worship.

For weddings the people had to resort to the Parish Church of either the bride or groom. Some came to Chittlehampton for baptisms and burials. In 1577 a child, 'William Tailor of Chitton-Ho', was baptised, and until the church was built, people came from Chittlehamholt, Head, Snydles and Ditchaton Water to be baptised. Some went to Warkleigh, some went to King's Nympton. In 1543, John and Cecile, the children of 'John Thomas of Hedchitant' (Edgington) (in a marriage entry of 1544 it is Chedant Hampton) were baptised. In 1599, Thomasina, daughter of 'John Rumbilo de Chitleam Holte', was baptised at King's Nympton and in 1602, Arthure, the 'sonne and heire of Mr Lewes Hatch of Hedde' (Head) was baptised.

Prior to the first Church Building Act of 1818, the building of a new church required a special act of parliament – a costly proceeding – and it was in fact much easier to build a Nonconformist chapel; when Chittlehamholt Church was first built it was referred to as the Chapel of Ease. When Chittlehamholt was provided with its own church in 1838, it was the result of the personal enterprise of Revd Thomas Bevan, who was resident at Warkleigh Rectory.

In 1835, Revd Thomas Bevan obtained the bishop's approval for holding services in the school-room of Chittlehamholt – the property of Revd Peter Johnson of Wembworthy. The bishop added that a building to be used merely and solely for divine service would be more satisfactory and when Bevan applied in the following year through the bishop's legal offices for a formal licence, he was told that he should obtain a petition from the vicar and inhabitants. This petition, dated October 1838, was signed by Lord Rolle, patron and lay rector of Chittlehampton; Robert Chichester, vicar; John Graddon and Richard Crocker, churchwardens; John Brown of Sandford (so described in the conveyance of the site which was his gift); Revd Charles Chichester and Amy Chichester, son and daughter of the vicar; Revd Peter Johnson, Revd Thomas Bevan, and John Huxtable, who was the only Chittlehamholt resident among the signatories.

The church was consecrated by the Bishop of Exeter on 30 October 1838 by the name of the Chapel of Ease. The architect was R.D. Gould of Barnstaple and it was described by Pevsner (*The Buildings of England, North Devon*, 1952) as 'aisleless, with lancet windows, lancet triplets at the W and E ends.' The first person to be buried in the churchyard was James Rice of Chittlehamholt. He died on 30 October 1838, aged 60. When Davidson visited the church in 1844 it had a barrel organ in a gallery at the west end, bearing the inscription 'Built gratuitously for this church by John Heard of Chittlehamholt 1838.' (Soon after constructing this organ, Mr Heard made a pair of musical bellows which he presented to the young Queen Victoria.) In 1848 John Heard repaired the Chittlehampton organ that Lord Rolle gave in 1809 for £6, and the original organ he built for Chittlehamholt church eventually gave way to a harmonium, and that in turn to a two-manual pipe organ. In 1964, the over-large pipe organ unfortunately fell into decay and was superseded by the present small pipe organ, which was installed by George Ismond & Co. of Taunton at a cost of £650. During the years of the Second World War there was a competition amongst the Congram children from Wards to see who would pump the organ. Whichever family member did this job got 7s.6d. a quarter.

The church was equipped with 300 seats (more than there are now because there was originally a gallery at the west end). The first perpetual curate was Revd Edmund Bennett, for whom Lord Rolle built a vicarage – the house now called Featherstones. The house ceased to be the vicarage in 1931 when Revd Arthur Hackblock became the rector of Warkleigh, Satterleigh and Chittlehamholt, using Warkleigh Rectory as the base for all three churches. In later years, John Pester carved the choir screen, the front cover and the gradine at the back of the altar, while the front of the gradine was carved by John's son Cecil.

There follows a report of the opening of the church from the *North Devon Journal*:

November 1st 1838
Consecration of the Chapel of Ease at Chittlehamholt

On Tuesday last the newly erected Chapel of Ease at Chittlehamholt, in the Parish of Chittlehampton, was set apart for its sacred uses by the Reverend the Lord Bishop of this diocese.

The Village of Chittlehamholt (from which the Chapel is about a quarter or half a mile distance) contains and is surrounded by a considerable population, who have hitherto wont to travel nearly four miles to Chittlehampton Parish Church. This inconvenience suggested to the principal owners of the soil of the Parish the necessity of a better provision for the Spiritual wants of the inhabitants and John Brown Esq. of Sandford generously offered a spot of land, both for the building and a burial-ground; and by the munificence of the Right Honourable Lord Rolle, who subscribed £200 and of the Right Honourable Lord Fortescue who contributed £100, aided by other Liberal donations and a Grant of £250 from the Commissioners for building Churches and Chapels, a very neat and substantial Chapel has been raised at the cost of about £1,000. The Building is 84ft by 25 within the walls, and the chancel 12ft by 8 and both the plan and the execution of the work did much honour to the taste and skill of the Architect Mr Gould, of this Town.

The Morning being fine, great numbers collected from the neighbouring Parishes to witness the ceremony; and about 11 o'clock, the hour at which the service was appointed to commence, the chapel was densely crowded, and hundreds afterwards came but could not gain admittance. Among the Clergy who accompanied the Bishop we noticed the Revd Thomas Bevan, Curate of Chittlehampton, Revd H. Luxmoore, Vicar of Barnstaple, Revd Richard Blackmore of Charles, Revd Zachary Hammett Drake of Clovelly, Revd Stawell of High Bickington, Revd Richard Bowden of Warkleigh, Revd John Wrey of King's Nympton, Revd Clay of Worlington, Revd Pelham Clay of Chawleigh, Revd James Arthur of Atherington, Revd John Russell of Swimbridge, Revd James Buckingham of Burrington, Revd Peter Johnson of Wembworthy, Revd W. Karslake of Dolton, Revd Karslake of Meshaw, Revd J.B. Jebb of Tawstock, Revd George Hole of Chulmleigh, Revd John Harding of Goodleigh, Revd Francis of Yarnscombe, Revd Davey of Chulmleigh, Revd Bond of Romansleigh, Revd R. Thorne of Bishopsnympton, Revd D. Baker of Bishopstawton, Revd T.H. Maitlands, Revd Clarke, Revd Melhuish and Revd R. Passmore of South Molton and several others amounting in all to about 35. The Misses Rolle of Hudscott, John Brown Esq., Thomas Wrey Harding Esq., Zachary Hammett Drake Esq., and many other influential residents of the neighbourhood formed part of the Congregation. On entering the Chapel, the Bishop and his Clergy alternately repeated the 24th psalm; and having reached the communion table, the petition, praying the Bishop to consecrate this chapel, was read by the registrar, signed by the Bishop, and ordered to be enrolled, the psalms, lessons and collects were read by the Revd Thomas Bevan. After the service had been completed, in the order which is set forth in the printed forms, the Venerable Archdeacon Barnes ascended the pulpit and preached from the 15th verse of the 10th chapter of the epistle to the Romans how shall they hear without a preacher...

In a parish, the length of which is several miles, and where the parochial tower is seen by many of the parishioners only as an object in the distance, it is clear that among them must be many who have been without the regular means of religious worship, not that you have been altogether denied the benefit of Christian precept or Christian example, for I know some who have laboured among you faithfully and you love and honour them for their works sake, but from the inconvenient distance of the parish church, some of you have been induced to resort to other places of worship to the danger of the unity of the Christian church. Ought you not, then, be thankful to those benevolent individuals whose piety and charity have provided for you and for future generations this commodious edifice in which we are now assembled. Not that I would have you to pay homage or worship to any God alone, to whose service this place is sacred, yet is it not forbidden to acknowledge with gratitude the kindness of our benefactors, while both they and we unite in ascribing all the Glory to God only, whose is the power and the victor, and the majesty, for all that is in the earth is thine O Lord, and of thine own have we given to thee. The Venerable Archdeacon then went on to advert to the leading doctrines of the Bible Mans fallen state – the redemption of the World by Christ – the doctrine of the Trinity – the necessity of the influence of the Holy Spirit, and urged upon his auditors to evince their adherence to these grand tenets of the Christian Faith by the continual homage of an obedient and Holy Life. After the conclusion of the sermon the Bishop offered a prayer and pronounced the Benediction. His Lordship, then preceded by his mace-bearer, and followed by the clergy and the registrar, proceeded to the ground at the side of the chapel and consecrated it to the purposes of a burial-ground, and ordered the Sentence of Consecration to be registered, and, having read over the prayer prescribed for the ceremony, the service terminated and the congregation dismissed. The occasion appeared to excite much interest among the villagers for whose benefit the building is designed, and we trust the pious object of the subscribers, through whose benevolence it is reared, will be realised in the increasing morality and religion of the inhabitants.

Chittlehamholt Chapel

The same John Brown who gave the site for the church also granted a lease for 100 years of the chapel site together with the chapel and other buildings lately erected therein, reserving for himself and his heirs, administrators and assigns the seat in the western corner of the said chapel adjoining the pulpit which was fitted up by the said John Brown. Chittlehamholt, which hitherto had no place of worship, now found itself in the same year provided with two, and that partly by the action of the same man. Suitable sites for church or chapel would have been difficult to find without the co-operation of John Brown, but that he should both aid the erection of a church beside his own house and fit up a seat for himself in the chapel was unexpected. The lease was conditional upon the payment of 5s. yearly and was upon trust that the lessees would:

... permit and suffer the said Chapel Buildings and Premises to be used for preaching the Gospel and for gathering a Church of Christ to be governed according to the rules of the New Covenant of Grace in Christ.

The reopening of Chittlehamholt Chapel, 13 November 1999. Seen here singing are Christopher and Tracey Thorne.

Organist Molly Thorne from Chittlehamholt Chapel.

Chittlehamholt Chapel, c.1920.

Below: *Warkleigh Church.*

Above: *Chittlehamholt, Warkleigh and Satterleigh choir, Warkleigh church, 1981.* Left to right, back row: *Diana Lethbridge, Dora Scrivener, Rosalyn Wright, Charles Phillpot, Rachel Davies, David Davies;* front row: *Joan Chevalier, Doreen Morgan, Ann Beckett, Franky Sheath, Ben Davies, Bernard Scrivener.*

Above, right: *Seen here outside Warkleigh Church, the Bishop of Crediton, the Rt Revd Richard Hawkins, who took a service here during October 1999.* Left to right: *Reg Pincombe, Charles Phillpot, Rt Revd Richard Hawkins, Revd John Bell, David Elworthy.*

Should it be used for other purposes, or remain unused for six months, John Brown had power to re-enter. The Tithe Apportionment of 1842 calls this building a Baptist chapel, but this appears to be a mistake, due no doubt to resemblances of doctrine and practice and to the novelty of the Brethren movement, which originated in 1830. The lessees were: William Crawford of Barnstaple (tea dealer); Robert Carter Chapman, Charles Alexander, Ambrose Powning (all of Barnstaple, ministers of the gospel); John Passmore and John Beer of Warkleigh (yeomen); Robert Gribble of High Bickington (minister of the gospel); John Willmott and James Gibbs of Barnstaple (deacons); and George Lovering of Tawstock (minister of the gospel).

John Brown junr granted a lease of an extended site in 1863 for 100 years from that date, the rent to be 10s. a year, with the same provisions and restrictions, including the right to the exclusive use of the seat adjoining the pulpit which had been fitted up by his father. The lessees this time were: Richard Baker of Satterleigh (yeoman); William Squire of Satterleigh (machinist); John Bragg of High Bickington (yeoman); William Westacott of Chittlehamholt (blacksmith); Henry Payne of High Bickington (shoemaker); John Bater of Chittlehamholt (yeoman); Richard Warren and Samuel Cole of Warkleigh (yeomen); William Beer of Warkleigh (thatcher); and George Gulley of Warkleigh (butcher). By 1909 there were only two surviving trustees capable of acting and one of these, Henry Payne, is described as 'formerly of High Bickington in the County of Devon, shoemaker.'

An article in 1937 states that Mr Elam Hammett was once presented with a wallet of 'treasury notes' by the members of the chapel in recognition of his faithful services in connection with the chapel Sunday school, of which he was superintendent for over 40 years. The late Mr R. Bater made the presentation.

During the second half of the twentieth century, the congregation decreased to single numbers and for a short time no services were held. It was thought that the chapel would be made redundant like so many other churches and chapels. However, with the dedication of the Thorne family from Chittlehamholt and Warkleigh Barton, this chapel has been rejuvenated with much renovation work having been done inside and out. At the special reopening service on 13 November 1999, the chapel was full to capacity.

Stafford Constable, now in his eighties, remembers that if there were any celebration events in the chapel, the food and teas would be prepared at Mr and Mrs Elam Hammett's home, Rose Cottage (now The Old Gate House). Stafford remembers that the food and jugs of tea would be carried from the house

to the chapel – a proper procession. The old school desks from the Chapel school were used as tables to eat the food on, and for seating on Sundays.

Warkleigh Church

The first mention of Warkleigh Church in the episcopal registers was made in 1276 when Sir Thomas de Wylelonde was presented to the living by Sir Walter de Ralegh. Edward Selly, the rector during the Commonwealth of the 1650s, was miserably harassed and forced to hide under the roof of his house. When apprehended he was ill-treated to make him disclose the whereabouts of his money. Once Selly was surprised at the parsonage house, and Christopher Stebbing, a trooper and one of Selly's own parishioners, dragged him downstairs by the hair of his head. Selly was then 80 years of age, but nevertheless he lived to repossess his benefice at the Restoration (1660).

One of the many bell-ringing certificates awarded to the Warkleigh Bell-ringers.

The south aisle was probably built in 1420 and still retains the fifteenth-century ceiling and carved bosses. The chancel – built before the aisle – was rebuilt by William Thorold in 1850, and the roof screen was removed and re-erected as a tower screen. This screen is excellent work of the renaissance style of about 1550. The blocked doorway to the rood loft remains in the north wall. In 1867, the roof of the nave was renewed to match the rebuilt chancel. An octagonal piscina survives in the aisle with foliage carving beneath. The church registers begin in 1538. The chalice and cover are Elizabethan, the work of T. Mathew of Barnstaple. The paten was made by John Elston in 1723. In 1553 there were three bells in the tower, two of which still remain as the present 5th and 6th. The 4th was recast in 1695, the 2nd and 3rd were added in 1901 to commemorate the reign of Queen Victoria, the gift of a member of the Thorold family. The present treble was given in 1929. The church was restored in 1869 and 1965.

When George R. Dampier Bennett was the rector in 1972, it seems he had influence from above to have the signposts re-worded in connection with Warkleigh church. There follows an extract from his newsletter at the time.

To a newcomer, Warkleigh is confusing. Coming up from Umberleigh to Home Down Cross and turning right the explorer seeking Warkleigh Church used to catch a glimpse of Warkleigh tower further on as he paused at the top of the hill by Broadmoor, only to be dumbfounded a few yards on by West Pugsley Cross signpost pointing leftwards to Warkleigh. This sent our newcomer further and further away from the church he was trying to visit. West Pugsley Cross signpost worried me so much as well as most of my visitors, that I drew a little sketch map and put on it my own idea of how the signposts thereabouts should be labelled, and submitted my sketch map to the Rural District Council and they most obligingly altered West Pugsley Cross to indicate Satterleigh instead of Warkleigh.

George Bennett goes on to say:

Perhaps some of our readers have got in their possession a copy of Spreat's engraving of Warkleigh Church, which shows so well this view, and bears the legend 'Warkleigh in the midst of a finely wooded country, placed on an eminence above a beautiful green meadow, it seems shut out from the world, and a fit abode of gentleness and peace.' (W. Spreat, Picturesque Sketches, 1842)

Spreat's drawing of the tower shows that even in those earlier times the tops of the lofty pinnacles had to be supported by unsightly ironwork. The iron bracings are now much lower down, near the bases of the pinnacles. Spreat's drawing shows six crocketings on each pinnacle; now there are only five. Presumably the large crockets had to be removed from their tops, thus making the pinnacles less lofty. The old drawing shows a vestry attached to the sanctuary of the main altar. This vestry was condemned as unfit for use by the rural dean in 1848 and was later removed, leaving the church vestry-less for 100 years until the ringing chamber was raised into its present loft, thus leaving space below for the new vestry.

The Old Warkleigh Rectories

The Old Rectory, Warkleigh.

The first Warkleigh Rectory was the house now known as Old Parsonage Farm, but Revd William Thorold, who was the rector from 1841 to 1888, said that the house was not grand enough for him and a new rectory was built on Revd Thorold's own land – this building is known today as Warkleigh House. On his death in 1888, the Thorold family retained the house and another rectory was built in front of Preston House – now the Old Rectory. In 1954 Ken Snow demolished the old Preston Farmhouse as Revd Cleavly wanted it taken down. At the time the

vicar owned the freehold of the property. While demolishing it, he found blackened and burnt timbers in the roof – a remnant perhaps of the fire which took place at Preston in 1875. The *Journal* takes up the story:

May 6th 1875
WARKLEIGH, SERIOUS FIRE *– We regret to report that Preston House, in this parish, has been almost entirely destroyed by fire. The property to which it belongs was purchased by the rector, the Revd William Thorold, some time since, and he determined on making extensive alterations and repairs in the mansion-house, almost amounting to re-building. The contractors for the work were Messrs. Symonds and Vicary, of Barnstaple, and they had nearly completed it – so nearly that the men engaged in the building have been lodging in the new part of the house for some time, and it was expected to be ready for occupation in a week or two. The workmen were there on Saturday last, and left about two o'clock. A farmer was going over his fields to see his cattle, when he was surprised to notice flames coming through the roof of Preston House. He gave instant alarm at the rectory and in the neighbourhood and the reverend owner and many besides were very quickly on the spot. A messenger was hastened off to Chittlehampton to fetch the fire-engine from that village, and with commendable celerity the engine was brought, and was efficiently manned.*

Ken remarked that it was a pity the building was demolished as, if a few hundred pounds had been spent repairing the roof slates, it would have been habitable. Ken describes Revd Cleavly as a comical character and can remember working at the rectory and seeing him skipping down the drive with a galvanised bucket in his hand, on his way to pick up the milk from Fred Brend at Old Parsonage Farm. The stones from the old Preston Farmhouse were taken down to Fishleigh Rock Garage which Ken was building at the time, and they were used as ballast for the forecourt. The little wooden hut which was used for prayer meetings at the rectory was also taken down – this hut was only accessible by going through the door at the end of the hall, through the kitchen, up the flight of stairs and across a gangway.

In 1984 the Warkleigh Rectory was sold and Revd Jim Davey was moved to King's Nympton Rectory, where he was still the rector of Chittlehamholt, Warkleigh and Satterleigh, but also had the added responsibility of George Nympton, King's Nympton and Romansleigh.

Warkleigh Bells
My father was a keen bell-ringer at Warkleigh Church from 1960. By 1963 he had become captain, having taken over from Charlie Bowden who had suffered a stroke. In 1991, after ringing the bells at Warkleigh Church, my father came home and suffered a fatal heart attack, aged 62. The bells are still regularly rung

Right: *The Warkleigh ringers in 1960. Left to right: John Darch, Harold Adams, Charlie Bowden, Revd Barker, Jack Matthews, Chris Lethbridge and Chris Clayton.*

Below: *The Warkleigh Bell-ringers, 2002. Left to right, back row: Ron Thorne, Alison Tranckle, Reg Pincombe, David Elworthy, Antony Gillanders; front row: Anne Thorne, Terry Sedwell, Nicholas Gillanders, Siobhan Smith, Colin Hammett.*

Below: *Satterleigh Church.*

Below: *Warkleigh School Prayer Book prize awarded to Alma Snow in 1934.*

Taking away the Warkleigh bells to be retuned, 1975.

by a band of local ringers under their captain, at the time of writing, Reg Pincombe. As such, it remains one of very few local towers rung by a team from within the local parishes.

While my father was a ringer, he kept a diary and there follow a few extracts:

I started to ring at Warkleigh in 1960 when Revd Barker was vicar, ringers were C. Bowden, R. Bater, H. Adams, J. Darch, C. Clayton, R. Darch.

Warkleigh ringers' first outing to Weymouth on Aug 3rd 1968. Coach left Chittlehamholt at 8a.m. First stop Colyton, Devon. Tenor 24cwt. We did not do very well on this peal. On to Weymouth for the day. Next stop in the evening at Upwey, Dorset. Tenor 9cwt. A very nice light peal which we rang quite well. Ringers C. Lethbridge, J. Darch, D. Elworthy, R. Bater, T. Sedwell, R. Pincombe, A. Parker, K. Barrow, R. Darch. Coach 13s.6d. per head. 36 adults 5 children. Stopped at Taunton for 1 hour for evening meal.

1968 – This winter an effort has been made to start a ladies team of ringers. So far we have Lorna Eastman, Jane Clayton, Marion Tucker, Pat Lock and Barbara Williams. We also have two new male recruits, A. Parker and B. Scrivener.

Nov 12th 1971 at Chittlehamholt Village Hall social and dance. Music supplied by the Ferguson Trio in aid of bell ropes. Event well attended. Many donations. Cost of band £10.50s.

Aug 5th 1975 – Annual outing to Looe with Steve Geens Coaches of South Molton. Rings made at Calstock, South Brent – South Brent very good. Ringers C. Lethbridge, L. Eastman, T. Sedwell, D. Elworthy, R. Bater, H. Petherick, B. Scrivener, D. Carter, A. Sage, H. Pidler.

An incident occurred during 1975 when the church bells were being removed from Warkleigh Church tower in order to be retuned. Captain Underwood, who at the time was watching with his wife from Church Cottage, saw this event unravel and relays the following story:

On a Saturday morning in the summer of 1975, I recall standing outside Church Cottage where we were living at the time, and saw the arrival of a lorry from an Exeter bell-foundry firm which had come to remove the bells from the tower at Warkleigh. They soon set to work and rigged up their equipment to get the bells down, and my wife and I came out of our cottage and watched with great interest what was going on. We could see they had put a big heavy wooden spar projecting from the window of the tower where the bells were housed and at the end of that was a pulley wheel. It was obvious that the bells were to be brought down to the ground in this manner. The men who came were obviously well-used to their type of work. Down on the ground was a winch – a revolving drum mounted on a stand at each end with a long wire wound around and a handle on each end – which allowed two

men to lower the bells. The work got under way and one of the bells appeared suspended at the tower window. Another pulley drew it out to the end of the spar into a position where it could be lowered to the ground. I recall that my wife and I were standing beside Mr Chris Lethbridge, the tower captain, who was generally present when these sorts of events were going on, for he was responsible for the church bells in the parish. The bell was hauled out by ropes through the end of the spar preparatory to being lowered down to the ground, and this operation commenced and the bell was lowered a few feet. Slowly the wire unrolled from the winch. The unwinding process was controlled by the brake and gradually the bell came down and then all of a sudden, there was a snap and, to our horror, the bell started to descend at a great rate. It wasn't a free fall but the bell was falling quite rapidly and the wire on the winch was peeling off the drum very quickly. The handles were whirling around and no one could touch them as they would break their arm. It seems that the cause of the accident was that the brake mechanism failed at the critical moment. However, it appeared that the right man was present as Mr Lethbridge leapt forward and grabbed a long spar of wood, eight or ten feet in length, and jammed it underneath the rotating drum, levering up on it to apply a braking action. He did this very effectively, pushing with all his force upwards to put more and more pressure on the drum, and slowly he brought the bell to a halt a foot or two from the ground. I think this was a remarkable thing to have happened and very fortunate indeed that Mr Lethbridge was standing there and knew exactly what to do. I'm sure the vicar and all concerned were very grateful to him for his quick thinking and ability.

An article follows from the *North Devon Journal* 1975, when the bells had been re-hung after tuning.

Bell-ringers set their sights on Warkleigh
Teams of ringers will converge on Warkleigh on Friday night to try out the bells of the parish church now rehung after tuning. The six-bell peal has some of the oldest bells in the country and has been in Whitechapel, London since August. The bells have been rehung on a new steel frame that, for the first time, will group them in a cluster. Previously the 2nd had been hung on its own. But there can be no more recasting for the three oldies. 'We would not be allowed to recast them because of their age and historic value,' said Mr Lethbridge the ringers' captain.

A poem follows about the bells in the parish, including the Warkleigh bells. It is thought to have been written by Revd Dampier Bennett in the 1970s:

A six o'clock from Warkleigh on the Hill,
The bells rang out across to Chittlehamholt.
Eight Chittlehampton bells pealed from the North,
High Bickington's sweet echo crossed the vale.
So gently broke the triple waves of sound,
On a still evening of enormous light,

That, when they ceased, I almost seemed to hear
From open church doors, village voluntaries.
A mile and more away the bells had called
From Hieritha, Mary and St John,
Come ye to church, my people, come and pray.
From changes back to rounds then tenors knoll,
The organ sounds old hundredth and we stand
To sing the lord we serve with cheerful voice.

Notes on the Warkleigh ringers from the *Parish Magazine*:

1997
On 4 September 1997, two half-muffled peals were rung in memory of Diana, Princess of Wales, who was killed in a car crash in Paris.

September 1999
The Warkleigh ringers won the shield and first certificate in class B at the Iddesleigh ringing festival on 25 September. The team, all members of our regular Sunday service band, were Anne Thorne, Alison Tranckle, Ron Thorne, David Elworthy, Colin Hammett and Reg Pincombe.

January 2000
Our new recruits all continue to make excellent progress and we look forward to the time when they will be able to join us for service ringing. Siobhan Smith, Anthony Gillanders and Nicholas Gillanders recently got their blue badges for competence and safety in basic ringing skills.

October 2000
Congratulations to Reg Pincombe who rang in his first quarter peal, 1,260 changes of plain BoB Doubles on 23 August. This was done to welcome Benjamin Steven Tranckle, Alison and Steve's recently born son. Although longer than our usual call change peal, and a different style, it was a very good quarter. The ringers were Anne Thorne 1, Dave Wilford (conductor) 2, Mandy Spearing 3, Ron Thorne 4, Terry Spearing 5, Reg Pincombe 6, with hindsight we should have rung a peal of 60 on thirds to complete the evening.

'The Warkleigh Bells', by the late George R. Dampier Bennett:

No 1   The newest, added in 1929 by Mears and Stainbank, Whitechapel.
No 2   Cast by Mears and Stainbank, the Whitechapel Foundry, London.
No 3   Cast by Mears and Stainbank, the Whitechapel Foundry, London.
No 4   Medieval bell, recast in 1695 by John Stadler of Chulmleigh.
No 5   Medieval bell, cast by Robert Norton of Exeter. Bears Latin inscription 'Misteriis sacris repleat nos' (DCA Johannis – 'may John's doctrine fill

us with holy mysteries' (St John I:I))
No 6   The tenor (10 cwt) medieval bell, cast by a Bristol founder in the fifteenth century. Bears Latin inscription 'Sancte Leo ora pro nobis' (St Leo pray for us) (Probably Leo the Great, Pope from 440AD).

An article on Warkleigh bells by Ron Thorne:

Warkleigh has a ring of six bells, hung in a steel frame by Fidler in 1975. This replaced a five-bell frame made by Stokes in 1889 with the second bell of the ring hung above this frame on two RSJs in 1929 by W. Aggett and Sons of Chagford. At this time, the ring was augmented from five to six bells. In the inventory of 1553 three bells are listed. The tenor bell was probably cast by William Warwick of Bristol between 1450 and 1480. The fifth bell of the ring is believed to have been cast by Robert Norton around 1430. The fourth bell by John Stradler dates to 1695. The three smaller bells were cast by Mears and Stainbank at Whitechapel in 1901 and 1929, completing the present ring of six bells and providing an interesting blend of old and new. The final augmentation was made possible by subscription for the whole parish and many friends. In its recent history, the tower was closely associated with Chris Lethbridge, who as well as teaching many people to ring, was instrumental in seeing through the 1975 re-hanging.

Satterleigh Church

There has probably been a church in Satterleigh since Saxon times, though it was first mentioned in 1288. The church of St Peter is a small structure consisting of a nave, chancel, south porch and a wooden bell cote on the western gable. It is built of local rubble with a modern slate roof. The font is fifteenth century and very similar to the one at Warkleigh. There is a richly carved ceiling of somewhat later date over the site of the rood, west of the screen. The screen itself has gone but the tympanum over it remains, painted in late-Georgian times with the Lord's Prayer and the Creed. The Ten Commandments are inscribed on large boards either side of the east window. The glass in this window was given as a memorial to James Gould of Knapp, Northam, patron of the living, and Maria Marianne his wife. They both died in 1857. The window itself was, like all the others in the church, renewed in the mid-nineteenth century.

The door is original, and is in its original wooden frame. Some of the bench ends carved with simple designs also date from the fifteenth century. Others in the chancel were carved to match them under the direction of Miss Salome Thorold of Warkleigh House, who is commemorated by a small brass plate affixed to one of the benches. The altar rails are Victorian but, together with the benches north and south, no doubt preserve the plan of the Restoration chancel. (Other examples preserving the old fittings may be seen at

Mr Bill Lewis, who gave this organ to Satterleigh Church. See notes on the Satterleigh harmonium.

Rosy Neil, watched by her sister Emily, plays the old Satterleigh Church harmonium at their home at Hillbrown, Chittlehamholt.

Cruwys Morchard and in St Martin's, Exeter – also in the care of the Churches Conservation Trust.)

On the north wall of the nave is a text which appears to be eighteenth century; and hat pegs of the same period are a happy reminder of the dignity of a past age. The reading desk and pulpit (which still has its sounding board) are seventeenth to eighteenth century. The royal arms over the door, dated 1726, are those which were in use from the accession of George I in 1714 until 1801, when the arms of France were discontinued by George III. They are (1st) England impaling Scotland, (2nd) France, (3rd) Ireland and (4th) Hanover.

On the north wall of the chancel is a mural tablet to Henry Byne of Satterleigh, who died in 1821. The arms are Byne impaling Thomas quartering Melhuish. The property came to Byne through his wife Mary Frances Thomas (daughter of Thomas of Drake's Place, Somerset), through the widow of her uncle William Melhuish. The chalice, paten and flagon formerly belonging to the church are inscribed: 'The gift of William Melhuish Esq. and Mary his wife to Satterleigh Parish 1766.' He died in 1770. The stone which once formed the entrance to his vault is fixed to the south wall of the church. A memorial to Robert Hacche Esq. (1699), now also fixed to the south wall, was formerly in the chancel floor. It bears the demi-lions of this ancient and widespread family.

There were also formerly memorials to Lewis Hacche gent., 1737, and to Robert Hacche, the younger gent., 1724. No doubt these, like many elsewhere, disappeared in a Victorian restoration, perhaps in 1852 when the chancel was repaired. In his will Lewis Hacche, minister of the Gospel (d.1673) desired to be buried 'in the little window of the chancel of Satterley Church'. In the churchyard is the base as well as a small part of the shaft of an ancient cross. The wooden lych-gate is a memorial to those who lost their lives in the First World War.

The bell-frame appears to date from the period around 1600. The bells are now almost unique in the county in still being fitted with the half-wheels which went out of fashion three centuries ago, when the whole wheel and its consequent half-pull made change-ringing possible. The first bell bears the inscription 'IOHNTHORN CH:WARDEN 1722' and was cast by Evans of Chepstow. The third is inscribed 'IOHN:THORN:GENT:IAMES:HENWOOD: RECTOR:I:C:W:1714' and was cast by John Stadler of Chulmleigh. The second bell is uninscribed but is late medieval and is one of the three bells recorded as being in the 'tower' in 1553. They are all very light, the third or tenor weighing only about 2½ cwts.

In March 1996 the church was declared formally redundant and passed into the care of the Churches Conservation Trust. Repairs have been carried out under the direction of the architect Kate Price.

The Satterleigh Harmonium
by Elizabeth Gibson

The little church at Satterleigh became very special to us when we were visiting the Neils at Highbullen and we always attended services whenever we could. In its farmyard setting, with the sheep grazing quietly nearby, time seemed to have stood still in such a peaceful place. Hymns were sung to the wheezing notes of an old harmonium played by Dora Scrivener – the tune which emerged was rather dependent on Dora's footwork. The notes were produced by air, blown through reeds and sometimes these could go a little astray. On one occasion she struck up a different tune to the one the congregation began to sing and she stopped peddling in confusion. Revd Bell gently reassured her with 'No Dora, it's us who have the wrong hymn.' After all, God would not mind and the harmonium's eccentricities were part of the charm of Satterleigh.

One Sunday, early in 1989, I joined the small congregation for evensong and found the harmonium replaced by a modern electric organ which had been given by W.H. (Bill) Lewis from Rose Ash who, until recently, was the organist at High Bickington Church. Mr Lewis' family lived at Chittlehamholt and Satterleigh Barton at one time. In 1989 the new organ was dedicated in Satterleigh Church; the inscription on the organ reads:

In memory of Bessie Nee Webber born at Satterleigh Barton 26th June 1884, this organ presented to St Peter's Church by her son W.H. Lewis (A Mus LCM) of Rose Ash, March 1989.

At the dedication service Mr Lewis treated the congregation to three musical items; the chorale prelude 'Jesus We Are Here' (J.S. Bach), 'An Old Time Tune' (Easthope Martin) and, very appropriately, 'The Finale from the Royal Fireworks' (Handel).

When I learnt that the harmonium was to be sent to a sale and would probably go to America, on a sudden whim I offered to give it a home. I came to an agreement with the churchwardens and on our next visit my husband and I collected it from Satterleigh Barton and brought it back to Hampshire. For ten years it stood in our dining-room and provided a great attraction, particularly at Christmas when the village carol singers came. Last year, when the time came for us to move house, it seemed right that the Satterleigh harmonium should return to its own corner of the country. We were delighted when

Jane and Martin Neil of Hillbrow, Chittlehamholt, agreed to have it and that it is now being played by their daughters Emily and Rosy.

Meethe Chapel

Meethe Chapel, at the bottom of Satterleigh Hill in the parish of Satterleigh, was opened on 30 September 1925. The ground for the site of the building was given by Mr Hubert Lionel Elworthy of Satterleigh Barton, and the stone was taken from the nearby Satterleigh Quarry. The first wedding in the chapel took place on 18 September 1951, when John Harris and Maggie Ley got married. Due to falling numbers and repair costs, the chapel had its last service on 19 December 1982, with the last preacher being Harice Pickard. The chapel was sold in 1984 and was then turned into a private dwelling.

Dot Ayre (née Bowden) remembers attending this chapel when it was opened in 1925. She says:

... there was always something doing down there; Sunday school and chapel Sunday afternoons and evenings. On Sundays when I was small, I used to go to Satterleigh Church in the morning, Meethe Chapel school in the afternoon, followed by a service, and very often Satterleigh Church again in the night. That was your Sunday. There was a stable next to Meethe Chapel and I

The opening of Meethe Chapel on 30 September 1925. Left to right, back row: *Percy Robinson, Archie Petherick, William Sing, Frank Seage, George Holland;* second row: *Revd Rickard, Marjorie Elworthy, Nelly Holland, Mary Petherick, Mrs Bendle, Gertie Stoneman, Ethel ? (the flower girl on the day the chapel was opened);* front row: *Emma Seage, Annie Sing, Ethel Stenner, Mrs Rickard, Ellen Stenner, Lucy Bowden, Ann Sing;* two girls: *Joyce Petherick, ?.*

can remember Mr Eastman from Capelcombe, King's Nympton, coming to tie up his horse and George Peters coming from Chittlehampton on his bike. I also remember attending Sunday school at the old Meethe Chapel that was situated just down the road on the site where the dwelling known as Meethe Gate now stands and was rented for 6d. per week – my Granny Clatworthy was the first person to live there when it was turned into a house.

Above: *Meethe Chapel outing. Left to right: Annie Sing, Lucy Stoneman, Freda Fewings, Dot Bowden, Kitty Wheaton, Nelly Holland, 1930s.*

Above: *David Elworthy holds the plaque that was removed from Meethe Chapel in 1982 when it was closed. David's family gave the ground on which the chapel was built in 1925.*

Above: *Meethe Sunday school, 1934. Left to right, back row: Elam Herniman, Freda Fewings, Wilson Holland, Jack Fewings, Morley Jones, Cyril Wensley; middle row: Raymond Holland, Edwin Fewings, Novello Fewings, Gwen Luxton, Evelyn Holland, Kenneth Stenner; front row: Donald Herniman, Jean Fewings, May Herniman.*

A preacher outside Meethe Chapel, 1951.

Wedding Gallery

Left: *The wedding of John Harris and Maggie Ley, who were married on 18 September 1951. They were the first couple to be married in Meethe Chapel.*

Above: *The wedding of Willie Sanders and Marion Congram in 1975.*

Above: *The wedding of Peter Evans and Elizabeth Moore, 1969. Left to right: Harry Congram, Greta Herd, Stan Evans, Margery Evans, John Horton, Peter Evans, Elizabeth Evans, Norah Moore, Fred Moore, Elizabeth Moore and Donald Moore.*

Right: *The wedding of Christopher Wright and Lisa Balmbra in 1996. Standing with them is Revd John Bell.*

Wedding Gallery

The wedding of Jessie Kingdon and John Hanson at Chittlehamholt church, thought
to be during the Second World War. The names of the two at the back are not known.
Front row, left to right: *Fred Clarke, ?, John Hanson, Jessie Hanson, Mr Kingdon, ?, Eddy Kingdon.*

The wedding of Norah Congram and Fred Moore in 1945.
Left to right: *Bill Moore, Elizabeth Moore, Doreen Handford, Jack Moore, Fred Moore,*
Norah Moore, Christine Congram, Harry Congram, Rose Congram and Lucy Barkwill.

Wedding Gallery

Left: *The wedding of Kathleen Wright and Owen Ford in 1954.*

Right: *The wedding of Colin Alford and Maureen Bowden at Warkleigh church in 1962.*

Below, left: *The wedding of Dorothy Pincombe and Raymond Holland at Warkleigh church in 1952.*

Left: *The wedding of Terry Sedwell and June Beer at Chittlehamholt church in 1965. Susan Lethbridge is seen giving them a lucky horseshoe.*

Right: *The wedding of Alan Bowen and Marilyn Baghurst at Warkleigh church in 1956.*

Left: *The wedding of Ivor Slee and Barbara Williams in 1984 at Chittlehamholt church. Left to right: Susan Lethbridge (bridesmaid), Barbara and Ivor Slee, Anne Thompson and daughter Erika (bridesmaids).*

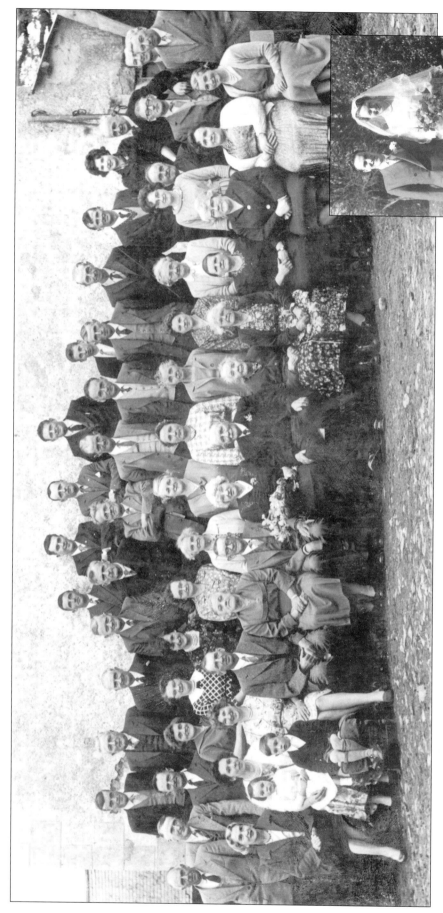

Above: *The golden wedding of Mr and Mrs Jim Thomas of Snydles Farm, Chittlehamholt, c.1965. Left to right, back row: Roy Cheriton, Gordon Cheriton, Reg Matthews, Dudley Middleton; third row: Terrence Ayre, George Ayre, Dick Gill, Reg Heard, Jim Ayre, Jim Sowden, Morley Burnell, Mr Huxtable, Stan Richards, Bill Jones, Terry Sedwell, Sonia Gill, Cecil Pester, George Jones; second row: Cecil Dockings, Bill Matthews, Mr and Mrs Venner, Mrs Middleton, Mrs Huxtable, Joyce Heard, Florrie Congram, Mrs Matthews, Mrs Burnell, Mrs Huxtable, Mrs Richards, Sabina Sedwell, Miss Huxtable, Harold Sedwell, Harry Bowden, Bob Bowden; front row: Mrs Dockings, Mrs Matthews and children, Mr and Mrs Bill Cheriton, Mrs and Mr Reg Cheriton, Florence and Jim Thomas, Mrs Jack Jones, ?, Mrs George Ayre, Mrs Bill Jones, Mrs Rhona Gill, Edith Osmand.*

Right: *The wedding of Chris Lethbridge and Diana Dicker, 19 March 1955.*

Wedding Gallery

*The wedding of Edward John Tucker and May Victoria Stone at Chittlehamholt church on 17 July 1937.
The photo shows them afterwards at the Village Hall. The names of the men on the top row are not known.
Left to right, middle row: Reg Bowden, Jim Clarke (the blacksmith), Wallace Clarke (Jim's son),
Fred Clarke (the blacksmith); front row: Mrs Jim Clarke, Mrs Fred Clarke, Edward Tucker, May Tucker,
Lucy Clarke, Mrs and Mr Fred Love. Fred is seen holding his daughter, Jill.*

*The wedding of Pat Lock and Cyril Jordan at Chittlehamholt church
in 1971. Left to right: Catherine Hill, Robert Hill, Steve Tucker,
Cyril Jordan, Pat Jordan, Phillipa Bennett, Richard Lethbridge.
Behind is Revd George Dampier-Bennett.*

*The wedding of Miss Alma
Snow and Stan Pearce at
Satterleigh church, 1989.*

Above: *Warkleigh Memorial at Cockram Butts Cross. Old stories handed down tell of a man appearing in the dark behind this cross with a glass wheelbarrow.*

Two war memorial scrolls sent from King George V to the family of Harold Pester from Fir Cottage, Chittlehamholt, who was killed during the First World War.

BUCKINGHAM PALACE.

I join with my grateful people in sending you this memorial of a brave life given for others in the Great War.

George R.I.

John (Jack) Congram from Wards, Chittlehamholt, whilst serving in the First World War.

Gv R1

HE whom this scroll commemorates was numbered among those who, at the call of King and Country, left all that was dear to them, endured hardness, faced danger, and finally passed out of the sight of men by the path of duty and self-sacrifice, giving up their own lives that others might live in freedom.

Let those who come after see to it that his name be not forgotten.

A.B. Francis Harold Pester
R.N. Division.

LET US ALWAYS REMEMBER
WITH PRIDE & GRATITUDE

HARRY BATER
HARRY GUARD
FRED LEE
JOHN MANNING
WILLIAM NEWCOMBE
HAROLD PESTER
GEORGE SLEE

THE MEN OF THIS PARISH
WHO DIED FOR ENGLAND
IN THE GREAT WAR.

Chittlehamholt War Memorial sited in the Village Hall.

Chapter 4

WARS

As in every parish up and down the country, the men of Chittlehamholt, Warkleigh and Satterleigh fought during the two world wars, and some didn't return. At the end of this chapter is some information on the men who died, which has been obtained from the War Graves Commission. Additional information came from newspapers, and from Brian Barrow who has carried out extensive research on many parishes in North Devon.

Although Jack Skinner and Elam Hammett came from the main village of Chittlehamholt, they were still in the parish of Warkleigh, and readers will see that their names are recorded on the Warkleigh memorial stone.

There follow a series of extracts taken from the local newspapers:

1st November 1917

The greatest sympathy is extended to Mrs Lee, eldest daughter of Mr and Mrs Wm Clarke, of Whitmore Lodge, Chittlehamholt, on the sad death of her husband, Pte Fred William Lee, who was killed in action on September 20th. His commanding officer, in a very kind letter of condolence to the widow and little boy, wrote in the highest terms of appreciation of Pte Lee's services, particularly noting that he was always among the first to render help to the wounded and to do all in his power to alleviate their pain. A memorial service at the church was largely attended.

16th May 1918

Mr Hammett, of Chittlehamholt, has been informed by the War Office that his son, Pte Elam Hammett, of the Dorset Regiment, with the Egypt Expeditionary Force, was killed on April 9th. A later official notice, however, reported that he was now 'missing believed killed'. In a letter the officer commanding has sent to tell Mrs Hammett of the circumstances, he says that during an attack, Pte Hammett was badly wounded, and that shortly afterwards the section of which he was a member was cut off, and so probably he is now a prisoner.

Harry Bater from Farrs Farm who was killed during the First World War.

March 29th 1917

A memorial service for Harold Pester (105 Royal Naval Division) who was killed recently on active service.

A requiem celebration of the holy communion was held in the Parish Church in memory of the late Francis Harold Pester, who for a number of years, was a chorister in the church. There was a large number of communicants. At Matins the vicar (the Revd C.H. Garland) read himself in. In the afternoon there was a memorial service. The vicar, taking as his text 'All souls are mine', made sympathetic allusion to the deceased, and spoke of his association with the parish. Revd Garland said Harold had lived nobly and died bravely, and, as testifying to the regard in which he was held by his officers and comrades, he had seen a letter from his officers, speaking of him in the highest terms and saying how much he was missed by all.

Francis Harold Pester

Number: R/105. Howe Battalion. Able Seaman.
Enrolled: RND 24/8/16.
Previous service: Army Reserve.
Entered: 12/12/15. Called up: 24/8/16.
Born: 29/8/92 Chittlehamholt, Devon.
Address: Fir House, Chittlehamholt, Devon.
Height: 5'6". Chest: M34". Weight: 140lb.
Complexion: Fresh. Hair: Black. Eyes: Blue.
Small scar on forehead. 4 vacc left.
Civil occupation: Carpenter apprentice.
Religion: C of E.
Swim: No.
Next of Kin: Father John F. Pester, Fir House.

19th September 1918

Mrs Manning, of Head Barton, Chittlehamholt, has received a letter from her son, Sergt J. Manning, saying he is slightly wounded and at a convalescent depot at Rouen, France.

Left: *John Snow serving in the Royal Navy during the Second World War.*

Right: *Ken Snow in the RAF during the Second World War.*

Below: *Raymond Snow, who was killed during the Second World War.*

Right: *A message sent from Buckingham Palace to sympathise with Mrs Snow of Greendown after hearing of her son's death.*

BUCKINGHAM PALACE

The Queen and I offer you our heartfelt sympathy in your great sorrow.

We pray that your country's gratitude for a life so nobly given in its service may bring you some measure of consolation.

George R.I

Mrs. E. Snow

Above: *Raymond Snow's memorial.*

Right: *The telegram sent to Mrs Snow of Greendown to inform her that her son Raymond had been killed on active service during the Second World War.*

POST OFFICE TELEGRAM

Celebration for the Return of the Chittlehamholt Soldiers in 1919

The parish meetings during 1919 give us an idea of the celebrations proposed on the return of the lucky soldiers. Mr T.R. Martin proposed, and Revd C.H. Garland seconded, that Warkleigh parish be asked to join with Chittlehamholt parish in a peace celebration. Mr J. Thomas stated his unwillingness to support this and proposed that the celebration be confined to Chittlehamholt. After some discussion Mr Martin withdrew his proposition and that of Mr J. Thomas proposed. It was then proposed that a committee of ladies comprising of Mrs Fred Clarke, Mrs Burgess and Miss Gladys Pester be asked to carry out a house-to-house collection. Also a sports committee was formed. Mr W. Congram kindly offered his adjoining field and the north end of the vicarage garden for all purposes. Also a dance was proposed to be held in the schoolroom.

The sum of money from the collection amounted to £14 with a promise of more to come. It was proposed that the sum of £12 be granted to the ladies' committee for the purpose of providing a dinner for the returned soldiers and a free tea for the whole parish. It was resolved on the motion of Mr Martin and seconded by Mr W. Congram that this committee ask the soldiers' knitting committee if they were willing to provide, from the balance they had in hand, a memento to be given to each of the men who had served from this parish. The vicar announced that he had arranged for two services to be held on the day of the peace celebration in Holy Eucharist; at 8a.m., and the special peace service at 3p.m.

At a meeting on 6 August 1919, Mr Harris produced a specimen photo frame he considered to be a suitable present and suggested that the name of the soldier along with the dates of declaration of war and signing of the Armistice should be engraved thereon. The chairman reported that the number of men who had served from the parish was 27, and that the available funds were sufficient to provide for a present for each man. It was resolved that Mrs Congram, Mrs Garland, Mrs Farr and Mrs Harris form a committee to purchase suitable presents and to make all arrangements for their presentation. It was also resolved that a vote of thanks be passed to Mr and Mrs Farr for their kindness in entertaining soldiers from this parish on the day of the peace celebration.

The question of the erection of a memorial in the village to those members of the parish who had fallen in the First World War was raised. It was agreed that in respect to the parents and relations a plain stone on a simple cross would be erected on a piece of ground near the Square or elsewhere. The chairman reported that from his investigations the erection of a suitable memorial would cost about £100 and reported that promises of subscriptions amounted to £29, this sum being insufficient to provide a large memorial. It was decided to erect a tablet on the outside wall of the school building. It was agreed that Mr J. Manning's name should be added to the memorial tablet, he having recently died in hospital of illness arising out of his military service. The drawing of the tablet was open to public inspection and it would take four months to complete. The tablet was eventually made – in cast bronze with relief lettering and framed in Forest of Dean stone – by J. Wippell & Co., Exeter. Mr W. Johns of the village fixed the tablet onto the school wall, and Mr J.F. Pester, also of the village, made an oak shelf for it. Revd Monro unveiled the War Memorial on 3 September 1921, after a service outside the schoolroom. After the school was closed in 1948, the memorial was removed and fixed onto the wall of the Village Hall, until, in 1981, when the old hall was pulled down and a new one erected in its place, the tablet was removed once more and now remains inside the present hall.

The following letter, courtesy of Mrs Margaret Bolt, gives information on Herbert Way, who served in and came through the First World War:

Herbert Way was born at Rags Cottage [now Shortridge Cottage], Warkleigh, on 24.2.1877. He was the sixth of ten children born to George and Jane Way. He would have been 37 in 1914.

I am not sure why he joined the N.Z. Army, but he was always saying what a wonderful country it was – even greener than England, and so much more space. He was wounded in the Dardenelles, and had a very pink artificial leg [fixed] from above the knee.

For many years he lodged with a Mr and Mrs Cockram at Portland Street, Exeter, until his last illness, when he came to live with his sister (Alice) Maud Eastman at Hacknell, Burrington.

I remember him as being able to walk very fast – especially on the way to a pub! – and having a fiery temper; the family nickname for him was 'Dancer'.

He was my Great Uncle.

Herbert Way died on 5 December 1951. His grave states that he was a veteran of the 'Great War, Private 10/1103 of the NZ Wellington Regt.'

Further extracts from the *Parish Magazine* follow:

3/1/1918

Quartermaster-Sergeant W.H. Mortimer, eldest son of Mr S. Mortimer of Warkleigh Barton, Umberleigh, has been offered and accepted a commission in the Dorsetshire Yeomanry. He is well known in agricultural circles throughout North Devon. He has seen considerable active service, having enlisted in The Imperial Yeomanry and served throughout the Boer

War, when he received a commission and was mentioned in dispatches. At the outbreak of the present war, Quarter-Sergt Mortimer enlisted in the Royal North Devon Hussars as a Private, and has served in the Gallipoli and Egyptian campaigns. In the course of which he has again been mentioned in dispatches. He is at present taking part in the action in Palestine.

7/3/1918

Lieut W.H. Mortimer, son of Mr S. Mortimer, of Warkleigh, has been promoted to Captain and Adjutant. He was formally Quatermaster-Sergeant in the Royal North Devon Hussars, and on receiving his commission was posted to the Dorset Yeomanry. Captain Mortimer is now serving in Palestine.

Captain W.H. Mortimer, eldest son of Mr S. Mortimer of Warkleigh, has been promoted to Staff Captain of the 12th Cavalry Brigade. Staff Captain Mortimer served through the Boer War with the Yeomanry, and went through the Great War – first with the Royal North Devon Hussars and afterwards with the Dorset Yeomany. He has latterly been serving with the Egyptian Expeditionary Force.

7/4/1921

Major W.H. Mortimer, Garrison Adjutant at Sarona, Palestine, died suddenly from heart failure in Palestine on February 21st. The Colonel's letter which announced the death said the deceased was loved by everyone, and was a very popular person. The deceased officer was a member of an old and esteemed North Devon family, being a native of Warkleigh.

William Owen was a native of Westbourne Grove, London. He was the son of William Price Owen and Lillie M. Owen (stepmother), of Watertown, and was the husband of Ellen Louise Owen. He is commemorated at Ypres (Menin Gate) Memorial, Ieper, West-Vlaanderen, Belgium, panel number 24–26–28–30.

Pte Owen is also commemorated on the granite cross at Cockrams Cross, Warkleigh, and a memorial is carved on a wooden board and mounted under the roof of the lych-gate to the church at Satterleigh.

The plaque in Satterleigh church reads:

In proud memory of William Price Owen. Private 72nd. Seaforth Highlanders of Canada, eldest son of William Owen Esq. of Watertown and London who laid down his life in the Great War at the second battle of Ypres, April 22nd–23rd 1915. Aged 35 years.
A gallant, brave and courageous life crowned with a soldier's death.

Alfred Somerville died in April 1917, and the following appeared in the Parish Magazine:

19/4/1917

Much sympathy is felt in the parish with the relatives of Alfred Somerville in his death. Six weeks before having attained the age of 18 he was called up for training at Swindon. There he fell ill, and died in hospital. During the short time he was there he won the regard of his comrades, who sent a wreath, with the inscription; – 'With deep sympathy, from the officers, non-commissioned officers, and men.' Sympathetic reference was made by the rector in his sermon.

November 18th 1927
CHITTLEHAMHOLT

On Armistice Day the usual service was held at the War Memorial, conducted by the Revd H.G. James (Vicar) who gave an address. A wreath of poppies, purchased with special collections at the Church and Chapel, was laid at the base of the Memorial by Mrs Pester. The hymn, 'O God, our help in ages past', was sung to the accompaniment of the violins played by Messrs W. and R. Heard. The sale of poppies was carried out by Mesdames Miller and Handford and Miss R. Pester. By the invitation of Lt-Col H.G. Leahy, OBE, the ex-servicemen of the parish were hospitably entertained at the Manor House to supper. A pleasant social evening followed. On Sunday a large number attended Divine service at St John Baptist's Church, including the ex-servicemen. The lessons were read by Lt-Col H.G. Leahy. An appropriate sermon was preached by the Vicar. After the service the ex-servicemen were individually introduced to General Sir Arthur Gay of Lapford who gave a short address.

Ken Snow talks of the war years when he spent time with his relatives at Hurstone Farm before moving to Greendown Cottage:

While we were living in Surrey, Mum and Dad and my two older brothers, Raymond and John [and I] used to regularly come to Hurstone Farm, Warkleigh, to see one set of relatives for a week, and then go on to Furze, Chittlehampton, to see other relatives. The week before the Second World War was declared, we were staying at Hurstone Farm. My older brother John was in the Navy Sea Scouts and was called up while we were down here. Mum and Dad went back to Surrey while Raymond and I were left at Hurstone.

Raymond got a job working for Charley Smith at Narracott Farm, Umberleigh, before being called up aged 18. He was killed aged 19.

I went to Warkleigh School for nearly 12 months and then, at the beginning of August 1940, Mum and Dad came down and stayed for a fortnight at Hurstone before we all returned to Surrey. My father built an air-raid shelter in the garden and we slept in it every night from the third week in August 1940 *until 14 December 1940. Some nights land-mines were dropped close by and it felt as though the shelter was going to cave in. Eventually, having had enough of the bombing, we all returned to Hurstone for a month. While we were there, Jack Pincombe from Pugsley let us live at Greendown Cottage which the Clinton estate owned. While I was spending my apprenticeship as a carpenter at Murch Bros in Umberleigh I was told the sad news of my brother Raymond's death. Fred Beer came into the workshop and said:*

Ken, I've got some sad news. Norman Smith *[the postmaster of Chittlehampton Post Office]* has just phoned up to say he's sending old John Gill over to your Mother *[at Greendown Cottage, Warkleigh]* with a telegram, so you better get over and see if you can get there before him.

The route John Gill took was from Chittlehampton up Winson Hill, Hudscott Plain, Four White Gates, and down Shilstone Hill, and I was coming down Drybridge Hill to the entrance as he was pushing his bike past Greendown Farm entrance, so I was able to take [the telegram] off him. Although Greendown is in Warkleigh parish, the Chittlehampton postmen used to deliver there and they still do today.

There follows a letter from Raymond Snow to his mother while he was serving in the war:

R.H. Snow
388117
HMLCT513
C/o GPO
London

Mon 30th Oct 1944

Dear Mother
Just a few lines hoping that this letter finds you all in the best of health, as it leaves me at the moment. Have you heard from John yet, as I have not. I would like his address so that I can send him a Xmas card. Has Ken been called up yet? I can't tell you where I am, but there is plenty of fruit here and the weather is about the same as when we were in England. I wish I could be home for Xmas to sample your elderberry wine.
How is everybody at Deason Court and Hurstone?
Well, Mother, I'll close now, as I must be careful what I say. So cheers, all the very best, keep smiling. My love to you all,
your son
Raymond xxxxx

Listed in the Parish Church in Satterleigh, those Satterleigh and Warkleigh parishioners and near relatives who answered the call of King and country in the First World War:

H.E. Baker	Royal Field Artillery	R. Squire	Royal Marines
J. Simmons	Army Service Corps	R. Hammett	Royal Flying Corps
E. Boucher	3rd Devons	J. Symons	North Devon Hussars
W. Simmons	Army Service Corps	C.W. Harris	6th Devons
W. Boucher	3rd Devons	A. Way	North Devon Hussars
J. Sing	Royal Marines	S. Harris	Royal Flying Corps
F. Boundy	Middlesex Regt	F. Westacott	3rd Devons
P.J. Skinner	Middlesex Regt	W.J. Harris	Royal Marine Artillery
R. Clatworthy	Royal Field Artillery	E. Herniman	North Devon Hussars
W.J. Skinner	6th Devons	W. Herniman	North Devon Hussars
W. Dockings	Royal Marines	F. Mears	3rd Devons
J. Smith	6th Devons	H. Moore	4th Devons
J.I. Elston	Army Ordnance Corps	W.H. Mortimer	North Devon Hussars
W. Smith	Army Service Corps	W.P. Owen	16th Canadian Highlanders
W. Guard	Royal Horse Guards	H.L. Owen MC	Machine Gun Corps
E. Snow	3rd Devons	W.L. Owen DSO MC	Queen's Own W Surrey
H. Gully	HMS Seagull	H.J.S. Owen	National Service
A.J. Somerville	National Service	E.J. Parkhouse	4th Devons
J. Gully	Home Defence	A.G. Shapland	1st Devons
H.J. Squire	1st Devons	C. Shapland	6th Devons
E.C. Hammett	Gloucester Regt	H. Simmons	13th Hussars

Above: *Bill Heard from Chittlehamholt was killed after the Second World War in an aeroplane accident.*

Right: *William (Bill) Bowden's Home Guard certificate.*

Right: *Wilson Holland standing outside Hilltown Farm when he was in the Home Guard.*

Above: *The Congram family during the Second World War, photographed at Wards Farm, Chittlehamholt.*
Left to right: *Raymond serving in the Tank Corps, Christine and Frank Congram and Harold Congram in the Chittlehamholt Home Guard.*

In the years when our Country was in mortal danger
William Albert Bowden
who served in the 6ᵗʰ Devonshire B.H.G. gave generously of his time and powers to make himself ready for her defence by force of arms and with his life if need be.

George R.I.

THE HOME GUARD
26 Dec 1944

Left: *Evacuee children at Butlers.*
Left to right: *Fred Moore, Peter Nicholls, Alfie Nicholls, and the Ready brothers.*

Bill Heard

Bill Heard was a Flight Lieutenant in the fleet air arms during the Second World War. He went right through the war and then took a commission to train pilots, being transferred to Singapore. On manoeuvres, his engine packed up. A parked transport plane blocked the runway and prevented him from landing and, after doing another circuit, the plane crashed. Bill's cousin, also called Bill Heard, was the local builder and, later, the postman/postmaster.

Raymond Congram

An article follows, which was written by Raymond Congram, who was brought up at Wards Farm, Chittlehamholt, and served in the Tank Corps during the Second World War:

I joined the Army in August 1942, reporting to a basic training camp at Bodmin, Cornwall. After six weeks, I went to Farnborough to begin training as a tank crew member, qualifying as a driver gunner. I was posted to a service unit – the Second Battalion Northamptonshire Yeomanry – in 1943 for training on the type of terrain we could expect on the Normandy landing. Sailing to Normandy on the second day of the D-Day landings, we were soon in action. We lost my first tank and my good friend. My unit suffered such heavy losses in this action that we were disbanded and the remainder of the men posted to other tank units who had also suffered heavy losses. I was posted to the 8th King's Royal Irish Hussars and saw action with them in France, Belgium, Holland and into Germany, where I lost my second tank, fortunately without loss of life. I was promoted to Sergeant and returned to England in 1946 to become a staff instructor to the newly formed Territorial Army based in York and Leeds where I ended my military career in late 1949.

Vincent Pester

Vincent Pester was brought up at Fir Cottage, Chittlehamholt, and served in the Second World War under the RAF Fighter Command as a mechanic.

He worked on the famous spitfire, fitting the Rolls Royce engines. The factory on the Thames estuary was bombed out twice when Hitler turned his attention to the fighter planes after so many German bombers were shot down over London. Vincent went to work on a fighter station where Douglas Bader was the commander. Vincent was the only mechanic to touch the engine of Bader's aircraft as he said, 'Pester, I get in some tight corners, and sometimes I've got to get maximum power and you're the only man I can rely on to do it.' Douglas Bader was a pilot who had lost both legs in a flying accident in 1931, and who got shot down over enemy territory and was taken prisoner of war. When parachuting, he buckled his tin legs and some more had to be parachuted in for him which he then used to escape and get back to England. Just before the D-Day landings,

Vincent was seconded to the American Air Force to service the engines of the flying fortress bombers.

The Home Guard

The Home Guard in Chittlehamholt village was made up of the men of Chittlehamholt, Warkleigh and Satterleigh. There were no group photographs taken, but individual shots have been found. My grandfather, the late Edward Dicker, who fought in the First World War, became a sergeant in the group. There follow memories from Wilson Holland, Raymond Ayre, Bill Bowden and Harold Congram. We shall begin with the memories of Harold Congram, as he talks about his time in the Home Guard:

Before the Home Guard was properly formed we were known as the Local Defence Volunteers with just an armband to note that we were being trained as a guerrilla force. We were about 30 strong and we had weekly get-togethers in the Village Hall – usually on Tuesday nights – for weapon training and arms drills. Our officers were Captain Hemms, who was an ex-tank officer, who unfortunately died of cancer before the war was over, and Colonel Wardell, who was head of the whole operation. The training officer was Sgt Major Tommy Rice. He was a good drill man, but if you stepped on his toes you'd better look out.

For some of our training we went to King's Nympton, where there was a searchlight battalion (the Oxford and Boxlight Infantry), and they used to provide a lorry to take us. We also used to do a lot of training in the Village Hall at Chittlehamholt.

I was a Corporal, and at one time I was in charge of the Browning machine-gun section. Sgt Edward Dicker was in charge of what they called the Northover team section which consisted of mortar attack devices with bottles filled with phosphorus and petrol with a strip of rubber in them for setting fire to things. You could sling about these bottles of burning material which burnt for quite a while once you lit them. This section was phased out after a while and Mr Dicker took over my Browning machine-gun section. I then went into wireless communication and intelligence with a walkie-talkie outfit provided. For rifle training we used to go to Stone Mill near Chawleigh and we used the old reading room, which now forms part of the dwelling called Coxhaven, for guard duty. At the time we were on duty the property was owned by Eddy Cox, a poultry dealer in the village and an agent for Spillers' Feed of Bristol. He didn't live in it, but used it as a store and had his poultry running about the place; it was a bit of a rats' castle.

From the outside, the horizontal elevation of the building has not changed very much: this part was the original reading room and the bit used for the guard room – where the side elevation stands – was a complete wilderness where Mr Cox's geese would roam, and before this, a shippen stood. My Uncle Aubrey Pester eventually bought the property in the 1980s from Mr Cox and renovated it as we see it today, naming it after Mr Cox (Coxhaven).

There were a couple of us on guard duty each night of the week. We spent the whole night in the old reading room, and after doing our shift we would get some sleep while the others took their turn. On occasions we had all-night exercises against the regular troops and neighbouring Home Guard. One evening, not far from where the Mole meets the Taw, the regular troops had crossed the river and gone into the woods. They infiltrated and got through to their objective. We knew they were there, but couldn't pin them down. They were very well trained and got through that night. We were trained primarily in guerrilla and harassing tactics; breaking up communications, etc. To start off we had British Lee Enfield rifles, but then they were all called in and we had American rifles. They caused a bit of a problem because they were a different size bore; a 300 instead of a 303. They weren't very accurate either. Sometimes we went to Northam Burrows handling live grenades with a ten-second fuse. If the crunch had come, I think we would have made a good account of ourselves.

My father fought in the First World War, in Gallipoli, for a while. He then went back to Egypt, fighting in the Nile Valley where he had a pretty rough time. He was a Corporal in charge of the machine-gun corps, as was my mother's brother, Cecil Pester. Bill Pester was there as well eventually. My father had appendicitis when he was in Egypt and was not fit for active duties so he was drafted to France where he ran a food tent. He stayed in catering until the end of the war.

Before Bill Bowden died in 2002, in his 91st year, he gave me his memories of his time in the Home Guard at Chittlehamholt:

When war broke out, I had to register with the Army, but as I was on the farm they never called me up, so then I joined the Home Guard. It became compulsory to join, providing you were fit.

I remember the night they thought the Germans were going to land; they kept us out all night. Lord Fortescue came to see us and tell us what to do. 'Kill every German you see', he said.

On Sunday afternoons we would practise shooting in Mr Thorne's fields at Holtgate. I had to be on guard duty three nights a week, and had to patrol the roads around Chittlehamholt. We normally went around in twos; I was usually with Wilfred Hancock from 'King's' Satterleigh. If it was a rough night, Sgt Dicker would have us in the Village Hall playing cards. He was the only real soldier amongst us.

One night we all met at King's Nympton Station for an exercise. We had to make a mock attack on Chulmleigh Home Guard by going through the woods and reaching the town at about 7 o'clock in the morning. On one exercise, the searchlight men from Hilltown thought they were going to wipe us out, but it didn't

come off and we managed to put up a fair struggle. After being out all night, Jack Pearce from the shop would give us a meal.

I remember coming home from Home Guard one night in the summer and I heard gunfire. I looked, and there was a German plane being chased by one of ours. Apparently it was brought down at Eggesford Forest, but I don't know if that was ever confirmed. Sometimes we could see German planes following the railway line, making their way to Wales. They managed to get through sometimes.

At the end of the war, all the Home Guard, including those from King's Nympton and Chulmleigh, were taken to a party at Winkleigh.

From the Village Hall minute-book:

War items Oct 29th 1940
On Oct 29th 1940, an application from Capt. Vaughn CC No 2 Company, 6th Battalion Devonshire Regiment H G for use of Chittlehamholt Village Hall for one night each week during the winter, for winter training of the Home Guard, was agreed to by the village hall committee. The fee to be five shillings per night for 2 hours.

The memories of Wilson Holland's time in the Home Guard follow:

There would be four of us on guard duty at night, and we took it in turns, with two being on duty while two were in the old reading room resting. We had to stay close to the Chittlehamholt telephone box in case any messages came through. There was a call one evening to say that a German aircraft had come down and we were to keep a lookout for a prisoner who was on the loose.

We had several mock attacks against other Home Guards. I remember once, King's Nympton platoon attacked us; we heard gunfire below Hills House Farm where a couple of the King's Nympton men were firing, but this turned out to be a decoy and the main part of the troop came from the other side, up through Shortridge Wood. At Hilltown, the searchlight section was manned by regular troops in three Army huts. As I lived close by, they knew me and on a Sunday night I used to walk past them down over the fields on my way to the Warkleigh phonebox to ring up my fiancée, Mabel. One night I walked past and there was a new chap on duty. He didn't realise that I regularly came past on a Sunday night and he stopped me with 'Halt, who goes there?' The following day the sergeant said to my father, 'you'll never know how close your son was to being shot last night.'

I remember the Americans sending over some rifles packed in some grease and a note inside saying 'Here they are, get on with it.' One time we had a day at King's Nympton Station. Alfie Beer, a butcher from King's Nympton, was in charge of the refreshments and had a huge pot of stew cooking for us. King's Nympton,

Chittlehamholt and Chulmleigh were the three platoons that formed the company.

Raymond Ayre's memories:

I was in the Home Guard with my father. Looking back, it seems pretty futile, but there was a time when it looked like the Germans were going to invade and the Home Guard were prepared to go out with their shotguns and get involved. However, that threat of invasion faded and Hitler didn't come.

I remember once, walking out of Clayton Farm after a farm sale of Mr Adams', and all of a sudden I heard machine-gun fire. A Spitfire had flown into the back of a German plane and both planes eventually came down over Beaford Moor. In the evening I went over there and saw both planes – not all those on board survived.

Evacuees

Peter Nicholls, who along with his brother Alfie was evacuated from London to Butlers Farm, Chittlehamholt, during the Second World War, tells of his experiences:

During the beginning of the war my brother Alfred, who was 12 years old, and I, at just five years, were put on a train along with hundreds of other children, all with labels on our coat collars and carrying gas masks. Miss Lewis, a teacher from our school, was in charge of us and stayed for quite a few years.

We came from Canning Town in East London which is close to the Royal Docks and was heavily bombed later in the war. Somehow – I can't remember how – we ended up staying with Mr and Mrs Congram of Butlers Farm with two other evacuees who were also brothers, I think their name was Reading. For various reasons, some evacuees couldn't settle and most of the others went back within a few years. My brother Alfred went back to London when he was 14 to begin an apprentice-ship as a sheet-metal worker. Mum took me back as well so I wouldn't be alone, but after about a month, according to Mum, I wanted to come back to Butlers. The bombing was very bad by this time, so Mum brought me back again and I stayed for another three years on my own until I was about ten.

Mum and Dad would send regular letters and parcels, and came down once a year for a visit. Dad couldn't always get away. I used to be told about two weeks before she was coming, and it was wonderful, but I used to get confused about who my real mum was. Mrs Congram, who I saw all the time, or this other mum, who brought me presents, etc. When Mum and Dad went back to London to carry on their war work in the factories, I used to see them off from Portsmouth Arms Station. I remember the train pulling away and going out of sight and it would be deadly quiet, with only the birds singing, and I would think how lonely I was and wish I was on that train. That's when I used to get

homesick. When I got back to Butlers I would go off into the stables or shed and cry my eyes out. I suppose that's when I knew who my real parents were. It got worse after Alfie went away. But, as time went on, there was plenty to do on the farm and I used to forget about it until the next visit.

Mrs Congram used to take me to Barnstaple now and then on a Friday – I think it was market day – and once we went into Ilfracombe where I got upset because the sand wasn't yellow like in my picture book. The noise of all the people and traffic gave me a headache.

Alfie, being older, was allowed to have a go at more things than me. He would follow Fred Moore, who lived on the farm, around like a sheepdog and was allowed to fire Fred's shotgun now and then, even though it knocked him off his feet. We were taught how to make bows and arrows from certain saplings, and see how far they would go. Fred was always way ahead.

I ended up staying five years at Butlers. Mr and Mrs Harry Congram became my family and I just grew up as part of them. As far as I was concerned, they were my parents, and I called them Mum and Pop. They treated me ever so well.

After a rainstorm, when the River Taw had turned a muddy brown, Pop, his son Bill, and Fred Moore would take us boys fishing for eels. We would dig for worms and thread them on a string which was then made into a bunch and used as bait, held down with lead weights. Once the eels took the bait, the line was pulled up and thrown onto the bank. That's when the fun started by trying to grab the slippery eel before it snaked its way back into the water. They were carried home in a perforated sack and then put into an earthenware basin where salt was poured on them to kill them. They were delicious when fried. I remember once, Alfie wasn't quick enough to get out of the way of the lead weight and it hit him on the head. We made sure it never happened again. He carried the scar for years.

When Alfie went back to London, I started following Fred around, I think I was trying to copy Alfie.

The most fearsome animal in my mind was the bull with the ring through its nose. I kept my distance. As I got older I was allowed to bring the cows in from the fields for milking – much to my mother's horror when she found out! Now and then the other farmers would bring their cows for siring, but in those days when I wanted to know what it was all about, I was told that it was to make little boys ask questions and I used to stamp off in a rage.

My brother got into catching moles and he used to skin them and hang them on the wall to dry out. You used to get more money if they were skinned. I couldn't get the knack of skinning them and when I took over from my brother after he left I used to give the moles to Mr Cox in the village and he would pay me. We also used to snare rabbits as well. (Fred Moore was a very good teacher.)

I remember the harvest was a great time; us kids always used to find something to do. Loads of rabbits would appear from the cornfields as we started harvesting and the five or six dogs that they had on the farm would catch them. Norah Congram, the daughter, used to shout out 'cooee' to the workers when it was meal time and the sound travelled across the valley. It was great seeing the hot tea in the urns being brought out with the pasties, apple pies and the real cream with a cloth spread out wherever we were.

Boxing Day consisted of shooting pigeons and rabbits and I can remember being very tired carrying them home. There were pigs too, but you had to have a permit to kill one during the war and you had to share it out to everyone because of the rations.

I remember an incident when a group of us went scrumping apples on a farm in Warkleigh, I don't know why I went with them because I could have had as many apples as I wanted on the farm. Anyway, to cut a long story short, the farmer came out and we all dispersed and ran into the cornfield and hid, thinking we had got away with it. My heart was pumping and I was so frightened I can feel it to this very day. I started to make my way home and thought I was so clever in going on a big detour back to Butlers. I got back into our own field and I was climbing over the gate when the farmer gave me such a wallop, I think he threw me over the gate. He had followed me all the way back from his farm. When I got inside Mrs Congram said 'you're quiet', and asked me why my ear was so red. I told her I had fallen over. The next day I made excuses not to go to school, but went in the end, and told the others I had got caught. I think one or two others had also. The headmistress called us all out and she said she'd had a complaint from a farmer and she gave us a strap in front of the whole class to make an example of us.

I can remember some American soldiers coming through the village in their jeeps, throwing sweets out to us, and also remember us doing PT in the road outside the school with the girls having to stuff their dresses in their knickers, which they didn't like.

Mostly I can remember staying on the farm when I came home from school. I didn't mix much with the other children in the village because there were enough things to do on the farm. I got on well with Fred Moore, who lived on the farm, and Bill Congram, the son. Fred was courting Bill's sister Norah at the time and to begin with I didn't realise what was going on. When they started going off together in the evening I used to say 'can I come as well?' and Fred would say 'No you cannot.'

I remember being part of the school plays in the Village Hall. I used to stutter a little bit at times and it used to help me. Miss Lewis always used to push me into things.

I was one of the last three or four from Devon to finally go home for good, and I think we all met at Exeter and went home together. Coming back to London was totally alien and frightening to me, seeing the rows and rows of bombed houses. I remember getting lost in my own street, not knowing which house I lived in. I became a nervous wreck, but I had cousins down the road who took me under their wing and

took me to school. There were twice as many children in one classroom than there were in the school at Chittlehamholt. I think there were 18 when I left, and they closed it soon afterwards.

Twenty-three years later I returned to Butlers with my wife and family, and I remember seeing Diana Lethbridge in her garden. I went up to her and asked if the Congrams were still at Butlers, and she replied, 'yes Peter they are.' That really threw me, and I said, 'how do you know me?' and she said 'I used to sit beside you in school.'

When we got nearer to Butlers we could see someone who looked like Gladys Congram leaning on the gate. She looked startled when she saw us and turned around and ran back into the farm. Then suddenly the family started to come out and old Mrs Congram held her arms wide out with a look of astonishment towards our son Steven who was almost ten then. She was saying 'Peter, Peter' and sort of looked around as I spoke to her and then she realised who I was. For a brief moment time had stood still for her because Steven was so like me at that age. As we went indoors, to my astonishment everything was how I had left it. The ornaments in the same place, the big wooden table, even the implements in the sheds were in the same place; it was like I had left yesterday and it seemed like the same cobwebs were still there and each room was the same. I thought going back I'd find things had changed, but Chittlehamholt was still cut off from the world and in its own time.

In conclusion, although I had no choice in what happened to me in the first place, it became a great part of my life, being an evacuee. I have no regrets whatsoever, and I'm certain Alfie would have said the same. Sadly, he died in 1991 and I miss him greatly.

The following memories were gleaned from talking with Jimmy Porter who, in 1941, with his brother Eddy, was evacuated from Dagenham in Essex to Chittlehamholt, staying with Beattie Newcombe (née Lugg) and her mother at Head Post Cottage until 1943:

I was born in Dagenham, which was right in the path of the bombers going up the Thames to London, and consequently Dagenham received a pasting from time to time. That's why we were evacuated, and schooling was erratic due to the raids.

I remember that my seven-year-old brother and I, aged 10½, were taken with hundreds of other children to a station in London and eventually arrived at Portsmouth Arms Station. We were taken to Chittlehamholt village with our name labels around our necks, carrying suitcases and gas masks, and lined up in the village Square. The farmers were all around the Square with their horses and carts and ponies and traps saying 'I'll have that one and those two.' It was just like a cattle market. The billeting officer, Mrs Pollard, came up to us and said that

Beattie Lugg and her mother would take us, so off we went down to Head Post Cottage.

On arrival, we were shown up some steep stairs to a bedroom at the back. Eddy and I slept together in a big double bed and that first night he cried his eyes out – he missed Mum and wanted to go home. I had to cuddle and console him, perhaps we both cried, I don't know. Later in our time there, the window from that bedroom was to become very enlightening; we saw herds of stags, rabbits, badgers, foxes and pheasants, all in the field beyond.

The day after we arrived, Eddy and I went to investigate our new surroundings; we walked down the hill to a lane on the left. This led to Callards Farm, which burnt down many years ago and was never rebuilt. We sat on a five-bar gate and saw two horses grazing. We threw pebbles at their rumps to get them galloping around. Mr Guard the miller from Head Mill, who was the tenant farmer under Squire Tanner and rented Callards for his cattle and sheep, saw us annoying his horses (we later knew them as Acty and Peter) and gave us a good dressing-down and told us never to mistreat animals again. He then showed us around the farm and all the other animals; this was to be the beginning of a close relationship with the Guard family, my interest in farm life, growing up and dealing with nature.

There was a water pump just inside the lane which supplied Head Post Cottage and Callards. The pump needed to be primed before you used it as all sorts would come out, including frogs. This water was collected by us in pitchers and supplied all our needs at the cottage. Our other chores included collecting logs and cutting them up and gathering sticks to make faggots for the fire; all this we obtained from an area we called 'our wood'. We also helped Beattie in her vegetable garden.

Although we were well looked after at Head Post, we spent most of our weekends with the Guard family on the farm at Head Mill. One of my interests there was looking after the free-range chickens and collecting the eggs. All the chickens and pigs were at the mill and the grain used to be brought in and taken to the top of the mill through the hatch and poured into the hopper. It would come down into two big stain grinding wheels and be ground up and cut through another hopper. Eddy and I used to help take the flour to King's Nympton on the horse and cart.

One day I got the shock of my life when a Ministry man came to slaughter a pig. They strung it up on a beam and slit it from top to bottom then let it down; the animal then got up, ran down the yard and collapsed on top of a dung heap. Eddy and I had the job of cleaning out all the entrails over a pump. The skins were given to Mrs Guard who used them for sausages, and they were lovely.

Hay-making time and corn cutting was a marvellous fun time for us at Callards Farm. We would help the men in the fields (perhaps hinder) making haystacks.

We were weaned on scrumpy which everyone drank from earthenware jars. The corn was reaped by hand scythe and sickle and stacked in bundles. Rabbits would run out in all directions, some we would catch and they became the next few dinners. I still remember the delicious stuffed roast rabbit.

I remember the farm had a big barn and in the roof there were owls. There were also rats and I would catch them and cut off their tails. I would set mole traps in the fields and take the animals to Mr Cox in the village; he would give me one penny for a rat tail, threepence for a moleskin and sixpence for an albino mole. I made my pocket money this way. I saved 66 shillings and spent it on Christmas presents on a trip to Barnstaple.

Some children had very unpleasant experiences as evacuees, but I had a very pleasant one. Children who stayed in London during the war survived on rations which they could only get by queueing at shops which weren't bombed. On the farm we ate rabbit pie, chicken on Sundays, blackberry and apple pie and lots of loganberries and blackberries from the hedgerow. Chittlehamholt was like another world to us and apart from the rationing you wouldn't know there was a war going on. I had a better education at Chittlehamholt than I would have had at home because in London all the schools had closed down. I sat the 11-plus exam in the Village Hall and the papers were sent to London, but I never received the results.

At one point Eddy and I were taken to Hudscott Manor, Chittlehampton, which had been turned into a children's hospital. We were told we had scabies; how we got it is unknown but Beattie had to have all her bedding fumigated. We did not go back to Head Post but were re-billeted with a Mr and Mrs Johns who lived at Sunny Mede. Mr Johns had an old Morris 8 car and occasionally he managed to get petrol. They also had two girl evacuees, from Birmingham I believe, and as the Johns were very strict, we were kept totally segregated. At one time we all went to a dance at King's Nympton and Eddy and I were told to walk there as there wasn't room for all of us in the car. On the way home we were allowed to stand each side on the running-board with our arms through the windows to hold on.

By now our mother was staying in the village with our youngest brother Derek who was 18 months old, and Father, a sergeant, who had just been invalided from the Army after Dunkirk, and came to stay for a while. The locals at the Exeter Inn just adored him and wanted him to stay, but he had been offered work with his previous employer who had got us a new house back in Dagenham. So it was back home again to a new school and the children there couldn't understand much of what I said because I had acquired a Devonshire accent. Nevertheless, the schooling I had received in Chittlehamholt put me ahead of the other pupils of my age and I became the school Vice Captain.

My experience as an evacuee in Devon taught me to

appreciate many things and installed a sense of responsibility that has kept me in good stead and remained with me all my life.

July 12th 1945 – An Evacuee Remembers
THANK YOU DEVON

We always thought of you Devon as a holiday dream,
Sandhills and glorious beaches, cut rounds and cream.
But you gave us a harbour of safety that dreadful September,
And the kindness of Devonshire folk we shall always remember.
Children from London bombed city loved life on a farm,
The sights and sound of the seashore far from hurt and alarm.
Others with friends and relations when war was declared,
Found peace in the Devonshire homes willingly shared.
Can we ever repay you Devon, our great debt?
Tho' we must return to our homes, we shall never forget.

Reports about the evacuees from the Chittlehamholt School log-books follow:

June 17th 1940 – *47 Boys have been sent to the village from London with two teachers in charge. A request for more desks to accommodate them [has been] sent to the education office.*

Oct 22nd 1940 – *15 dual desks have been sent from West Ham Education Department as there was not sufficient furniture here to accommodate the evacuee children.*

Feb 24th 1941 – *20 children have been evacuated to the area from the Connaught Road School in Bristol.*

Jan 20th 1941 – *Mr Wilson, one of the West Ham teachers, has been transferred to Warkleigh School.*

Oct 31st 1941 – *Six Plymouth evacuees admitted.*

Nov 20th 1941 – *36 children evacuated from Bristol. Miss Barker, the teacher, came with them.*

May 8th 1945 – *VE Day. School closed owing to announcement on the radio declaring a public holiday.*

Terry Sedwell was evacuated to Chittlehamholt during the Second World War, and is one of those evacuees who remain in the parish today. He lives with his wife June at High Down, Warkleigh. He recalls:

I was born in Barking in Essex in 1931 and I was an only child. When war broke out, I was eight years old and I can remember practising with the gas mask in school and my father building an air-raid shelter in the garden. I think we must have used it

but I can't remember any bombing, I think we more or less evacuated ourselves before the worst of it had started.

Our next-door neighbour used to teach at a place called Westham and part of the school – I think it might have been two or three classes – was evacuated to the Chittlehamholt area. After that, Mother got in contact with her and we evacuated ourselves privately, so to speak, and she got digs for us and we came to Devon. When the war broke out I think I was staying with my Aunty in Sittingborne, Kent, and remember practising with the gas mask there. I think we came to Devon in 1940, 12 months after the war actually started. My mother and grandmother came with me, and my father stayed home. He was working in the Admiralty at the time, his real job was in the head Post Office in London, but he was transferred to the Admiralty, I suppose because of the war. He used to operate the morse code, taking and sending out messages.

I can remember arriving at South Molton Station on the Great Western Railway from Paddington, and we were picked up by car and were posted at Higher Watertown. There were people called Passmore who lived there and we were only allowed to stay there for less than a week because they had a daughter who was getting married at the same time and so they wanted the rooms. We then moved on to Whitmore Lodge with Mrs Lock and I went to Chittlehamholt School from there. We finally moved to Snydles with Mr and Mrs Thomas around 1942–43 and I became involved in the farming. Eventually I got married and started to farm at Beers Farm.

Just before the war ended our house in Barking was bombed. Father happened to be on night work when our house was bombed and when he came home in the morning the house was flat. He was offered temporary accommodation until the house was rebuilt. The only time I went back was in 1946 and I returned to Chittlehamholt after a week. My mother and grandmother returned to our house after it had been rebuilt around 1947. In 1957–58 father sold the house and they all came down to South Molton to live.

During the war I remember the ARP (air-raid precautions) wardens in Chittlehamholt – similar to Mr Hodges, the character in the television series 'Dad's Army' – they were trained for fighting fires and dealing with casualties. If a bomb dropped and a house caught fire they would be trained to deal with it. They had training evenings and I can remember going up there as a casualty and being taken out on a stretcher and bandaged up. They had women in there as well, including Mrs Mackenzie – wife of Captain Mackenzie, one of the head wardens – and several others from the village. The ARP used old stirrup pumps for putting out fires, and they used to stick it in a bucket of water and pump as hard as they could but it wouldn't have put out a big fire. When the war was over there were sports and a big tea behind the chapel.

Mary Turner (née Martin), who was born at Hurstone Farm, Warkleigh, always laughs at the fact that, while children from cities were evacuated to Devon, she was evacuated from Warkleigh!

During the war, a German aircraft being chased by a British plane was forced to lighten its load, and dropped five phosphorus incendiary bombs. Two bombs landed in fields at Deason Farm, one on Warkleigh Barton and two at Hurstone – one of which has never been found. It is thought that this bomb landed in a wet field and sank into the ground so no one knew where to begin looking for it. The other bomb went into the vein of the reserve water supply, giving it a funny after-taste. The Martins were forced to get water from Deason Cottage.

As it wasn't known at the time exactly what type of bombs had fallen, the authorities wouldn't let the Martins stay in the house and the family were evacuated to the farm at Highbullen where Mary's aunt and uncle lived. The menfolk were allowed into Hurstone during the day to look after the stock, but it was a fortnight before the family were allowed back.

Christine Stuckey (née Congram) remembers the arrival of the evacuees during the Second World War in Chittlehamholt:

I remember before the war, there were 32 of us in Chittlehamholt School and that went up to 94 when the evacuees arrived. It did spoil the education of the local children. The evacuees brought two or three teachers with them including Mr Realy and Mr Wilson. To do something to occupy the [suddenly larger] population of children, they started a youth club and that's where I learnt to dance. Mr Realy played the piano and Mr Wilson was a dance teacher.

I don't think we were old enough to understand the seriousness of the war, and all those children being taken away from their parents and not knowing where they were going to go. Anyone that had an empty bedroom in their house was obliged to take some evacuees. We had two boys and they cried the first night, and Mother couldn't find out what was wrong. It turned out that they had promised to look after their sister but they had been parted. That must have been dreadful for them and when the authorities looked into it she was with Mr and Mrs Coles from Cobbaton.

Nuclear War

The biggest threat to us these days would be a nuclear war. Even as far back as 1964, Warkleigh and Satterleigh Parish Council were making plans for such an event and appointed the following committee: Chairman, Mr W. Holland; Vice-chairman, Mr F. Brend; Clerk, Major H. Owen; Post Warden, Brig. F.G.A. Parsons; Billeting Officer, Mr F. Pepper; Farm Warden, Mr H. Elworthy; Morale, Revd A.H. Jones; Special Constable, Mr R. Heard; RDC Representative, Mr W. Hancock; Food Supplies, Mr G. Tipper; Water and Sanitation, Mr A. Bowen; Transport, Mr C. Judd; First Aid, Mrs A.H. Jones; Welfare, Mrs F. Pepper; Patrol Wardens, Messrs G. Snow, H. Snow, A. Gardener, J. Sowden, C. Lethbridge, C. Morgan, Capt. L. Whitty, Miss P. Cole.

Commonwealth War Graves Commission

The table below gives some further detail about just some of those men from the area who were killed in both world wars. All entries have been taken directly from the Commonwealth War Graves Commission.

Commonwealth War Graves Commission: Casualty Details, First and Second World Wars.

Rank:	Private	Additional Information:
Initials:	E.C.	Son of Elam and Annie Hammett of Rose House,
Surname:	HAMMETT	Chittlehamholt, Umberleigh, Devon.
Forenames:	ELAM CHAPPLE	
Unit Text:	2nd/4th Bn.	Cemetery Location Information:
Regiment:	Dorsetshire Regiment	The Jerusalem Memorial stands in Jerusalem War
Service No:	30130	Cemetery, which is 4.5 kilometres north of the walled
Age:	19	city. The cemetery is situated on the neck of land at
Date of Death:	9th April 1918	the north end of the Mount of Olives, to the west of
Commemoration:	JERUSALEM MEMORIAL,	Mount Scopus, close to the the Hyatt Hotel and the
	Israel, Panel 30.	Hadassa Hospital.

Rank:	Gunner	Additional Information:
Initials:	G.	Son of Alex and Annie Slee, of The Village,
Surname:	SLEE	Chittlehamholt, Devon.
Forenames:	GEORGE	
Unit Text:	241st. Siege Bty.	Cemetery Location Information:
Regiment:	Royal Garrison Artillery	Duisans and Etrun are villages in the Department of the
Service No:	82411	Pas-de-Calais, about 9 kilometres west of Arras. The
Age:	29	cemetery lies in Etrun but takes its name from the nearer
Cause of Death:	Died of wounds	village of Duisans. It is one kilometre north of Duisans
Date of Death:	23rd May 1917	on the D339 road off the Route nationale N39 (Arras-St
Commemoration:	DUISANS BRITISH	Pol), in the angle of the Arras Habarcq road and a track
	CEMETERY, ETRUN,	leading to Haute-Avesnes.
	Pas de Calais, France. III. N. 40	

Rank:	Private	Additional Information:
Initials:	H.	Son of Edwin and Sophia Bater, of Farrs Farm,
Surname:	BATER	Chittlehamholt, Chulmleigh, Devon.
Forenames:	HARRY	
Unit Text:	1st Bn.	Cemetery Location Information:
Regiment:	Devonshire Regiment	Gorre is a hamlet 2.5 kilometres north of Beuvry, and
Service No:	30280	4 kilometres east of Bethune. Leave Beuvry on the D72,
Age:	20	cross the railway and then the Canal d'Aire on the way.
Cause of Death:	Died of wounds (gas)	The cemetery is 150 metres from the church in Gorre,
Date of Death:	16th March 1917	to the left of the D72 (Rue de Festubert).
Commemoration:	GORRE BRITISH AND	
	INDIAN CEMETERY,	
	Pas de Calais, France, VII. E. 3.	

Rank:	Private	Date of Death: 15th February 1916.
Initials:	J.	Commemoration: LOOS MEMORIAL,
Surname:	SKINNER	Pas de Calais, France,
Forenames:	JACK	Panel 99 101.
Unit Text:	11th Bn.	
Regiment:	Middlesex Regiment	
Service No:	G/83	Additional Information:
Age:	23	Son of James and Lily May Skinner, of South View,
		Chittlehamholt, Umberleigh, Devon.

Rank:	Driver	Date of Death: 11th September 1918
Initials:	T.H.	Commemoration: CHITTLEHAMHOLT
Surname:	GUARD	(ST JOHN THE BAPTIST)
Forenames:	THOMAS HENRY	CHURCHYARD, Devon,
Unit Text:	'D' Bty. 150th Bde.	United Kingdom, In North part.
Regiment:	Royal Field Artillery	
Service No:	223719	
Age:	24	Additional Information:
Cause of Death:	Died of wounds received in action	Son of John and Annie Guard, of Longwells,
		Chittlehamholt. Born at Court Mills, Yarnscombe.

Rank:	Private	Additional Information:
Initials:	A.G.	Son of John and Margaret Shapland, of Shortridge,
Surname:	SHAPLAND	Warkleigh, Umberleigh, Devon, who had three sons and
Forenames:	ARTHUR GEORGE	four sons-in-law serving in His Majesty's Forces.
Unit Text:	1st Bn.	
Regiment:	Devonshire Regiment	Cemetery Location Information:
Service No:	7872	The Thiepval Memorial will be found on the D73, off
Age:	30	the main Bapaume to Albert road (D929).
Date of Death:	25th July 1916	
Born:	Swansea	Cemetery Visiting Information:
Enlisted:	South Molton	Each year a major ceremony is held at the memorial on
Commemoration:	THIEPVAL MEMORIAL,	1st July.
	Somme, France,	
	Pier and Face 1C.	

Rank:	Sergeant	Additional Information:
Initials:	L.W.	Son of Mary Ann Loveband of 21, St Leonards Rd,
Surname:	LOVEBAND	Exeter, Devon, England, and the late Revd Matthew
Forenames:	LIONEL WILLIAM	Thomas Loveband. Born at Warkleigh Rectory, Devon.
Unit Text:	6th	
Regiment:	Australian Light Horse	Cemetery Location Information:
Service No:	740	The cemetery is approximately 5 kilometres south-west
Age:	29	of the city centre in an area known as Sabara (Arabic
Cause of Death:	Killed in action	for prickly pear).
Date of Death:	27th March 1918	
Commemoration:	DAMASCUS COMMON-	
	WEALTH WAR	
	CEMETERY, Syria, C. 86.	

Rank:	Private	Supplementary notes: Formerly 13649, Hussars.
Initials:	H.	
Surname:	SIMMONS	Additional Information:
Forenames:	HARRY	Son of Mr J. and Mrs S.C. Simmons, of Lower Beers,
Unit Text:	9th Bn.	Warkleigh, Umberleigh, Devon
Regiment:	West Yorkshire Regt (Prince of	
	Wales's Own)	Cemetery Location Information:
Service No:	20052	Mudros is on the island of Lemnos. East Mudros
Age:	22	Military Cemetery is situated on rising ground about a
Cause of Death:	Died of nephritis	kilometre north-east of the village of Mudros next to the
Date of Death:	18th December 1915	Greek Civil Cemetery.
Enlisted:	South Molton	
Commemoration:	EAST MUDROS MILITARY	There is also a memorial carved on a wooden board and
	CEMETERY, Lemnos,	mounted under the roof of the lych-gate to the church at
	Greece, III. E. 146.	Satterleigh.

Rank:	Major	Additional Information:
Initials:	W.H.	Son of Samuel and Ellen Mortimer of Warkleigh,
Surname:	MORTIMER	Umberleigh, Devon.
Forenames:	WILLIAM HENRY	
Awards:	Mentioned in Dispatches	Cemetery Location Information:
Regiment:	Dorset Yeomanry (Queen's Own)	Ramla (formerly Ramleh) is a small town 12 kilometres
Age:	46	south-east of Jaffa.
Cause of Death:	Died of heart disease	
Date of Death:	21st February 1921	
Commemoration:	RAMLEH WAR CEMETERY, Israel, V.26.	

Rank:	Private	Enlisted: Barnstaple
Initials:	A.J.	Residence: Warkleigh
Surname:	SOMERVILLE	
Forenames:	Alfred James	Cemetery information:
Regiment, Corps etc.	Gloucestershire Regiment	Commemorated on the granite cross at Cockrams Cross,
Battalion/etc:	15th (Reserve) Battalion	Warkleigh, also carved on a wooden board mounted
Number:	7/6882	under the roof of the lych-gate to St Peter's Church,
Died Date:	26/03/17	Satterleigh.
Born:	Umberleigh, Devon	

Rank:	Able Seaman	Additional Information:
Initials:	R.H.	Son of John Walter and Edith Violet Snow of
Surname:	SNOW	Greendown, Warkleigh, Devon
Forenames:	RAYMOND HOWARD	
Unit Text:	H.M.L.C.T. 513.	Cemetery Location Information:
Regiment:	Royal Navy	Oostende New Communal Cemetery is located in the
Service No:	P/JX 388117	town of Oostende on the Stuiverstraat, a road leading
Age:	19	from the R31 Elisabethlaan. Travelling towards Brussels
Date of Death:	1st November 1944	on the R31 the Stuiverstraat is located 500 metres after
Commemoration:	OOSTENDE NEW COMMUNAL CEMETERY, Oostende, West-Vlaanderen, Belgium. Plot 9. Row 6. Grave 21.	the junction with N33. The cemetery is located 800 metres along the Stuiverstraat on the right-hand side of the road.
		Cemetery Visiting Information:
		This cemetery is open at all times.

Chapter 5

SCHOOLS

Both Warkleigh and Chittlehamholt had a school until 1948, when they were closed due to falling numbers. Juniors were transferred to Chittlehampton, and the seniors to South Molton. Today it is interesting to note that the juniors from the parishes can go anywhere; King's Nympton, Chittlehampton, or Umberleigh, and the seniors to Chulmleigh or South Molton. There follow interviews with past pupils, a schoolteacher and extracts from the log-books.

Warkleigh School Notes
by the late Robert Bovett from his book, Historical Notes on Devon Schools, *published in 1989.*

According to the information recorded by the Charity Commissioners in 1824, a small sum of money, given in about 1766, and another later gift had been made up to the sum of £40 by Denys Rolle on condition that it was applied to support a school under the superintendence of the rector, and that by the date of the enquiry, payments were being made to a schoolmistress to teach eight children to read.

By a deed of 1846, the rector of the time for the United Parishes, Revd William Thorold, gave to the minister and churchwardens a piece of glebe land in the parish of Warkleigh, on the roadside and lying between the road and the then rectory (now Old Parsonage Farm), for a site for a school to be conducted upon the principles of the National Society. As is often the case, the terms of the deed do not apparently indicate the actual intentions of the donor and a clue to what transpired is given in information supplied by the donor himself in 1879 and quoted by the Charity Commissioners in their report of 1910.

Warkleigh School, c.1917. Left to right, back row: ?, ?, Jack Adams, Harold Stenner, ?, Albert Crook, Fred Bowden, Reg Bowden; third row: Beaty Harris, ?, Daisy Crook, Gerty Balman, ?, ?, ?; the second row includes: Lissie Medland, ? Parkhouse, Dot Bowden, Dora Balman, Lizzie Crook, ?, ?, ?, Muriel Swan; front row: Harold Crook, ?, Charlie Bowden, Bill Bowden, ?, Cyril Shapland.

Miss Salome Thorold from Warkleigh House, 1936.

Above: *Warkleigh School 1927.* Left to right, back row: *Harold Cook, Jimmy Hooper, George Parkhouse, Reg Bowden, Dick Tucker, George Shapland;* third row: *Margaret Medland, Ella Turner, Hilda Tucker, Murial Swan, Joyce Shapland, Lizzie Crook, Minnie Balman, Dot Ayre;* second row: *Sonny (Jack) Fewings, Ned Herniman, Leslie Medland, Gwen Herniman, Sonny Clarke, Arthur Parkhouse, Tom Tucker;* front row: *Ernest Herniman, Jim Tucker, Wilson Holland, Wilson Parkhouse, Charlie Colman, Frank Gregory.*

Warkleigh School 1917. Back row, left to right: *George Balman, William Bowden, Charlie Bowden, ?, ?, ?;* third row: *?, Harold Stenner, Jack Adams, teacher Iva Headon (on the end);* second row: *?, ?, Beaty Harris, Dora Balman, ?, ?, Leslie Medland, ?, ?, ?, ?;* front row: *Cyril Shapland (boy sitting on box), Fred Bowden, Reg Bowden, ?, ?, Wilson Parkhouse, ?, ?.*

To Builders and Contractors
Warkleigh

A new school and teachers' residence is proposed to be erected in the parish of Warkleigh, plans and specifications for the same may be seen at the present schoolroom. Tenders for the above to be sent to the Revd William Thorold, Warkleigh Rectory, on or before the 5th day of June next. The committee of management do not pledge themselves to accept the lowest of any of the tenders.
Dated May 9th 1873, Warkleigh.

The above refers to the clearing, in 1876, of a payment outstanding in respect of the conversion of some outbuildings into a school, and subsequent developments appear to confirm that a school was provided in 1846 by adaptation of outbuildings belonging to the rectory for the purpose of a school.

By another deed of December 1873, the rector granted further land on three sides of the original site, of considerably larger area, for the purposes of the school, and it was following this conveyance that the first school was demolished and a new school, properly built, with a separate teacher's house, in 1876. These new buildings were erected at a cost of £590 with a Government grant, proceeds of a parish rate, voluntary contributions, and £26 from the diocese.

The school building is typical of the period, solidly built of stone, the schoolroom and the smaller infants' classroom forming the shape of a 'T'. It is curious that the window of the infants' room facing the road is of a different style from the windows at either end of the schoolroom, and a possible explanation is that it had been provided in the adaptation of the outbuildings for the first school building, and was reused in the new building.

The two ecclesiastical parishes, for some while united as one rectory, were combined as one civil parish of Satterleigh and Warkleigh in 1894.

The school, by virtue of its association with the National Society as required by the trust deed, was described and conducted as a National School until it came under the LEA after the 1902 Act, whereafter it continued as a Voluntary Church School. It became a junior school in 1946 when the seniors were moved elsewhere, and was closed in 1948.

Molly Wilkey (née Heard), at the time of writing in her 88th year, was born in Chittlehamholt and later became a teacher at Warkleigh School. She talked to me about her time there:

I started off teaching just before the Second World War as a trainee at Chittlehampton. I was there for two years, cycling every day, until a position of teacher came up at Warkleigh School. Not being 18, I wasn't old enough to take the position – I was only 17½ – but they still transferred me because Miss Harding, the head teacher, wanted me as I had a little knowledge that none of the other applicants had.

After six months I became what they call unqualified. At that time there was no chance of going to college, so I took all my exams externally and qualified through a correspondence course. After the war, there was such a shortage of teachers that they allowed men who had several different qualifications to come into the profession. I actually qualified because of my two music diplomas which came under the heading of a qualification. I did very well, but as I didn't stay at grammar school long enough to take my GSE – I ended up doing it the hard way, but I made it in the end.

The condition of Miss Harding's headship at Warkleigh School was that she should be the organist of Warkleigh and Satterleigh churches, it being a Church school. She peddled away, but she was no player and as soon as I arrived she offloaded it onto me as fast as she could, and I was very grateful. Miss Harding lived in the Warkleigh schoolhouse along with Miss Cable who was headmistress at Chittlehamholt School. I think they both came from Sheffield and both jobs must have come up at the same time.

I remember coming back from playing the organ in Satterleigh Church one day. I had just bought a new bicycle with hub brakes and they weren't very reliable. I met Miss Thorold from Warkleigh House carrying her case and walking in the middle of the road on one of the corners. I couldn't stop and I went bang into the hedge beside her. She wasn't a bit alarmed, and all she said was 'My dear are you alright?' How I didn't knock her down I don't know.

It was quite a happy school; some of the children were monkeys and got up to some games, but it was a different sort of naughtiness than today – then it was just

Above: *The Bowden boys from Oakford Cottage, Satterleigh, outside Warkleigh School, c.1921. Left to right, standing:* William (Bill), Charlie; *sitting:* Fred.

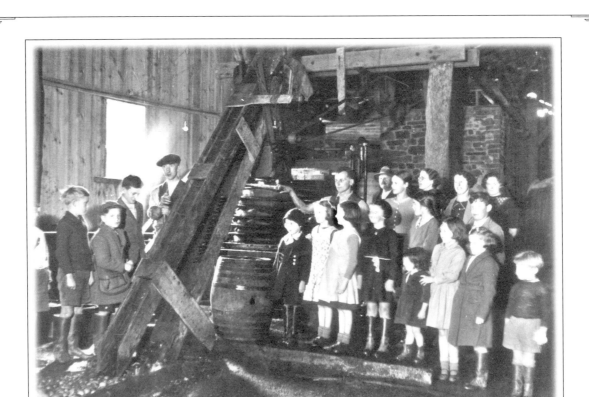

The Warkleigh schoolchildren pay a visit to the Hancock's cider works at King's, Satterleigh, c.1937.

Warkleigh School, 1935. Left to right, back row: Sonny Clarke, Gladys Ware, Edward Herniman, Ronald Ware, Ruth Symons, Alma Snow, Morley Jones, Gordon Parkhouse, Margaret Medland, Freda Fewings; third row: Douglas Gratton, Harold Snow (standing behind Douglas and Harold is Ella Turner), Harold Frayne, Leslie Medland, Claude Eastmond, Gwen Herniman, Novello Fewings, Evelyn Holland, Gwen Clarke, Christine Smith, Ray Snow, Gwen Ware, Lesley Lock, John Pincombe; second row: Percy Gratton, Jo and Jessie Symons, Rachel Parkhouse, Dorothy Clarke, Cissie Tucker, Effie Snow, Gwen Luxton; front row: Stanley Symes, Kenneth Stenner, Ronald Herniman, Fred Herniman, Cyril Symes, Ray Holland, Trevor Snow, Leslie Pincombe.

innocent fun, but today it's bullying, hitting and robbing. There's a culvert that goes under the road and feeds the water from the Old Rectory pond, and the children got down there one day and blocked it all up and flooded the road; we had to call the Council out. Another time they pushed paper through the ventilator under the cloakroom floor and tried to set fire to it.

Dorothy Ayre (née Bowden), now 84, and her four brothers Reg, Charlie, Fred and Bill, all lived at Oakford Cottage, Satterleigh, and went to Warkleigh School. She remembers:

I went to Warkleigh School when Miss Harding was the headmistress. She lived in the schoolhouse with Miss Cable who was headmistress at Chittlehamholt School. Miss Cable walked to Chittlehamholt every morning and as she set off before we got to school and didn't get back until after we had gone home, we didn't see much of her. Dorothy Diamond was my first teacher and I also remember some of the others; Iva Pester and Ruth Pester from Chittlehamholt, Ruth Buckingham from Furze Barn, Chittlehampton, and Molly Heard who was starting teaching when I left school.

Miss Salome Thorold from Warkleigh House took a keen interest in the school, and she used to come down every morning to take our pennies to pay into the penny bank; we had a card and gave her money which she payed into the TSB savings account in South Molton. I used to earn a bit of money from various people including old Mr Elworthy of Satterleigh Barton. If I did anything for him he would give me sixpence, and if you had got that money to put into the penny bank you thought you had a fortune. At dinner time on Fridays I used to fetch Miss Harding's eggs for her from Mr Charlie Harris at Highdown. I used to get something for that, and at the same time, if old Mr Phillips from Chittlehampton, who used to deliver the newspapers, didn't have time to go up there I took the paper up and he'd give me 1d.

When Miss Thorold came into the class, we all stood up and said, 'good morning Mam'. When Revd Hackblock came in on Friday mornings to take us for scripture we used to say, 'good morning Sir'. Now when the children pass you, they call you by your christian name, no 'Sir' or 'Madam', that's all gone; times have changed.

I can remember our school and Chittlehamholt School paying a visit to Cleave Copse to see Mr Peel's museum of stuffed wild animals, all of which he had shot when he was a big-game hunter. Mr Holland from Hill Town took us in his longtail cart.

When the Second World War came, the vicar gave a canteen to Warkleigh School. Dinners were cooked there for both Warkleigh and Chittlehamholt Schools. Bill Skinner from the Exeter Inn and Spencer Vivian from Chittlehampton (who did a paper round in the area), are both known to have picked up the containers to take to Chittlehamholt School.

Memories of Warkleigh School
Interesting extracts from the log-books.

June 18th 1915 – *Closed school for one week for Hay Harvest.*

Jan 7th 1919 – *Scholars reassembled this morning, all present. Miss Thorold has kindly presented two more pairs of shoes for the children who come to school with wet boots to be able to change them.*

June 12th 1919 – *The assistant is granted leave this afternoon and the infants are kept in the big room. There is a small attendance, many of the children are gone to the fête at Chittlehamholt.*

Dec 21st 1920 – *After this morning's session, Miss Thorold presented war savings stamps to 19 children who had made the greatest number of attendances early during the year. Mrs Thompson presented chocolates and sweets to every child present.*

Dec 5th 1921 – *The prizes gained in the needlework competition between this parish and Chittlehamholt are: 1st prize 10s.0d. Mary Adams; 2nd prize 5s.0d. Dora Balman; 3rd prize 2s.6d. Doris Moore; HC 2s.6d. Irene Moore; C 2s.6d. Gertrude Balman. Thus it will be seen that this little school has had the distinction of winning all the prizes offered.*

Dec 21st 1921 – *Miss Thorold presented Edward Holland with two shillings as a reward for a perfect attendance and each of the six children who pay into the penny savings bank with one shilling. The children afterwards had great fun in scrambling for sweets and nuts provided by the teachers and every child received a cracker.*

Sept 8th 1922 – *Miss Iva Pester, the infants' teacher, left today. Miss Ruth Pester commenced as monitress.*

Nov 6th 1922 – *Miss Olive Pester commenced today as assistant in the infants' department.*

May 24th 1928 – *Empire Day. The children assembled in the playground and sang the National Anthem and other songs and saluted the flag.*

Sept 12th 1932 – *Miss Heard started as a supplementary teacher.*

May 24th 1933 – *Fred Herniman absent, he has broken his collar bone.*

Sept 18th 1933 – *Miss Dorothy E. Snow commenced duties at this school today as a student teacher.*

Mar 20th 1934 – *Freda Fewings left school today and commenced duties as monitress at Chittlehamholt School.*

Warkleigh School, 1939. **Left to right, back row:** *Trevor Snow, Harold Snow, Cissie Tucker, May Herniman, Joyce Allen, Effie Snow, Ivy Lock, Ray Holland, Leslie Lock;* **third row:** *Clarice Allen, Dorothy Pincombe, Maggie Ley, Jean Fewings, Crystal Hancock;* **second row:** *Donald Herniman, Harold Gratton, Bill Pincombe, Les Pincombe, Edwin Fewings, John Turner, Fred Herniman;* **front row:** *Harold Holland, Joan Herniman, Ella Ley, Marjorie Pincombe, Muriel Herniman, Gwendoline Jones, Norman Hancock.*

Warkleigh School, 1936. **Left to right, back row:** *Percy Gratton, Claude Eastmond, Gwen Ware, Ruth Symons, Novello Fewings, Chris Smith, Gwen Herniman, Leslie Medland;* **third row:** *Douglas Gratton, Trevor Snow, Nancy Bird, May Herniman, Evelyn Holland, Cissie Tucker, Maggie Ley, Ken Stenner, Ronald Herniman;* **second row:** *Charlie Harris, Les Pincombe, Crystal Hancock, Dot Pincombe, Jessie Symons, Jo Symons, Jean Fewings, Doreen Holland, Joan Herniman, John Turner, Raymond Holland;* **front row:** *Albert Harris, William Pincombe, Fred Herniman, Donald Herniman, John Bird, Edwin Fewings, Harold Gratton.*

Left: *The old Deason School.*

May 3rd 1935 – *After singing Jubilee songs the children were presented with Jubilee mugs by Miss Thorold. The school closed this afternoon for the Jubilee.*

July 31st 1935 – *The school was closed all day for the annual flower show.*

Sept 20th 1935– *The school was closed for Barnstaple Fair.*

Feb 19th 1936 – *Cissie Tucker absent due to ringworm.*

Jan 19th 1938 – *Novello Fewings absent suffering from measles. Edwin and Jean also excluded from school. Maggie Ley absent due to suspected measles.*

Sept 27th 1938 – *John Pincombe fell in the road near the school during the dinner hour and cut his knee very badly.*

Oct 5th 1938 – *All the children were fitted for gas masks this morning.*

Feb 7th 1945 – *Harold Holland, who has been absent on account of bronchitis, has now contracted measles. John Midwinter, an evacuee, also absent since he is billeted in the same house.*

The final entry in the log-book states:

Feb 2nd 1948 – *I have today been informed that my services are required at George Nympton School and that there must be a temporary closure of this school. The four pupils will travel by the school bus to Chittlehampton Junior School. This school has therefore closed at the end of the afternoon session for an indefinite period.*

Janet Judd recalls her days at school:

In 1944 the headmistress of Warkleigh School, Miss Harding, retired when the 11-plus pupils went to South Molton Secondary School to complete their education. Mrs Vickers was then appointed, followed by Mrs Keeley, who taught there until 1948 when she was moved to Mollands to cover for a teacher on sick-leave. The school consisted of just four pupils at that time; Pearl Buse, myself and my sister Sybil, and Tony Hancock. Tony started school at not much over 3½ years of age. He used to arrive at school, sitting in front of his sister Crystal on her horse, Gaddocks. Mrs Ford cooked our school dinners in the canteen, assisted, if memory serves me correctly, by Effie Snow. After the closure of the school, we caught the South Molton school bus to Chittlehampton.

Novello Gregory (née Fewings) recalls some of her school memories:

I used to live at Oldridge Farm on the B3226 South Molton main road. My two sisters and two brothers and I walked the three miles to Warkleigh School every day, quite often we never needed coats because the weather must have been lovely. Miss Thorold bought some macs for the school so that children like ourselves who came from a long way away could wear them home if it started to rain. I remember bringing two pints of milk daily in my satchel to provide hot chocolate at break times. If Miss Thorold wasn't very well, the whole school sometimes went up to sing to her. Miss Harding the headmistress gave me the school accounts to take up to the Rectory on a Friday afternoon, and I can remember her giving us all hot chocolate at break time if it was very cold.

Outside activities consisted of lots of sports, and annually we danced the maypole in the school playground, with the children voting for the May Queen. Miss Thorold would come down and give us all a fairly big bag of sweets.

At Christmas time we had a tea in the school, given by Miss Thorold, and the mums were given an orange and a jar of jam.

I will always remember when Miss Thorold died in 1938. Miss Harding gave me a prayer book – which I still have today – because I was the only child in the whole school who went to the funeral, and she made me write 'for attending Miss Thorold's funeral' inside it. At assembly she pointed out that more children could have attended as she was so good to the school.

Kathleen Ford (née Wright) recalls some memories of her childhood at Chittlehamholt:

I started school in 1938 before I was five years old. I walked with my two older sisters, Audrey and Olive, from Simmons Farm – a distance of 2½ miles. We always had plenty of company because David Harris from Presbury, Peter Bater from Westerground and Hanson Hammett from Kinnings would walk with us. When we got to Farrs Farm, Cynthia and Hadrian Balman would join us, plus all the evacuees later in 1940 – I remember Tom Brown from Westerground (we called it Westernground in those days) and the Butwells from Farrs.

A while after I had started – probably some time during 1939 – I can remember having to look after a little girl called Diana Dicker (now Lethbridge) who didn't like school. I remember playing dolls with her. Her mother would bring her to school in a red knitted suit one week and a green one the next. Being the third of five children, I envied her lovely knitted suits. Diana was my first schoolfriend, and we are still good friends to this day.

There were no school dinners then and Mrs Slee (George and Ivor's mother) used to make us a drink of cocoa. Diana and I used to take our sandwiches to eat at her home at dinner times. Another alternative was to take a potato with us and cook it on the black stove – it used to take all morning to cook! Then along came school dinners cooked by Mrs Turner at Warkleigh School – I can still remember her treacle tart and lovely roast dinners.

Miss Cable was my first teacher and I had many letters from her after she retired. My sister Olive and I had music lessons after school on Tuesdays with Mrs Doidge – because I went first and had to wait for Olive, I used to go back to school and help Miss Cable mark the exercise books – all those sums! After school was over we walked the 2½ miles home – just imagine all those shoes we wore out! When I tell my grandchildren how far we had to walk, they can't believe it. I have even taken them on our school route by car, just to show them!

Mr Cox lived opposite the school and he never complained at the noise we children used to make. We were allowed to play outside the school in the road and I can remember him setting off to feed his sheep at Rowcliffes and Highbullen (down Mucksey Lane) with a bucket on each arm and weaving in and out as we were playing our games. We always had to take our gas masks to school – big trouble if we forgot them – my hide-away in case of bombs, etc. was Woodside, at Miss Beer's house.

After the war was over, and the evacuees had left for home, Diana and I and others went to the South Molton Secondary School in Old Barnstaple Road. We passed our exams for the Technical College, but I had to stay at Simmons to work on the farm. We soon got involved with the Annual Flower Show and the Young Farmers' Club which was enjoyed by everyone. (I don't think we learnt very much, but we certainly had a good time!) From an early age, we attended Sunday school each week at the chapel in the village and afterwards we had to visit Great Auntie Mary Venn (on Dad's orders!) who lived at No. 2 South View. When I was older I used to help Mr Constable with the younger Sunday school children and also played the organ for singing choruses and hymns from Golden Bells. There were two shops in the village and every Saturday we had to take the horses to Mr Wallace Clarke, the local blacksmith, to get their shoes replaced. We were certainly never bored!

My memories of Chittlehamholt will be with me for ever.

Deason School

There was also a school at Deason in Warkleigh, built in 1846. The building still remains in Deason Court and is the property of Mrs Ruby Kingdon. The plaque is still imbedded in the wall and bears the following inscription:

1846
This schoolroom was erected by I. Stevens of Warkleigh for the Education of the poor children of Warkleigh and the Neighbourhood.
T. Burgess
Subscribers   I. Beer, I. Passmore

Deason School plaque.

It was a free school, supported entirely by Mr Stevens, farmer of Deason. The school was used on Sundays by the Bible Christians, but how long this chapel school lasted is not known. Perhaps the competition lead to the improvement of the National School.

Chittlehamholt School
Notes by the late Robert Bovett

There is evidence that there was a school in Chittlehamholt by the year 1834, when, as quoted by Revd J.H.B. Andrews in his history of the parish (*TDA*, 1961), the parish records mention a school-room owned by Revd Peter Johnson also being used for services and which he intended to convey to trustees. However, the schoolroom was in the same ownership in 1842, according to the Tithe Award, and in fact was not transferred to trustees until 1873.

From 1856 onwards, the school is referred to in the directories as a National School, and the same sources from 1883 state that the school had been built in 1850. From the evidence of the Tithe Map, however, it is fairly certain that the building as it was in 1842 still comprises the main part of the present building and any work at that time must have been in the form of extensions or remodelling.

In 1873 the school premises were conveyed to the vicar and churchwardens and it was required by the terms of the deed that the school should be 'in union with the Church of England.' There is no reference to the National School. The school was closed on 25 April 1874 and reopened on 26 January 1875, the hiatus being accounted for no doubt by a necessary reconstitution of the school to conform with requirements of the 1870 Act. The first necessity was the appointment of a teacher with the appropriate qualification.

In 1899, according to the log-book, a classroom was added to the original schoolroom and this was evidently partly by extension and partly by reducing the length of the schoolroom. In 1913 a further class-room was added, which was brought into use in September, thus making three rooms in all.

Chittlehamholt School group, c.1920. Left to right, back row: Kathy Skinner, Ruth Pester, Dora Latham, Ivy Johns, Lewey Turner, Eve Beer; third row: Walter Heard, Bill Thorne, Bill Johns, Percy Coles, Ern Coles, Fred Turner, Walter Bird, Lionel Hammett, Herbie Beer, ?, ?, Reg Heard, Arthur Luxton, ?, ?, Aubrey Pester, Frank Heard, Leslie Thatcher, Norah Thatcher; second row includes: Maggie Latham, Gerti Clatworthy, ? Turner, Jessie Kingdon, Lily Beer, Molly Turner, Annie Slee, Annie Crooks, Florence Pester; included in the front row are: Percy Johns, Jack Luxton, Arthur Smith, ? Latham, Arthur Luxton, ? Clatworthy, ? Clatworthy, Ron Chapple, Eddy Kingdon, Vincent Pester.

Left: Christine Stuckey proudly holds the clock which was presented to her mother on the occasion of her marriage in 1920 by teachers and scholars of Chittlehamholt School where she was a teacher.

Right: A clock presented by teachers and scholars to Florence Congram, teacher at Chittlehamholt School, on the occasion of her marriage in 1920.

After the 1902 Act the school continued under the LEA as a Voluntary Church School. It became a primary school when the seniors were removed in 1946 but remained in existence for only two more years and closed in 1948.

The old school building still stands on the north side of the road going west about 100 feet from the centre of the village. It is a long low white-rendered building, now a dwelling known as The Old School.

CHITTLEHAMHOLT SCHOOL AND THE GREAT BLIZZARD – JANUARY 29TH 1947.

by Muriel Moore (née Wright), who was born at Simmons Farm

No doubt many people over the age of 55 [in 2002] will be able to remember where they were and what they were doing on that day, because it was the day of one of the worst blizzards, if not the worst, of the twentieth century.

I was a young girl of seven at the time and, together with my elder sister Vera who was 11, attended the local primary school at Chittlehamholt, a small village in the heart of the North Devon countryside. The school consisted of six pupils, who were all given a thorough

grounding in the '3Rs' by Miss Parker, the head-mistress, and we daily walked the two-and-a-quarter miles each way.

It happened to be threshing day at home that day (it would have been called thrashin' or drashin' in our part of the country) and it was always a very busy time for all the family: Dad organising the various jobs, and Mum, with my elder sisters, preparing food for all the helpers, mostly neighbouring farmers. No electricity or mod-cons in those days – dinner was cooked in the clay oven-in-the-wall, and it was always roast on thrashin' days. All the water would have been carried from the well, a good 100 yards away, so it really was a hectic day. Although the weather must have looked quite bleak in the morning, my sister and I walked to school as usual. We wore gloves, pixie hoods and warm coats, but tights or long trousers were definitely not in fashion in 1947.

Miss Parker watched the deteriorating weather at frequent intervals and eventually decided that we ought to set out for home. There were no telephones to warn our family that we were on our way, and my parents admitted many times over the following years that they were so busy coping with the problems that the blizzard was causing to the thrashin' that it quite slipped their minds that we weren't at home!

The marriage in 1920 of John (Jack) Congram of Wards Farm, Chittlehamholt, and Florence Pester of Fir Cottage. The photograph is taken outside the cottage known today as September Cottage. The lady on the far left on the back row is thought to be Mrs Allanson, the vicar's wife. Left to right, back row continued: *Ernie Jackman, Rose Congram, Henry (Harry) Congram, John (Jack) Congram (bridegroom), Florence Congram (bride), Cecil Pester, Bill Pester, Ivy Pester;* middle row: *Revd Allanson, William Congram, Mary Congram, Elizabeth Pester, John Pester, Olive Pester;* sitting: *Vincent Pester, Aubrey Pester, Annie Congram, Gladys Pester, Ruth Pester.*

By the time we set off from school, the snow was well covering the road and the wind was swirling the powdery flakes into our faces, making it very difficult to get our breath. I can remember constantly telling my sister that I couldn't and didn't want to walk any further, but she kept bullying me to keep going, at one stage persuading me to walk backwards while she guided me along the ever-deepening, snow-covered road – I still know the exact stretch of road where we did this. Luckily, we later rounded a sharp right-handed bend which meant the wind was not quite so directly in our faces, and a little further on we met the threshermen on their 'poppity-pop' Marshall tractor, who had abandoned work to head for home. At that point, we still had at least a mile to go, but we were then able to walk in the tractor's tracks and eventually arrived home with our faces and legs red raw, shivering and completely exhausted. Our journey had taken hours! My sister still recalls how she thought she was never going to get me home. Miss Parker later wrote a letter of apology to our parents for not sending us home sooner. She was a very dedicated teacher and we all loved her, but I've often wondered if she could have slept very well for several nights after the blizzard, for she would have had no way of knowing whether we had arrived home safely. There were no telephones around in those days and the roads were cut off for some time.

29 January 1947 is definitely one childhood threshing day that I will never ever forget, and certainly one that I was lucky to survive.

Vera Geatches (née Wright) remembers her childhood years:

I was born at the beginning of January 1936, a year when our country saw three kings on the throne, Europe was heading for a war and, in our countryside, farmers were struggling to make a living, not a good time for a fourth daughter to arrive at Simmons Farm. I developed into an extremely shy, serious and studious child, sandwiched between confident extrovert sisters. My memories are chosen at random – some happy, some not so happy – but all part of my early life at Simmons and Chittlehamholt School.
So here goes...

Agreeing to have my long dark curls cut, in preparation for starting school, and being rewarded with a farthing.

Being in constant fear of the loud, forceful teacher who had arrived at our quiet little school with the swarms of evacuees. What a nightmare for a timid five-year old!

Discovering the delights of reading and books. The glass-doored bookcase in the big classroom was my passport to a different and wonderful world; my imagination knew no bounds.

Soldiers stopping outside the school in an armoured vehicle and handing down sweets to all of us. Could they have been Americans?

Being cornered and kissed in the playground, don't worry, I was probably about seven and it was part of a game.

Outside Chittlehamholt School, 26 March 1947. Left to right, standing: George Sanders, Robert Bater; *sitting on John Fry the pony is Tommy Allday, with Mrs Tickle the dog. Holding the pony is Bill Heard the postman/postmaster with Muriel Wright and Margaret Guard behind.*

Right: Dorothy Snow, Chittlehamholt schoolteacher.

Chittlehamholt School, c.1927. Left to right, back row: *Reg Thorne, Arthur Luxton, Wilfred Holland, Stafford Constable, John French, Gerald Passmore;* fifth row: *Norah Congram, Eva Walden, Betty Passmore, Florrie Latham, Beattie Lugg, ?;* fourth row: *Arthur Lugg, Albert Latham, Doris Hall, Gerti Latham, Muriel Constable, Bill Beer;* third row: *Aubrey Headon, Reggie Turton, ?, George Slee, ?, Bill Congram, Harold Congram, Leslie Heard (standing above Leslie is Lennard Holland);* the second row includes: *Clara Butcher, ? Waldon, ? Waldon;* the front row includes: *Audrey Holland, ? Latham, Bessie Slee, Harry Webber, Stan Medland, Elam Herniman.*

Left: *Inside Chittlehamholt School, 26 March 1947. John Fry the pony had called to say goodbye before leaving for London Zoo. Seated at the front desk are Robert Bater and Margaret Guard, and behind are Tommy Allday (just visible on the far left) and Muriel Wright. Standing next to teacher Dorothy Parker are Vera Wright and George Sanders. Sitting with the pony is Mary Courtney.*

Very few toys to remember at home, but we had lots of fun with a rubber ball and invented games bouncing it against the barn wall. Standing on the swing in the tree and sending it higher and higher.

Hating the drudgery of farm work, playing was a luxury, but there were highlights too; harvest time with tea in the field and riding home on top of the last load as darkness fell.

Milking my cow in the field, collecting warm eggs from the nest, having a pet bantam hen to call my own; picking apples, collecting nuts and finding mushrooms in the damp fields.

Being first in the race up the field to tell Dad the war was over at last.

Taking it in turns standing against the dairy door to recite poems: my favourite one entitled 'Errands'. Does anyone have a copy I wonder?

Crossing the river on the swaying clapper bridge, then finding wild strawberries on the railway bank in the hot June sunshine.

Rare picnics by the river, paddling in the cold water, dresses tucked into knickers, and the pebbles were so hard on our feet.

1945 and outings in the Hillman Minx. Too many of us in the back seat and usually at least one of us was sick. Wishing we'd never set off.

Wishing that just for once I could have new clothes instead of hand-me-downs.

Feeling sorry for myself that my birthday was so near Christmas and having to pretend not to notice that my cards and presents were second-hand.

Back at school now and remembering those regular nature walks, maybe teacher's excuse to get out of the classroom; I've had good reason to thank her for learning about flowers, trees and wildlife, when our own children were growing up.

Seeing the snowflakes whirl outside the window whilst taking the 11-plus examination at Barnstaple Girls Grammar School, and a few days later making the traumatic journey home from school with Muriel in the 1947 blizzard.

My last day at Chittlehamholt School; after a year's piano lessons, being given the honour of playing the hymn at the end of lessons. Eight verses of 'Now the day is over' played very slowly and I fear with no musical talent.

To sum up, childhood for me came to an abrupt end when I left home to go to Barnstaple Girls Grammar School. The changes in home and school life were momentous and very frightening, but I survived and grew to love Grammar School. I guess I was never really part of farm or village life again although it was good to know it was always there in the background for me.

Life for me at present is spent in retirement with my husband Ray in south-east Cornwall. Our four children have all left home and our two young granddaughters, aged four and three, are enjoying a very different kind of childhood. It is my hope that their memories will all be happy ones.

Further articles from the newspapers follow, covering the activities of the schools:

June 24th 1898
Miss A.C. Phillips, of Chittlehamholt, has been appointed mistress of the new school at Week Cross by Chulmleigh School Board. It is proposed to open the School on July 4th.

November 18th 1927
Wilfred Holland, a scholar attending Chittlehamholt School, has been awarded second prize, a box of paints, value 7s.6d., in a colour work competition for children under 11 years of age. A hanging lamp has been presented to the School by Miss Cable, having been purchased with the proceeds of the last children's concert.

December 28th 1928
Doris Hill, a scholar at Chittlehamholt School, has been successful in winning one of the ten-shilling prizes offered by the Empire Health Week Committee for the best essays of 'Why is cleanliness the first law of health?' Through the kind invitation of Miss Cable (headmistress), a pleasant afternoon was spent by parents and friends at the school. The children's splendid work was on view, and they rendered some excellent songs and plays to the credit of their teachers. On breaking up each child received a nice present, through the generosity of Mrs de Legh.

May 19th 1933
The monitress and scholars attending the Chittlehamholt School have presented to the Revd and Mrs Hackblock a parting gift of book-ends and a teapot-holder as a slight token of the love they have for them. Mr and Mrs Hackblock have always been very interested in the welfare of the children who are all sorry to lose such good friends. Recently Mr Hackblock gave a beautiful picture of the 'Babe in the Manger' to the School, and this, besides being in itself a joy to see, will be a constant reminder of the Rector when he is no longer with them.

Nora Congram's work at the examination, held in March at Barnstaple, reached a sufficiently high standard for her to be considered in the apportioning of special places at the Grammar School.

May 14th 1937
Christine Congram, a pupil at the day school, has passed the scholarship examination recently held at Barnstaple. Christine was 10 in March.

January 12th 1945
CHITTLEHAMHOLT
A very enjoyable time was spent at the School, when Miss Cable (the retiring headmistress) invited parents and friends to a 'Christmas' afternoon. A huge Christmas tree was decorated with toys and gifts of all kinds, given by the children. They were sold, the proceeds, over £5, being given to the Aid to Russia Fund

Chittlehamholt School, 1936. Left to right, back row: *Ivor Slee, Catherine Medland, Phyllis Ridd, Joan Headon, Bill Congram;* third row: *Harold Frane, George Medland, Peter Bater, Muriel Couch, Joan Skinner, Georgina Passmore, Evelyn Medland, Neville Guard, Aubrey Headon, Raymond Congram;* second row: *Margaret Medland, Alethea Skinner, Pam Guard, Molly Hulland, Christine Congram, Mary Ridd, Audrey Wright, Olive Wright;* front row: *Ken Guard, Reg Crook, Ronnie Hulland, William Beer, Derek Pearce, Cecil Headon, ?, Frank Congram, John Headon.*

Chittlehamholt School, 1938. Left to right, back row: *Harold Frane, Georgina Passmore, Catherine Medland, Joan Skinner, Ivor Slee;* third row: *Molly Hulland, Christine Congram, Peter Bater, Evelyn Medland, Anne Clements;* second row: *Ronald Hulland, John Headon, Lorna Martin, Olive Wright, Margaret Medland, Alethea Skinner, Audrey Wright, William Beer, Graham Clements;* front row: *Derek Pearce, Reggie Beardon, Cecil Headon, Frank Congram, Gerald Pearce, Reggie Crook.*

for Children and a Children's Hospital. The children also wished the value of the presents, which are always given by Miss Cable, to be used for the same good causes. Mrs Worthington and Mrs Bryant thanked Miss Cable for her great kindness, and loud cheering voiced the feelings of everyone.

The following extracts are taken from the Chittlehamholt National School log-book:

Jan 26th 1875 – *I, Ada N. Webb, reopened this school today after it having been closed since April 25th 1874, admitting five children.*

Feb 9th 1877 – *School closed in the afternoon, all the children were invited to a tea in the Manor House given by Mrs Bater.*

Mar 27th 1877 – *Very poor attendance. Several boys being kept at home tilling potatoes.*

May 7th 1877 – *School closed in the afternoon, today being Chittlehamholt Revel.*

Jan 27th 1879 – *Mary, Elizabeth, Lucy and John Clatworthy, also Sophy and John Westacott, have left and gone to the Chapel school.*

April 1st 1887 – *The school has been closed owing to the spreading of scarlet fever.*

Sept 2nd 1887 – *The Hernimans, Clatworthys, Medlands and Harrises have been kept at home on account of typhoid fever in the village.*

May 3rd 1889 – *John Lewis, Annie Slee and Ada Clarke admitted.*

April 10th 1891 – *Admitted Henry Congram.*

Mar 25th 1892 – *Admitted Annie Congram.*

May 13th 1892 – *Admitted James Lewis.*

Mar 29th 1895 – *Admitted John Congram.*

Mar 12th 1897 – *Admitted Gladys Pester.*

Chittlehamholt School, 1931–2. Left to right, back row: Leslie Heard, ?, Lucy Clarke, Elam Herniman, ?; fourth row: Bessie Slee, Joan Headon, Georgina Passmore, Phyllis Ridd, Nora Congram; third row: Clara Boucher, Mabel Latham, Lily Skinner, Vera Guard, Pam Guard, Joan Skinner, Rosemary Clarke; second row: Harold Congram, Aubrey Headon, George Slee, Raymon Congram, ?, Bill Congram, Stan Medland; front row: Peter Bater, Christine Congram, Ivor Slee, Alethea Skinner, ?. The War Memorial can be seen above Clara Boucher's head. When the school was closed it was removed and it is now fixed inside the Chittlehamholt, Warkleigh and Satterleigh Village Hall.

Mar 29th 1897 – The Chapel school was closed on Friday last, consequently 21 children have been admitted into this school. They appear to be in a very backward state.

Nov 23rd 1900 – Scholars on books 72. Present today, 26 boys and 35 girls.

1903 – Admitted Iva Pester.

Oct 4th 1904 – Florence Pester has commenced duties this morning as a monitress approved by the County Council.

April 6th 1906 – Gladys Pester has left having a labour certificate, although only 12 years old.

Mar 5th 1907 – Staff: E. Townsend (certified trained), E.M. Townsend (supplementary), Florence Pester (probationer).

July 17th 1908 – Florence Pester has been notified that she will be apprenticed as a pupil teacher here for two years and will receive instruction from the head teacher.

Sept 18th 1908 – Miss Edith May Townsend of the schoolhouse has been presented with a silver coffee pot by the scholars and a silver sugar basin by the managers on the occasion of her marriage to Mr John Smoldon of Fullabrook, Chittlehampton.

Dec 9th 1910 – I have excluded Tom Beer from school as he is suffering from ringworm.

Sept 1st 1911 – On behalf of the staff and scholars, the mistress presented Miss Florence Pester with a silver-mounted handglass, brush and comb, as a token of affectionate regard, which she has universally won during her work at the school for the past seven years, on the occasion of her leaving.

May 24th 1912 – Today being Empire Day, the children left the school at 3.30, forming a procession to the vicarage where they gave a short display of marching and sang some patriotic songs.

May 27th 1913 – In recent years this school has been full, so that the work has been carried on with difficulty. A new classroom is at present being built.

Sept 22nd 1913 – The new classroom was formally opened by the Bishop of Crediton.

Nov 15th 1915 – Iva Pester has commenced duties here today as monitress.

1917 – Miss Florence Pester commences work here today as an uncertified teacher.

April 19th 1918 – Iva Pester resigns her position as a monitress today to take up a post as a supplementary teacher at Warkleigh School.

June 8th 1925 – George Slee, aged three years four months, admitted.

1928 – Ruth Pester has been appointed as supplementary teacher.

Nov 29th 1928 – Raymond Congram, Albert Latham and Aubrey Headon came to school too late for a mark this afternoon.

April 8th 1929 – Joan Headon and Phyllis Ridd admitted.

Mar 20th 1934 – Freda Fewings began duty as monitress.

June 10th 1937 – In the afternoon, the children visited South Molton Cinema to see the Coronation film of King George VI and HM Queen Elizabeth.

Jan 17th 1937 – Miss Dorothy Snow commenced duties as an uncertified teacher.

Feb 6th 1939 – Admitted Diana Dicker who has been poorly and so unable to commence school at the beginning of the term.

Oct 22nd 1940 – Ronald Stewart, Terence Bucklem, James Conway and Kenneth Guard absented themselves from afternoon school to follow the hounds and reached school at 3.

Aug 6th 1943 – The school spent a part of the afternoon picking blackberries for the WI jam making.

Beattie Newcombe (née Lugg), 84 at the time of writing, was born at Head Post Cottages. Although it is now all one cottage at the time of writing, it used to be divided into two cottages.

Beattie remembers taking Vera Guard (now Ayre), who lived down the road at Longwells, with her to Chittlehamholt School each day. Beattie also walked to school with Eileen Govier (now Radford) who lived at Head Barton. Eileen's parents would bring her up to Head Post Cottages every morning so she could walk to school with Beattie as she didn't like passing Head Quarry on her own. Head Quarry was fully operational in those days and Beattie recalls a lot of work going on there. After school, Beattie would walk Eileen right back to Head Barton, and used to go there to play with Eileen on Saturdays. When Beattie left school, Eileen wouldn't walk to Chittlehamholt School on her own, so she switched to Umberleigh School, catching the train at King's Nympton Station. When Eileen's parents bought her a pair of sandals, Beattie admired them so much that they bought her a pair as a 'thank you' for walking Eileen to school for so many years. Beattie thought this was a marvellous present to receive as no one had very much money in those days.

Beattie recalls that every day her headmistress from Chittlehamholt School, Miss Cable, would walk from the Schoolhouse at Warkleigh where she lived to the village, even though she owned a car. Beattie remembers her having a Baby Austin. Beattie and her friends would walk and meet Miss Cable, and although she never told them not to do it, Beattie could tell that it wasn't what she wanted them to do.

When they passed the Exeter Inn on their way to school, Tom Martin the landlord would come out in the middle of shaving and tease Beattie and her friends, saying things like 'you've been kissing the boys again.'

Beattie remembers going over to have dinner with her aunt and uncle – Mr and Mrs Jimmy Skinner – at South View Cottages after school. She remembers 23 December 1927 when the cottages were destroyed by fire; it was so cold that day, her mother wouldn't let her go to school. Mr and Mrs Skinner then went to live at Ilfracombe. After that, Beattie had to have her dinner with her cousin, Bill Skinner. He and his wife lived in the house today known as The Old Forge, which was then three cottages.

A year younger than Beattie, Stafford Constable remembers that Chittlehamholt School was badly heated and a lot of the children had chilblains. There was no lighting either. Before dinner, grace was sung – 'Be present at our table Lord, be here and everywhere adored.'

Reg Heard, who was ten years older than Stafford, told him that A.J. Coles, better known as Jan Stewer, once taught him at Chittlehamholt School, and that when there was a Chapel school it was reputed that the boys from the Chapel and Church schools would fight at dinner times and then go home as happy as larks. Stafford remembers the attendance officer for the Church school was Mr Westcott, who used to travel in a pony and trap.

Chittlehamholt Chapel School

A letter below, taken from the *North Devon Journal*, suggests that the Chapel school started in 1817 and school records show it closed in 1897 with the admission of 25 children from the chapel school to the National School in March of that year:

Chittlehamholt Chapel School

SIR, – The above school was started under the auspices of Mr G. Muller, of Bristol, 15 years ago, and has been conducted ever since for the purpose of combining purely Scriptural with ordinary instruction. Will you kindly insert the following report in relation to it, with the above statement, in your next issue.
I am, sir, yours respectfully,
JOHN PASSMORE.
Newton Board School, Bishop's Nympton.

Education Department, 3rd January 1888
SIR, – Adverting to your letter dated 6th October last, I am directed to inform you that my Lords have received a report on the Chittlehamholt Chapel School from HM Inspector, who recommends that the school should be recognised as efficient both in regard to the premises and instruction. He states that the room is a good one, and the appointments are fairly good. The children are in good order, and well taught so far as their instruction goes.
I have the honour to be, sir, your obedient servant.
J. SMITHER.
R.L. Riccard, Esq., Clerk to the Union, South Molton.

Below: *Waiting for the school bus outside the old Post Office, Chittlehamholt, 1972.* Left to right: *Susan Stewart, Julie Sedwell, Linda Guard, Bridget Guard, Colin Stewart, Andrew Guard.*

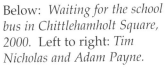

Below: *Waiting for the school bus in Chittlehamholt Square, 2000.* Left to right: *Tim Nicholas and Adam Payne.*

Above: *Waiting for the school bus in Chittlehamholt Square, 2000.* Left to right: *Tom Bowman, Russell Coomber, Shaun Winson, Matthew Coomber.*

Down the Pub

The Exeter Inn, Chittlehamholt, with the petrol pump still in use, c.1960.

Bill Boucher outside the Exeter Inn in the 1930s.
In 2002, his daughter Laura Stenna is 100 years old.

The Exeter Inn darts team, 1971–2, seen here competing at the Town Arms, South Molton. Left to right, back row: *Gerald Herniman, Fred Moore, Gerrald Woolacott, Sonny Chugg;* front row: *Frank Congram, Jim Medland, John Darch, Brian Gover.*

Mine host.
Landlords David and Debbie Glenister.

Peter Griffin with his dog, Amber, in 2001.

Bill Congram with his dog, Titch.

Chapter 6

BUILDINGS PAST & PRESENT

The last 40 years have seen a steady flow of new houses being erected in the parishes. With the help of old maps, we can identify buildings which no longer exist in the parish. Other houses have been knocked down in more recent times and therefore photographs of them exist.

Martin Neil remembers when his family arrived in Chittlehamholt in 1963. He says that the only modern house was Silver Birch bungalow. Before this was built, there stood a lovely thatched cottage on that site – of which we have photographs – which was divided into two dwellings.

In the early 1900s and beyond, a mason called Bill Johns was responsible for building many houses, including Hillbrow, Sunnymead, and The Beacon in Satterleigh, which has since been rebuilt.

In the 1970s the only modern buildings in Warkleigh were The Magpiery, Stoneycroft and Undercleave. A large number of buildings were erected in Chittlehamholt in the 1970s, some of which were built by the late Michael Lynch of Braunton. These include Russons, Farriers, Lambarts, Chapelgate and Highwinds. There has been a dwelling built recently a few feet away from the original site of Russons Farm. Other buildings which were erected in the 1970s are Barnclose, Meadowside, Middleham, Fairview, Thornlea, Tower View, Johns (which is now called Roseland) and Lloret in 1969. In the 1980s, in Warkleigh, The Embers was built, and the 1990s saw the erection of Broadview within the grounds of Broadmoor Farm, Grandison in the grounds of Pugsley Farm, and a barn conversion at Warkleigh Barton. The 1980s and 1990s also saw the building in Chittlehamholt of The Launds, Misty Meadow and Northview, which has since been divided into two dwellings – one half is the present Post Office and the other is called Foxes Walk.

In 2002 we have highly skilled builders, decorators and carpenters living in the parishes, namely David Gillanders, Mac Lightwood, Richard May and Willie Sanders, who built his own bungalow, The Launds.

The rest of this chapter concentrates on the history of some of the older buildings in the parishes, past and present.

The Exeter Inn

The Exeter Inn is a sixteenth-century coaching inn. The road through Chittlehamholt at that time was the main Barnstaple to Exeter road, so the inn is appropriately named. It must have been quite a sight, all the coaches arriving in the village, with perhaps a sound on the coaching horn as they approached the Exeter Inn, and then changing horses before proceeding on to Exeter. At Cobbaton there is a house called Travellers Rest which was once a pub. No doubt this provided a welcome rest for the horses after climbing Codden Hill.

Shaun Faley, 2001.

Stand-in barmaid, Lynne Maud, at the Exeter Inn, 2002.

Chittlehamholt Manor.

Extension of the Exeter Inn in 1981.

Below: Inscription inside a leather bible presented to Thomas Henry Bater of the Manor House, Chittlehamholt, by his relatives at Butlers to mark his birth in 1877.

Above: Peter Sheath having one more for the road.

Harry Congram drinking in the Exeter Inn, 1970s.

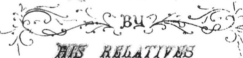

PRESENTED TO

THOMAS HENRY BATER,

(son of Thomas Bater Esq. Manor House, Chittlehamholt.)

BY

HIS RELATIVES AT

BUTLERS FARM.

FEBRUARY 26TH 1877.

I love them that love me; and those that seek me early shall find me. Prov: VIII. 17.

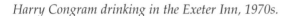

Liberal fête at Chittlehamholt Manor, 1960. Left to right, standing: Margaret Adams, Mrs Lennard, Jeremy Thorpe MP; sitting: Marian Tucker, Pat Lock (Liberal Queen), Joyce Pinn.

Some of the older inhabitants of Chittlehamholt do not remember a second inn, but there was supposed to have been a cider house on the site of Silver Birch bungalow called the Carpenters Arms.

In 1850 John Jenkins was the landlord of the Exeter Inn alongside his wife, Elizabeth. By 1893, William Clarke became landlord with his wife, also called Elizabeth. A case reported in the *North Devon Journal* states that in 1893 a carpenter called John Smith was summoned for having been drunk and that William Clarke, landlord of the inn, was summoned for permitting drunkenness. The outcome of the case was that John Smith was fined 5s. plus costs, while William Clarke was fined £1 plus costs. It was hoped that this would serve as a caution to the young publican.

The *Kelly's Directory* stated that by 1914 Tom Martin was landlord. Some of the older residents of the village remember him and by all accounts he was quite a character. A newspaper report gives us an account of Tom's son, Lionel, coming of age in 1924, when a large number of relatives and friends celebrated in the schoolroom. The health of Mr Martin was proposed by the vicar, Revd C.H. Garland, and that of the host and hostess by Mr Cockram.

Tom Martin also farmed, and George Slee remembers milking his cows on Saturdays. He also had some ground at the Manor and a couple of fields opposite the council-houses. Aubrey Headon can remember him and his mates being asked by Tom Martin to catch moles, for which he gave them a penny a tail. Aubrey recalls that most boys had mole traps then. After showing Tom the tails, the boys would put them back in their pockets and then produce the same ones the next week. However, he soon got wise to this. Tom Martin also did a bit of taxi work around the village.

Bill Congram recalls that the Exeter Inn was part of the manor estate at one time and when it came on the market in 1918 it included 20 different lots. The Exeter Inn was not included in the main catalogue, but was sold at the conclusion of the sale and, according to the *Journal* of the time, was secured by Mr B.T. James for £550. Bill Congram recalls Starkey Knight and Ford, brewers of Tiverton, buying the pub at one stage, and it is assumed that Tom Martin simply carried on the lease.

November 15th 1918
Chittlehamholt, North Devon
To Brewers and others.
Messrs Blackford and Son, favoured with instructions from the owner, will offer for sale by public auction at the Royal and Fortescue Hotel, Barnstaple (immediately after the sale of Chittlehamholt Manor) tomorrow, Friday 15th November 1918 at 4pm, all that well known, much frequented, fully licensed freehold public house, The EXETER INN in Chittlehamholt village where for a continuous period a lucrative business has been carried on. For viewing, please apply on the premises and further

particulars of the auctioneers or Messrs Cross Wyatt and Co. solicitors, South Molton.

The next landlord was Bill Skinner and, like Tom Martin, he also did some taxi work in the village, and introduced the petrol pumps at the pub.

Around this time, Bill Congram and Ray Turner can remember a character called Bill Boucher who used to work at Whitehall and lived where Trevor Snow lives at the time of writing, at The Nook in Warkleigh. He used to come up to the Exeter Inn on his pony Judy and was a frequent visitor. Bill Congram recalls that one evening Bill Boucher left the pub at 9.30p.m., and as it was a nice warm evening, the regulars stayed chatting outside after last orders at 10 o'clock. Suddenly they heard the clip clop of Bill Boucher's pony and saw Bill raise his hand and say 'Goodnight gentlemen'. Apparently, after leaving the pub at half past nine, Bill's pony decided to turn left at the Square instead of going on into Warkleigh. When Bill realised what was happening, he decided he may as well continue around the circuit and found himself going past the pub again. Bill Congram recalls that it was a long time before Bill would admit what had happened. Raymond Turner often saw Bill Boucher jump on his pony outside the pub and almost fall off the other side. The pony would side step across the road to help him balance before heading for Warkleigh – more or less – and tip him off when he got home.

Leo Ford was the next landlord, followed by Bob and Gwen Williams and then John and Jacky Tattersall. Growing up at the time, I became good friends with their son, Chris, in the 1970s. It was at this time that John changed the name of the pub to Uncle Tom's Cabin – the name of his previous pub. When John and Jacky left, Jim and Joy Chapman took over and restored the name to the Exeter Inn. I remember spending the night in the pub a few times while babysitting for their daughter, Penny. It was around this time that Heather and Steve Petherick came to the village. Heather became a teacher at South Molton comprehensive school – I was in the second year at the time and she became my form teacher (2P). Heather has fond memories of the Exeter Inn:

Friday night was darts night in the Exeter Inn, and many a young man went to fling a few arrows. In fact, at one time we had two teams; the Exeter Inn (the more experienced players) and Joy's Boys (named after the landlady, and consisting of the local lads). Willie Sanders and Bill Isaac were the comedians of the B team, although Pete Isaac was the better player, and he never got banned from three local pubs for having soda-syphon fights like some!

Dorothy and Charlie Bunting took over from Jim and Joy, and they ran the pub more as a 'spit and sawdust' place. In 1978 Noel Dunstone, who lived behind the pub, got stuck in the snow at Portsmouth Arms and phoned the pub for assistance. Charlie Bunting thought it would be great to form a rescue party, so off he went after lunchtime closing with a gang of about ten including Steve Petherick, Bill Isaac and Willie Sanders. The snow was thick, but they slithered down the hill in Tony Lynche's Escort van. After meeting Noel on the Exeter road, they started homeward past the Fortescue pub and back to Ken Guard's in the van, but then had to walk. As Charlie started to climb the hill to the village, his energy began to wane and when he eventually collapsed, the boys had to get a sheet of galvanise from a nearby hedge and they dragged him through the snow. After a struggle they made it past Highbullen, and, as they turned the corner and Charlie spotted the lights of the pub, he sprang up and marched off towards his goal, leaving his 'huskies' behind exhausted.

In 1980 Norman and Margaret Glenister took over the pub. They still own it although their son David is the sole landlord alongside his wife Debbie. Debbie cooks the meals – catering for the Devon appetite for meat and teddies – and they look after us locals very well.

I remember being in the pub when Norman Glenister came to view it. A few of the locals were sitting in the corner (at the only table that was arm's length from the bar!) and everyone was very concerned about Norman's 'clutch bag' – men didn't carry handbags, not down here. Norman got a lot of teasing about his handbag. In fact it was offered to my husband as a gift but he refused. Bill Isaac accepted it instead – he thought it might keep his baccy dry when he was out hedging.

The Exeter Inn today also has a cricket team and they have won many games. Below are the results from a game they played against Chittlehampton in May 2001:

Chittlehamholt beat Chittlehampton by 53 runs.
Chittlehampton: Andon 29, Billington 13, Huxtable 1, John Ashford 8, Murcu 4, Battle 2, Fuller 2, Ransome 2, James Ashford 19, Hickman n.o. 0, extras 10; total 90. Bowling: Bowman 7-0-13-2, May 9-2-16-1, Glenister 7-0-35-4, Wadling 5-0-16-2, Roy May 2-0-2-1. Chittlehamholt: Page 1, Landfish 17, Wadling 34, May 35, Broman 3, Cufford 9, Bowman 1, Glenister 6, May 3, Page n.o. 2, Crebin 1, extras 31; total 143. Bowling: Andon 6-1-11-2, James Ashford 9-2-19-1, John Ashford 7-0-18-1, Fuller 6-1-23-1, Battle 4-0-11-0, Huxtable 3-1-12-1, Hickman 3-0-11-1, Murch 2-0-9-1.

Chittlehamholt Manor

The site of the Chittlehamholt Manor is quite outstanding. The parks which stretch away in front of the house contain many noble trees, and the ground falls away to woods which form a border between the pastureland and the River Taw. Approaching the house down the main drive, magnificent views of the river can be seen in both directions. The back drive leads up from the extensive farm buildings to the small Parish Church. The house has been added to on four separate occasions. The original would seem to have been a farmhouse with a wagon shed attached. This now forms an unusual inner hall with a tiled floor and ornamental pillars supporting the ceiling. The back part of the original house is today the kitchen quarters. In about 1850 the present front of the manor was added – this began with an extension of the building from the outer wall of the wagon shed and comprised a new passage hall, staircase, and two front rooms with bedrooms above. About 20 years later another addition was made to the front of the house – a large drawing-room and a small lobby, with cellars underneath and bedrooms above. The lobby turned the corner at the far end of the house and in the 1930s, during the late Revd Carter's occupation, another staircase and a morning-room, with a bedroom above a small pantry, were built. This completed the Square of the house by joining to the old back door and kitchen quarters. A small utility courtyard remains in the centre of the Square, in which the old drinking well is still in existence. The approach to the house is attractive with an oblong courtyard flanked on one side by the back of the old stables, on another by the end part of the old house, on the third side by the outer wall of the wagon shed and on the town side by the 1850 Georgian-style front door and library wall. The eaves in the front of the house have some curious carved wooden decorations of vines and grapes, while a fine magnolia tree grows beside the drawing-room bay windows.

According to records, the Pollards already owned the manor in 1617 when it was conveyed to Lewis Pollard by his father. Lewis was created a Baronet in 1627 and his son, Sir Hugh Pollard, became controller of the household of Charles II. The house now known as The Manor was then a small house called Fraynes, excellently situated and considered at the time to be a desirable place for a manorial residence, which in time it became. The Manor then passed to the Bridges family, whose heiress brought it to the Hughes. A Mr Bridges-Hughes sold it to John Willcocks in about 1799, and in about 1810 it was purchased by John Brown of Sandford and remained in the family for 108 years. In 1863 John Brown junr married Caroline Louisa Davy of Crediton in Chittlehampton church. John Brown died six years later, aged 40, and there were no children from the marriage (although some years previously he had become the father of a girl, whom he acknowledged, who had descendants in another part of the country). The young widow erected a headstone with railings around it which can be seen just to the right as you enter Chittlehamholt churchyard. Caroline later married Robert Madge, and as was reported in the *North Devon Journal* of 1871. Mrs Madge repeated her kindness from the previous year to her poor neighbours by making a considerable and very welcome distribution of blankets and other articles of warm clothing, thereby earning the thanks and blessings of the recipients and ensuring to them seasonable relief and accession of comfort during the approaching winter season. In the same year about 60 persons sat down to a substantial dinner in the schoolroom on the occasion of the presentation of a magnificent silver epergne to Mr and Mrs Robert Madge of the Manor House, which was supplied by Mr Wm Huxtable, jeweller, South Molton, and which bore the following inscription:

Presented to Mr and Mrs Robert Madge, Manor House, Chittlehamholt, by friends and tenants as an acknowledgement of their kindness as landowners and their benevolence to the poor.

On 8 June 1875 Robert Madge died. On the day he had ridden out with the otterhounds in the morning and in the evening he rode up to the hayfield to see his men at work. A cart, which was being laden with hay, moved off and his horse made a slight jump, by which he was thrown out of the saddle and fell on the ground upon his back. He was confined to bed and, as he did not get any better by 9 o'clock, a message was sent for his medical attendant, Mr Harper of Barnstaple. As the distance was far to ride, there being no trains running at that hour of the night, he did not arrive until past midnight, only to find that death had occurred at about half-past eleven. The valuable horse that Mr Madge had ridden at the otter hunt in the morning and which the messenger rode in on the same night to fetch the doctor was found very ill next morning, no doubt from the hard pace at which he was ridden, and died in the course of the day. Again there were no children by this marriage. It is said that Caroline's second marriage was unhappy and that she took refuge in their farmhouse at Farrs from the violence of her husband. Robert Madge lies in the churchyard without a memorial.

Caroline married again, this time to Thomas Bater of Farrs who died in 1904, by whom she had one son. When Thomas Henry Bater was born in 1877 he was presented with an inscribed leather Holy Bible by his relatives at Butlers. Thomas Henry's birth is recorded in the *Journal*: 'Bater – Jan 15th 1877 at the Manor House, wife of Thomas Bater of a son.' His coming of age in 1898 is recorded in the *Journal* with 150 people sitting down to a dinner in the schoolroom and a presentation being made to him by Mr Heard, which consisted of a handsome gold lever watch with the following inscription: 'presented to T.H. (Thomas Henry) Bater esq. by the tenantry and friends as a mark of respect Jan 15th 1898', and this was accompanied by an illuminated address and list of subscribers. In connection with his birthday, the following Monday a tea was given to all the children in the parish, followed by an invitation dance from 7p.m. to 3a.m. The number present was about 250. The music was supplied by Messrs Saunders and Smolden. A

magnificent arch was erected in the village by Messrs Heard. On the Saturday and Monday anvils were fired at intervals during the day and everyone appreciated Mr and Mrs Bater's great kindness in giving them such an excellent treat and Mr Bater junr had the heartiest good wishes of all present.

In 1918 the manor was sold in parcels, the present Manor House being the sole relic of the manor, set amongst the trees which the John Browns planted. Mrs Bater's son, Mr T.H. Bater, then on active service, gave instructions for the sale. It is interesting to see what the manor owned at that time.

At the same time and place Mr Blackford offered the Exeter Inn, Chittlehamholt, which was secured by Mr B.T. James for £550. Messrs Cross Wyatt and Co. of South Molton were the solicitors concerned.

Notes on Chittlehamholt Manor by Diana Lethbridge:

My parents, Edward and Florence Dicker, and my grandparents, Isabella and Arthur Gooding, came to Chittlehamholt Manor with Revd and Mrs H. Carter in 1930 from Suffolk. The Revd Carter was retired but continued to take services in the area when needed.

I was born in 1933 and can remember my grandfather being gardener at the Manor, tending the walled garden (which I wasn't allowed in!) where he grew peaches, nectarines and had a lovely asparagus bed. He was employed at The Manor for 30 years.

My father was chauffeur to the Carters, driving a Wolseley car. He also mowed the lawns and tennis court, groomed the horses and milked the house cow.

The indoor staff consisted of a cook, parlour-maid, chambermaid and kitchen maid.

In 1947, Mr and Mrs Eric Lennard, with their foster daughters Anne and Barbara, moved to Chittlehamholt Manor which they ran as a smallholding. Mrs Lennard JP ran a herd of Guernsey cattle and eventually became Chairman of the Devon Branch of the Guernsey Cattle Breeders Association. Amongst the numerous organisations which she served were North Devon Cruse, Beaford Arts Centre, Chulmleigh and District Abbeyfield, and WRVS, but she was best known for her service to the Family Planning Association of which she was Chairman for four years in the 1960s. Although Joan Lennard led a very busy life, she still made time to serve on local committees such as the WI and the Conservative Association Flower Show, and it was during the time she was chairman of the Parish Council that Launds Playing-Field came in to being.

Cleave Copse, Warkleigh

Cleave Copse was built in 1911. The first owner, who commissioned the building of the house, was Mr Charles Victor Alexander Peel FRGS, FZS. He was a big-game hunter, naturalist and author. A son of Mr Charles Peel of North Rhode, Cheshire, he was educated at Eton and on leaving went on a world

Left: *Cleave Copse.*

Below, left: *Arthur Gooding, aged 90, gardener at Chittlehamholt Manor in 1963.*

Below: *Servants at Chittlehamholt Manor, c.1938. Left to right: Iris Parkhouse (parlour-maid), Doris Carter (kitchen maid), Lily Skinner (parlour-maid); front: Mary Harris (cook).*

Chittlehamholt Village Hall as it looked before it was demolished and replaced in 1981.

The opening of the new Chittlehamholt Village Hall in 1981 by Revd Tim Jones, retired vicar. Left to right: Mrs Jones, Squadron Leader John Beckett (Chairman of the Village Hall), Mrs Bartlett, Chris Bartlett (Chairman of the North Devon District Council), Revd Tim Jones. Courtesy of the North Devon Journal.

tour; the beginning of his big-game hunting career. The children of Chittlehamholt, Warkleigh and Satterleigh used to go on school trips to visit his collection of stuffed animals which he kept at Cleave Copse. Some of his hunting trophies can be seen at the Royal Albert Museum in Exeter.

Mr Peel's literary offerings include *Somaliland*, which is regarded as a definitive work on the country; *Through the Length of Africa*, *Hunting Polar Bears*, *The Zoological Gardens of Europe* and *Wild Sport in the Outer Hebrides*. The latter – in which Mr Peel made a close study of the animal and bird life of the area – gives a graphic description of what is known as the wildest place in the British Isles. He was also the author of a successful novel, *The Ideal Island*, and wrote extensively for the naturalist and sporting press. Some of his camera work denoted a mastery of that art also. Mr Peel was a big-game hunter practically all his life, and he wrote extensively from 1894.

The Peel family spent much of each year in Africa, but entertained extravagantly at home, so needed a small practical house with a high degree of internal ornamentation, set in sporting countryside.

When Cleave Copse came up for sale in 1995, the paper described it as:

... like Alice Through the Looking Glass, *as the front door opens into a most surprising wonderland – quite unexpected for an Edwardian house of such modest proportions the property occupies an idyllic setting at the end of a private drive off a quiet lane and surrounded by its own gardens and grounds set in more than 18 acres with its own lake, stream, woodland and paddocks. It also boasts a separate lodge cottage.*

At the time of writing, the current owner, an American lady named Sarah Hicks, has the house on the market for £800,000. She bought the property in 1996 and has since carried out many improvements including renovating the lodge cottage, creating a conservatory, terracing, extensive wood decking, installing a covered gazebo and spa bath and illuminating the side of the house with floodlights.

Church Cottage, Warkleigh

Church Cottage, Warkleigh, dates from 1589, the year after the Spanish Armada. A document in the Devon Record Office describes a gift to the parish by William, Earl of Bath, of a newly erected house to the south part of the churchyard and described as the Church House. The Church House was probably a mixture of church hall and inn from 1589 until 1735, and then became the parish poorhouse until about 1840. By 1858 it was a cottage and was sold to the Hon. Mark Rolle, becoming part of the Rolle estate.

It remained in estate hands until 1958, when it was part of Warkleigh Barton, which had been sold by the Clinton estate.

The cottage stands in a peaceful location backing on to the church and facing south, overlooking a valley, fields and beyond to woodland.

The Warkleigh Hotel

The property which was once the Warkleigh Hotel is now a private dwelling known as Woodleigh. It stands on the B3226 main road beside the River Mole, within a few yards of the Watertown footbridge. Below is an advert from 1875 regarding the letting of the hotel, followed by an advert from the sale of 24 acres of prime oak coppice growing in Satterleigh Barton, and finally an advert for the sale of the property in 1892.

TO INNKEEPERS
TO BE LET, with immediate possession, the WARKLEIGH HOTEL, in the Parish of Warkleigh, together with a large Garden and two Meadows adjoining, situated on the River Mole, midway between Southmolton Road Station and Southmolton. Tenders for the above will be received by the owner Mr John D. Young, Barnstaple, up to Friday, April 30th, 1875.

OAK COPPICE FOR SALE
SATTERLEIGH, Devon
MR JOHN BLACKFORD has been instructed by Messrs John and Richard Baker, to Sell by Auction, at the Warkleigh Hotel, on Tuesday, the 22nd day of February inst., at Three o'clock in the Afternoon, about 24 Acres of Prime OAK COPPICE, now standing and growing on Satterleigh Barton, and marked and burled out in 24 Lots. The above is well situated for removal, as the Coppice adjoins the turnpike road about four miles from South Molton Road Station, and the like distance from South Molton. A Person will be in attendance to show the Lots on the day previous and on the morning of the Day of Sale. Dated Auction Office, 8, Barnstaple-street, South Molton. 8th January 1876.

WARKLEIGH Devon
Eligible Freehold Property for Disposal
MESSRS BLACKFORD & SON are favored with instructions from the Owner, J.D. Young, Esq., to offer for Sale by Auction, at the 'Ring of Bells Inn,' South Molton, on Thursday, 4th August next, at 4 o'clock in the afternoon, the fee single and inheritance of all that desirable fully Licensed Hotel called 'THE WARKLEIGH HOTEL,' together with the Coach House Station, and other convential outbuildings and productive Meadow, Orchard, Garden and Appurtenances hereto belonging, containing about 2 Acres, now and for many years in the occupation of Mr John Howe, as tenant thereof.

The above is conveniently situated adjacent to the main road, leading from South Molton to the South Molton Road Station, L & S.W.R. 5 miles from the former and 4 miles from the latter. The Buildings are in excellent repair, and capital trout salmon fishing is afforded by the river Taw flowing as its eastern boundary. The district is also frequently hunted by Fox and Otter Hounds as well as Harriers, and the whole as a moderate investment offers a rare opportunity to limited capitalists

To view apply to the tenant, and for further particulars to the Auctioneers, South Molton.

Dated South Molton, July 19th, 1892.

Russons

Russons Farm and cottage stood many years ago. It was accessed by going down the track beside Woodside Cottages. Close to the site now stands a recently built house, owned and built by Mr and Mrs Brant. Further down the track stands Rowcliffs (used as holiday accommodation) which is now owned by the Highbullen Hotel. The main entrance to Rowcliffs comes in past the hotel. In the late 1970s and until the 1980s, Rowcliffs remained empty and started to deteriorate until Highbullen bought it. It is interesting to note that Highbullen owned it in 1923 when the estate, with its 14 or so properties, including Russons, was sold. In the sale catalogue Russons is described as a block of accommodation land with buildings, the tenants being Mr W.R. Herniman and Mr Herbert John Kingdon, the lane being in hand. The buildings included a stone and slated barn with a bullock house and cart linhay with loft over, and the remains of a burnt-down cottage. The story which has been handed down through the generations is that the cottage burnt down when a lady left a candle burning while going up to the village. I searched the newspapers for 1923 and before for an account of the story, but there was no report. In the sale papers of Rowcliffs and Russons both properties are said to have a right of way for all purposes along the lane leading to Chittlehamholt.

Chittlehamholt, Warkleigh & Satterleigh Village Hall

In 1931, a hall was built in Chittlehamholt village. Harry Congram gave the field called Dry Meadow on a lease of 1s. per annum for 999 years. Bill Congram, Harry's son, recalls being one up on the other lads as his father gave the ground. Raymond Ayre can remember in the early days of the hall, when there was a club night twice a week. A few of the elders would be in charge, including Jack Congram, Fred Moore and Bill Turner. Claude Eastmond played the piano and there was the opportunity to play skittles, darts, table tennis, a game of cards, etc. All ages came along. There is no knowledge of a hall before 1931

and prior to this social gatherings were held in the schoolroom, examples of which are shown below, taken from newspaper reports:

January 16th 1925
A very successful fancy dress and balloon dance has taken place in the schoolroom in aid of the choir funds and the provision of stage curtains. The room was very prettily decorated with fairy lights, festoons and holly by Mrs Garland and the Misses Ashdown. The costumes were of a pretty and varied character, and the judges, viz. – Mr and Mrs Ashdown, Mr and Mrs Malcolm and Mrs Leahy had a very difficult task in awarding prizes. The successful competitors were: Ladies – most original costume, Miss N. Skinner (Christmas tree); prize given by Miss Leahy. Best costume, Mrs R. Pester (night); given by Mrs Beaumont. Gentlemen – Mr C. Pester (pierrot); given by Mrs Ashdown, Mr R. Dockings (king of diamonds); given by Mrs Malcolm. Children – Molly Turner (danger signals); Gertrude Latham (black cat). Hearty cheers were accorded the judges and donors of prizes. An iced cake, given by Mrs Garland, was won by Miss D. Harris. The Misses O. Harris and R. Pester supplied the music, while Mr C. Pester was MC.

Oct 28th 1927
The harvest thanksgiving services have taken place in St John Baptist's Church. The sacred edifice was effectively decorated by lady members of the congregation. A well-attended tea in the Schoolroom was presided over by Mesdames Congram, Pester, Thomas and Harris. The evening service was largely attended, the preacher being the Revd H. James (Vicar). In the evening a dance, which was well attended, took place in the Schoolroom, Miss R. Pester being the pianist. The collections from the weekday services and the morning services on the following Sunday, with the profits from the tea and dance, are to be given to the North Devon Infirmary, to which deserving institution the fruit and vegetables have also been sent.

Village hall Queen January 31st 1957
In 1957 a village hall Queen was elected. The honour went to Mrs W. Harris who sold the most threepenny trinkets for village-hall funds; her total amounted to £11.0s.6d. Other totals were Miss Margaret Heard (£6.10s.), Miss Muriel Wright (£1.2s.), Miss Mary Martin (£1.2s.) and Miss Margaret Guard (15s.6d.). The crowning ceremony was performed by Mrs J. Carter and the queen was presented with a silver and turquoise necklet and earrings and a posy of anemones with silver ribbons by Maureen Thorne. The other four contestants received boxes of handkerchiefs.

The committee minute-book gives more information about the early years of the hall. The first committee members were Messrs F. Bryant, W. Bater, V. Pester, E. Kingdon, F. Heard, J. Congram and J. Clarke. It was decided that, to start with, the hall would be opened every night and the times for opening would be 6.30 to 10p.m. in the winter, and 7.30 to 10p.m. in the summer, and that the members of the committee would be the stewards and would arrange between themselves who should be present each evening. Mrs Medland was the first cleaner; she cleaned and tidied up the hall every day and attending to lights and fires for 5s.0d. a week. She also scrubbed and cleaned the hall four times a year, and any other time when required, at 5s.0d. a time. In 1932 Mr Bryant proposed, and Mr J. Congram seconded, that there would be a broadcast speech by HRH the Prince of Wales on 27 June and a wireless would be provided in the Village Hall for anyone who wanted to listen. This hall was to last for a good 50 years until in 1981, its exact 50th year, it was pulled down and rebuilt by S.H. Hulland, builders from South Molton, and the architect was Mr Len Eves. The new hall was opened by the late Revd Tim Jones, who was once a vicar of Chittlehamholt, Warkleigh and Satterleigh. Time goes very quickly as we know and we now find that in 2002 the present hall celebrates 21 years. In 1992 a further extension was built on to this hall and the adjoining field was bought, allowing space for adequate parking.

Heather Petherick's memories follow:

The original Village Hall in those days was small and built of wood. It could – and often did – hold about 100 at a squeeze.

Hunt balls, Conservative balls, Bell-ringers' balls and ordinary dances were always an occasion as a special bar had to be erected with a wooden frame covered with black polythene. [It was] a little chilly on a cold night, and when it rained the drips could be used to water down the whisky in your glass!

It was decided to raise funds for a new parish hall – headed by Chris and Di Lethbridge – and the fund-raising events began in earnest: Bingo with Bernard Scrivener as caller, dances, discos, film shows, slide shows, coffee mornings, socials, jumble sales, etc. I used to be on the door at discos because, as a local teacher at South Molton, I would know the local lads and was quite happy to sling out any who were argumentative. No one argued with a woman in those days.

I must also mention the children's parties in the Village Hall during the 1970s and '80s. My children loved them. Sam Heath and Ray Hobbs with his accordian provided entertainment. One game I recall was Farmer Brown. Two teams of 15 sat facing each other on chairs and each team was given a part to play; Mr Brown, Mrs Brown, sheepdogs, cows, sheep, chickens, ducks, etc. Ray would read a story about the Brown family and if your part was mentioned, you ran to the top of your line, around the outside and down to the bottom and back to your seat. Points were awarded for the first team back to their seat. I always felt sorry for the person at the end – usually a well-built person – who played the Devon bull. Their chair got swung around, usually with them in it, as people galloped past.

The children thoroughly enjoyed the game, along with the wonderful tea that followed.

Warkleigh & Satterleigh Social Centre

After Warkleigh School was closed it stood empty for some while, apart from during the monthly distribution of library books. Eventually it was purchased by the parish in 1953 and a social centre was formed for Warkleigh and Satterleigh. Regular whist drives and socials were held, and evening classes too; sewing with Christine England, square dancing and folk dancing under the tuition of Tony Foxworthy, play reading, etc. The centre was eventually sold in 1980 and turned into a private house. There follow some articles, below and overleaf, from the local newsletter of events which took place in the social centre:

November 1965
The annual Harvest Social was an even greater success this year and it was indeed gratifying to have such a good attendance. Our little social centre had a welcoming, festive air due to the beautiful floral arrangements by Mrs Tony Gardener and Miss Hayes. Mr and Mrs Bill Hammett kept the fun going in their usual happy manner and our best thanks go to them for all their hard work. Also our warmest gratitude to everyone who contributed so generously and to the ladies of the committee for their part in providing sandwiches, etc. and doing all the back-room jobs. Thank you all for coming, the more the merrier was certainly true. The first whist drive was held on Tuesday October 26th, and there was the usual friendly and jolly atmosphere. Mrs Jones and Miss Hayes provided the prizes and refreshments. Prize winners were as follows: Ladies: 1st Mrs D. Herniman, 2nd Mrs L.A. Shapland, 3rd Mrs W. Lindsay, Consolation Miss G. Hayes. Gentlemen: 1st Mr E. Snell, 2nd Mr E. Luxton, 3rd Mr W. Bowden, Consolation Mr R. Kingdon. Competition: Mr R. Kingdon.

Luggers, Chittlehamholt & the Luggers Lodger

At one time there was a dwelling called Luggers – part of the walls still remain just above Presbury Farm. Harold Congram can remember the tramp who took refuge in the building during the 1930s when it was barely habitable. The locals nicknamed the man the Luggers Lodger. His real name was Cole and he was thought to have come from the Ashreigney area. He often went over to Butlers, where they gave him cheese and cider. Harold remembers as a child being told to keep away from him, although he was harmless enough. At the time there were quite a few people on the road and they used to go to the Union in South Molton, where they

─── *Village Hall* ───

NEW HALL.

Social Centre Opened at Chittlehamholt.

FINE ACHIEVEMENT.

After over two years of steady effort, the inhabitants of the parish of Chittlehamholt have realised their ambition in securing a Village Hall. Mrs. de Legh was prominent in the initial steps, in September, 1928, and to her, as to Mrs. W. Pollard, of Whitmore, Chittlehamholt, who has acted as Hon. Secretary, the parish is much indebted.

At a public meeting the proposal was taken up with enthusiasm. A Committee was appointed, with Mr. W. Pollard as the President, other members being Mr. and Mrs. de Legh, Mr. and Mrs. Martin, Mesdames A. C. Thomas, Pester, Johns, J. Congram, J. Clarke, T. and W. Bater. As a result of concerts and dances, subscriptions, a grant from the Carnegie Trust Fund, and nearly £70 from a fete and bazaar (held at Whitmore, by kind permission of Mr. and Mrs. Pollard), the total of £260 involved by the provision of the new Hall has practically been secured. The new Hall is situated in Dry Meadow, close to the village. The site was generously given, for the nominal acknowledgement of 1s per annum, by Mr. H. Congram, whose gift is greatly appreciated.

The Hall is a wooden structure of pleasing design, with exterior of asbestos, and red asbestos tiles. It measures 60 feet by 20 feet. The interior is lined with matchboarding, and lighting is with oil lamps. The Hall has been admirably fitted up, and Messrs. Pester and Johns erected the building in a capable manner.

Generous gifts include:—Pianoforte, Mrs. de Legh; three large hanging lamps, Mrs. Beaumont; bracket lamps and sundries, Mrs. W. Pollard; curtains, Mrs. Radcliff and Mrs. H. Carter; 12 bridge tables, Mrs. Bryant.

OPENING CEREMONY.

The new Hall was opened on Friday by Lieut.-Col. T. Gracey, of Northcote Manor, Burrington. There was a good attendance in spite of very inclement weather. Mr. W. Pollard presided, and those also on the platform were Col. Gracey, the Rev. and Mrs. H. Carter (Chittlehamholt Manor), Mesdames Pollard and de Legh.

Col. Gracey congratulated the parish on their achievement in providing a hall practically free from debt. The new building would add greatly to the social amenities of the neighbourhood. He apologised for the unavoidable absence of Mrs. Gracey.

Thanks were accorded Col. Gracey, on the motion of the Rev. H. Carter, seconded by Mrs. Owen. A vote of thanks to the President and Committee was voiced by Mrs. Beaumont, seconded by the Rev. A. Hackblock.

ENTERTAINMENT AND TEA.

Two very enjoyable entertainments, organised by Mrs. Pollard, were given during the afternoon and evening. The programmes embraced pianoforte selections by Mrs. Ahmad, who was also the accompanist for the songs, an amusing sketch by the Misses Barton, songs by the Rev. B. Vaughan, Miss Hilary Rootham (Barnstaple), Miss Barton, Mr. W. W. Holdup (South Molton), Mr. J. Harris, and monologues and stories by Mr. R. W. Pitman (High Bickington).

There was a largely attended public tea which Mrs. T. H. R. Martin superintended. She had the assistance of Mesdames Congram, F. Clarke, Heard, Pester, French, Anson and Martin, and Misses Congram, Newcombe and French. Mr. E. Stone also rendered very valuable help.

A children's bran-tub and quoits was run by Messrs. Vincent Pester and Frank

Heard; skittling, Messrs. G. Clarke, Kingdon, T. Bater and J. Congram; bowls, Mr. Johns; sheep weight judging, etc., Messrs. Thomas, Pester, W. Bater and Martin. There were competitions for a fine salmon given by Mrs. Owen and cakes given by Mrs. Ratcliffe and others.

For the very successful dance which concluded the day's programme Mr. C. Pester was M.C., music was supplied by the Dartonia Band, Mrs. W. Heard superintended the refreshments, and Messrs. J. S. Thomas and J. F. Pester were other helpers. There were several interesting competitions, the prizes for which were distributed by Miss Bater (Farra).

Results:—Spot dance winners: Miss M. Boucher and Mr. K. Wythe, Miss Pickard and Mr. White. Balloon waltz—Miss M. Latham and Mr. G. Moore. Draws:— Tea service given by Mrs Bryant won by Mrs. Johns; case of pipes, given by Mr. P. Couch, won by Mr. R. Medland; iced cakes, given by Mrs. Owen and Mrs. Ratcliffe, won by Miss G. Hill and Mr. Bussell (Chulmleigh) respectively; salmon, given by Mrs. Owen, won by Mr. Snow

Right: *An invitation card for the opening of the new Chittlehamholt Village Hall in 1981.*

Left: *The demolition of Chittlehamholt, Warkleigh and Satterleigh Village Hall in 1981.*

Above: *The old Village Hall. Also visible in the photograph is a wooden construction with black wrapping, which was used as a bar for dances.*

Above left: *The present Village Hall with its Union Jack and bunting to celebrate the Queen's golden jubilee. This hall celebrated its 21st birthday in 2002.*

Left: *An account from the local newspaper regarding the opening of Chittlehamholt, Warkleigh and Satterleigh Village Hall in 1931.*

knew they could get a good meal.

Bill Congram recalls being told when the Luggers Lodger was in residence. The lodger once had a falling out with Mr William Harris on whose land it stood and the lodger had to go. Bill then remembers him lodging at the old farmhouse at Featherstones.

Below are details of the sale of just one of the farms and four cottages which were known as Little Shortridge and no longer exist.

1927 WARKLEIGH, NORTH DEVON
2½ miles from Umberleigh Station
Cockram, Dobbs and Stagg have been instructed to offer for Sale by Auction at 'Unicorn Hotel' South Molton, on Thursday, 18th August, at 3pm., Desirable FREE-HOLD FARM, called 'LITTLE SHORTRIDGE', comprising about 99½ Acres good Meadow, Pasture, Arable and Orchard Lands (mostly good Meadow and Pasture), with four Good COTTAGES and sufficient OUTBUILDINGS.
Possession of all, except the Cottages, will be given at Lady-Day next.
To View, apply Mr A. Cockram, 'Great Shortridge' (adjoining the property).
Further particulars of the AUCTIONEERS or of Messrs CROSS, WYATT, VELLACOTT & WILLEY, Solicitors, Southmolton and Barnstaple.

Ken Snow, a retired carpenter and wheelwright, talks of his career and a few of the buildings he has worked on in Warkleigh:

I started my apprenticeship with William Sanders & Son, builder of South Molton, in Easter week 1941 when I was 14 – I lived at Greendown Cottage in Warkleigh at the time. I cycled to South Molton in the morning, having to be there and on the lorry by 7 o'clock as we were going to Minehead to erect Nissen huts and searchlight sights. We got back at 8 o'clock at night. That first day, all I had to do was hang doors on each end of the Nissen huts and I soon got fed up and jacked it in.

I got a job at Murch Bros in Umberleigh and served four years of my apprenticeship there before being called up. I spent some time in this country and was then sent to India where I spent three years. When I returned I finished my apprenticeship at W. Isaac & Sons, Braunton, and then registered with the Ministry of Works and started out on my own.

Glebe Cottage, Warkleigh.
We worked on this building in 1966 when it was called Rectory Cottage. The Revd Jones applied to the diocesan parsonage board at Exeter to have the cottage restored, but when they came to check they didn't have any record of the cottage being there. It appears that the rector at Warkleigh had the cottage built in 1912 for a gardener, and paid for it himself. The cottage had been empty for 17 years. We rebuilt the front wall, repaired the roof, the

chimneys and windows, built the new extension at the back and put in a new bathroom, larder and coal store. When it rained, it went straight through the cottage – there were 4 inches of mud inside when we started work and so we also put in a septic tank and drainage, etc.

Edgington House, Warkleigh
We worked at Edgington House from 1966 to 1973 for Mr and Mrs Whitney. We re-roofed the sheds first; we took off the thatched roof of one open-fronted shed and replaced it with timber and galvanised iron. In the house, we re-roofed and repaired the floor. We also concreted the lower yard, built a retaining wall and converted the stable into a milking parlour because Mr Whitney had some Jersey cows. We then updated the groom's flat over the stable and coach-house with Mr Whitney creosoting the roof timbers as we uncovered them.

Warkleigh House
In 1952, when Mr and Mrs Pepper bought Warkleigh House, we did a few jobs – mainly decorating – before they moved in. Mr Pepper used to write for comics including The Lion, Hotspur, The Tiger, *etc., and sometimes he would walk around the house in a daze and wouldn't answer when I spoke to him – I suppose he was working on his stories. In 1965, when Mr Featherstonehaugh bought the property, we re-roofed the house and the stable block. Through the entrance hall there was a floor with soft wood which we took up and laid oak to match each side. Wilson Holland remembers that when the Thorolds lived here they had two gardeners and two indoor staff. Jimmy Simmons the under-gardener used to take the laundry in a pony and trap to the Satterleigh council-houses to a Mrs Luxton.*

Warkleigh House was at one time run as a country house hotel and Janet Judd, who came to live in Warkleigh in 1944, recalls that it was owned by people called Ferguson and was later bought by a family called Bullard who also bought Higher Beers, renaming it Warkleigh Farm House. It was during the ownership of Frank and Margaret Pepper that they kindly allowed Janet and her friends to use the tennis courts on Tuesday evenings. They formed a tennis club and were able to buy tennis balls and eventually replace the net.

Highbullen

Highbullen is a splendid Victorian Gothic mansion built by William Moore of Exeter in 1879. Walter Heard's father told him that Highbullen was either going to be built where it is now or in a field known as Broadley just along the road from Holtgate. In 1923 the estate was sold and shown below is a summary of the lots – it is interesting to note how much Highbullen then encompassed.

Following the sale of Highbullen in 1923 at the Bridge Hall, Barnstaple, the local papers give us

A view of Hope Cottage, Combrew, Sunnybank and Sunny Cottage. This row of houses is traditionally known by the older members of the village as Rattle Street because of the sound of the men's hobnail boots on the cobbles.

Chittlehamholt Square, early 1900s.

Below: *Drakes Farm, Chittlehamholt, before it was pulled down in 1969 and replaced with a bungalow.*

The old cottages which were pulled down. Silver Birch bungalow now stands on the site reputed to have been the Carpenter Arms. Mrs Slee is standing outside.

Oakford Cottage as it was before a new house was erected on the site.

An old photo of Lower Spiecott when it was thatched.

the following information. First submitted as a whole, the property was withdrawn at £17,500. The mansion was submitted separately and also withdrawn. Mr T.R.H. Martin of Chittlehamholt purchased two pasture fields of 13½ acres adjoining Edgington House for £575 and a 12-acre arable field fronting on the Barnstaple road privately after the sale; these were the only lots sold.

A year later, *The Western Times* stated that Highbullen was coming on to the market again with the following results, after the sale at the George Hotel, South Molton:

Whitehall dairy holding, 17 acres withdrawn at £850. Whitmore (small farm) 31 acres sold to Messrs Sparkes, Pope, Matthew and Thomas of Exeter for a client for £1,550. Hills House Farm, 81a 2ro. 30pk to the tenant Mr G. Tucker £1,550. Rowcliffs and Russons Farm, 54 acres withdrawn at £850 and afterwards sold at private treaty. Four accommodation pasture fields respectively, together with four enclosures of pasture and woodlands and quarry occupied by Mr H.J. Kingdon sold to Mrs Clarke of Chittlehamholt for £745. Newland mixed farm, 87 acres withdrawn at £1,500. Snapdown and Snapdown Wood, 51 acres withdrawn at £833. The Hermitage, 18 acres to the tenant Mr E.E. Herniman for £810. Woodleigh, a riverside residence and four acres with 14 acres of accommodation land to the tenant Mr J. Hulland for £936. South View Cottages, Chittlehamholt, to the tenant Mrs Elstone for £300. Edgington Cottage was sold privately to Major Beaumont for £325.

During the war, a private school was evacuated to Highbullen. After the war, 'Barbers By-Products of Chardstock' used Highbullen Farm as a knacker's yard, either dealing with the animals on the spot or transporting them to Chardstock. Three German prisoners were employed in the grounds, travelling daily from Winkleigh.

When Colonel Caws and family lived at Highbullen they ran it as a hotel. The guests were mainly coach parties with a Hants and Dorset coach coming in on a Monday, staying two nights and then going on Wednesday. Every week a Ribble coach would come in on Wednesday, just staying for one night, followed by a Hants and Dorset one, which would stay until Saturday.

Since arriving in 1963, the Neil family, headed by Hugh and Pam, turned this mansion into a very successful hotel where many personalities, including Sir Laurence Olivier, have come to stay. Their son Martin now takes a leading role in running the hotel and spoke to me about the early days:

In 1963 my father and mother bought Highbullen. In that bad winter things couldn't have been worse – it was in a very run-down state; there was no mains water or electricity, and it was very grim and cold. Being in Highbullen was like being in Siberia. As an eight-year-old boy, I thought my parents were mad to buy it. I had a battery as a bedside light and there were bats hanging from quite a few of the ceilings. I had been brought up in London where there was plentiful heat, lighting and electricity and easy access to a phone; all the things I took for granted living in a city just weren't there at Highbullen. The building had a huge amount of potential though, and it took a lot of time and money to get it to a state where it was habitable and usable.

The hotel we owned in London was debt free by the early '60s and, although the plan was to buy a cottage outside London and have a bit of family time at weekends, Mum and Dad ended up buying Highbullen. As soon as they'd bought Highbullen, they had plans and ideas for doing it up and so family life never really happened as planned; the business always came first and family time was taken here and there. It's always been that way.

With Mum and Dad getting older, I started to see a lot of opportunities at the hotel that we weren't taking advantage of so I re-focused my energies on the hotel. In 1985 I bought Whitehall from Brigadier and Mrs Parsons as I thought it would be a useful addition to what we were offering at Highbullen. This automatically meant I had more of a commitment here than before. Jane and I finally moved down permanently and have been here for the last 15 years.

The main launch-pad for the business was the restaurant and the cellars. Most of the business at first came from the local community, and because that was doing well, we started to fill the bedrooms and obviously expanded. Once the business was built up, we had to keep adapting because country house hotels are now very hard to make financially viable, and many go out of business. There's such a big choice of holidays now that we have to keep bringing in new amenities and facilities just to keep the same amount of people coming. The temptation is for people to jump on a plane and have a cheap holiday abroad. Although what we charge at Highbullen is very good value by British standards, you could probably get a week's package holiday abroad for the same price as a four- or five-night stay. That's what we're up against; if we don't have the facilities we'll go out of business, but if we borrow money to buy the facilities, we still risk going out of business; you're damned if you do, and damned if you don't.

If the weather in North Devon was nice 365 days a year, we wouldn't need so many new facilities; you've got to get people to leave their nice comfortable homes and drive to North Devon, and they're not going to do that just to sit indoors and stare at the rain. Because people eat well at home these days, and supermarkets offer a fantastic variety of food, you've got to offer more than a blazing log fire and a nice evening meal. We've got a golf course, tennis court, indoor swimming pool, gymnasium, etc.; things people haven't got at home, which makes our hotel more of an attractive proposition. There is of course a direct link between any developments we undertake and local jobs; if we don't have the customers, we don't need the staff. At the time of writing we've started on a £1.5 million expansion of the hotel which will turn it into a mini Gleneagles Country Club, creating a new centre with an indoor putting green, pool, gym and restaurant. With better year-round business, we'll be able to offer more permanent jobs.

A large cross-section of people come to stay at the hotel, and for every 1,000 people that come through the door, you get a few celebrities. We've welcomed Sir Laurence Olivier, who wrote part of his autobiography here, and more recently ex-president Giscard D'Estaing of France, author Wilbur Smith, and supermodel Elle McPherson, whose unlikely appearance at the railway station caused quite a stir. I couldn't get a taxi for her, so I gave her a lift to Tiverton Parkway. When she walked into the station, every pair of male eyes was directed towards her.

I have been acting for 30 years, splitting my time between acting and running the hotel. I've had roles in 'Dr Who', 'Minder', 'International Velvet', and Carlton's children's series 'Bernard's Watch'. At the time of writing, I have started filming the third series of 'Down to Earth' in which I play estate agent George Roebuck. Some of this is filmed in the office of Webbers in Torrington. Sometimes the acting and hotel work merge; last year I ended up serving 'Down to Earth' actor Warren Clarke. As the restaurant was very busy, he wanted to eat in his room so I popped his meal in the boot of my car and drove it over. He was so embarrassed that he had dragged me away from the hotel.

Right: *Taylors Cottage, Chittlehamholt, seen through the woods.*

Below: *View of Chittlehamholt village. The men in the picture are thought to be Fred and Jim Clarke, standing outside Cobblestone Court where they had their blacksmith business from the early 1900s onwards.*

Chapter 7

BUSINESSES PAST & PRESENT

There were several tradesmen in Chittlehamholt village 80 years ago, and people who grew up at that time can give us a clear picture of that fascinating bygone age. Raymond Ayre, who used to live at Haynetown, talks of the hive of activity the village was and the sounds emanating from all the professions which no longer exist. One tradesman was a tailor called Mr Elam Hammett, known as Tailor Hammett. He ran his business at The Old Gate House in the Square – in those days it was called Rose Cottage. Mrs Hammett ran a grocery shop from here and Mr Hammett had his tailoring business around the back. A photograph of Tailor Hammett and his family, taken c.1908, shows articles in the shop window.

Mrs Hammett's grandson, Hanson, remembers being told that sugar and suchlike for the shop arrived in big sacks which used to be weighed. The men in the area would drop orders into Mrs Hammett on their way to the pub on Saturday nights, and Mrs Hammett would measure and price the goods ready for the men to collect on their way home.

On retirement, Mr and Mrs Hammet lived at the house known at the time of writing as The Old Forge, which was once one of three cottages. Hanson recalls that even after his grandfather retired, he would still take in tailoring and would mend any clothes people wanted repaired. Raymond Ayre remembers one night he was gaming about with his best suit on when he fell and tore his trousers. He was worried that his mother would notice when she put his clothes away, so that night Raymond put his own trousers away and then sneaked them out to Mr Hammett's on Monday. Mr Hammett asked, 'Boy, what have you been up to?', to which Raymond replied, 'I've ripped my trousers and I don't want Mother to know.' Mr Hammett replied, 'I'll make a good job of them, come back tomorrow night.' He did do a good job, and Raymond's mother never saw the join in the trousers. Raymond can't remember whether Mr Hammett charged him for the repair, but he knows that he never

told anyone about it. Whenever they caught each other's eye in chapel, Raymond felt they both knew something no one else did.

Mr Elam Hammett was born in Burrington in 1864 and came to Chittlehamholt in 1876. At 12 years old he was apprenticed to Mr E. Copp's tailoring business. During an eight-year apprenticeship, six years were served for food only – no wages. The seventh year he was paid a shilling a week, and the last year he received 1s.6d. a week. Elam went on to run his own successful tailoring business.

He married Miss Annie Chapple of Chittlehamholt on Christmas Day 1886 – the bride's 21st birthday – with Revd Yauldren officiating. They had eight children – five boys and three girls – but only two sons and one daughter survived. Their son Elam was killed in the First World War, in which their eldest son Ralph also served. Ralph had his own prosperous tailoring business at Crewe. Their son Lionel lived at Kinnings Farm, Chittlehamholt, and their daughter, Mrs Ernest Herniman, lived at Cawsey Meethe.

On Christmas Day 1936 Mr and Mrs Hammett celebrated their golden wedding anniversary – it was also Mrs Hammett's 71st birthday. Newspaper reports describe a family gathering and a wedding cake surmounted by orange blossom. Other decorations included white heather and five doors, each with a gold ring to represent ten years.

When the Hammetts sold the shop, Mr and Mrs Percy Couch took over. Percy worked for Lethbridge's, the bakers in South Molton, and also delivered the bread in the village. After this period, Maurice Thorne can remember a Mrs Cockwell living there. Maurice would buy paraffin for his mother

Photograph above: *The Hammett family with their shop and tailoring business at Rose Cottage, known today as The Old Gate House. The door in the picture has since been replaced with a window. Standing in the doorway are Elam and Annie Hammett with their children (left to right) Minnie, Elam, Lionel and Donald.*

Builder Willie Sanders from Chittlehamholt.

Steve Petherick, agricultural engineer
from Chittlehamholt.

Potter Eileen Jones of the Chapelgate Pottery,
Chittlehamholt.

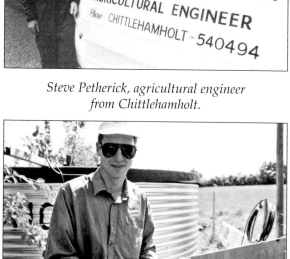

David Gillanders, builder from Warkleigh.

Painter and decorator Mac Lightwood
from Chittlehamholt.

Veterinary surgeon Heather Hammond from
Chittlehamholt gives Diana Lethbridge's cat
Lucy an injection.

Visiting greengrocer John Lucas serving
Margaret Thorne from Chittlehamholt.

Alan and Marilyn Bowen from Snapdown,
Warkleigh, with their holiday caravan business.

and remembers that inside the wall was just like a glass cabinet which opened.

Brothers Fred and Jim Clarke were once the village blacksmiths. They operated from Fred's premises, known at the time of writing as Cobblestone Court, although at the time – 80 years ago – it was called Combrew. Ken Guard recalls Fred Clarke scraping out a piece of red-hot coal from the anvil, holding it in the palm of his hand, and lighting his pipe with it.

Harold Congram can remember Lt Col Leahy who lived at the manor. He was thought to be a Cavalry Officer but Harold doesn't know how he became one because he was as nervous as a kitten. He was an awesome character who could often be seen walking in the village with a stick which had a spearhead attached to the end for personal protection. He would get the spear sharpened in Clarke's the blacksmith.

When conker time came around, the local children would enjoy going up to the smithy to see if they could pick up a horseshoe nail, which was the ideal tool for piercing a hole through the conkers.

Fred dissolved the partnership and later became the village postman, delivering the *Western Times* on Fridays. He also did a bit of taxi work with his pony and jingle. Fred's wife was the local midwife.

Jim continued the blacksmith business and put up a new workshop and forge in his garden on the other side of the road to where he lived. Appropriately, this house is called The Old Forge, although I remember that back in the 1970s it was called Avening. The house next door is called Farriers and was built in the 1970s a few yards away from where the forge and workshop once stood.

Jim's son, Wallace, helped his father in the smithy and in the evenings did cycle repairs and sold bikes.

At one time, Warkleigh had a blacksmith's shop. The late Bill Bowden couldn't remember one during his lifetime, but recalled his father saying how he used to bring the horses from Satterleigh Barton to the cottage now known as Warkleigh Cottage, which used to be the forge. *Kelly's Directory* confirms that John Simmons was the local blacksmith.

The two sets of the Heard family were carpenters, wheelwrights, undertakers and threshing contractors.

Walter Heard, in his nineties at the time of writing, talks of his grandfather as an agricultural engineer who made machinery and bought grass machines and hay-turning equipment and hired them out to the farmers who could not buy them. Walter's father William, like his father before him, was a machinist and built a reed comber. He was known to people as Uncle Heard. Bill Congram remembers being told that

Visiting window cleaner John Russell, a regular cheerful face around the parish. John is often heard singing whilst doing his job.

Uncle Heard went down to Braunton before he made his reed comber and saw one working there. He got the idea for building one from this, but didn't get too close to the design in case there was trouble about the patent of the machine. Walter and his brother Frank, with the help of his father, then built a second reed comber which later caught fire. Bill Congram recalls that the second one was a much better machine and had self-aligning bearings which went like a Rolls Royce. Bill said, 'I was the first one to cut the cords when they tried out that machine.' Uncle Heard got into the business of threshing corn with steam engines and threshers. Squire Moore helped him, financially, to buy the equipment and Jack Nott went into partnership with him. Later, Walter and Frank Heard took on the business. Threshing days, which altogether involved around 12 men, were busy days in the harvesting calendar. The farmers had to provide the coal for the steam engines and had to make a trip either to Portsmouth Arms Station or King's Nympton with their horses and carts to get the special steam coal. Walter and Frank went from farm to farm, with each farmer helping the other.

Harold Congram, who is in his early eighties in 2002, remembers there was a lot of timber felled at Satterleigh in his school-days and it was hauled by a steam tractor pulling a wagon to Umberleigh to be sawn up in Murch Brothers' sawmill. That same tractor is still running and was recently featured in a magazine called *Old Glory*. It used to stop outside Chittlehamholt School and stoke up steam. It was difficult to get her and the wagon around the corner at Manor Cross, so they used to come the other way, past Entrance Cross. One time they had a slip of timber outside the church and never came back to pick it up. After that the road was widened.

The Pesters, like the Heards, were carpenters, wheelwrights and undertakers – there was enough work for both families to make a living. Harold Congram remembers being told that before his grandfather, John Pester, moved to Fir Cottage and built a bigger carpentry workshop, he was living in the cottage known at the time of writing as Searles, where he built a workshop. The same Searles building still stands and in 2002 is used as a general garage. Harold's sister, Christine, remembers that when Bill Heard lived at Searles she saw him on a nice day when the doors were open, making coffins. Christine's grandmother, Elizabeth Pester, used to make the pillows for the coffins and Christine remembers seeing her doing this and lining them with white material.

When not farming, Richard May from Farrs Farm diversifies into his carpentry business.

Maurice Thorne of M & M Plants, Chittlehamholt.

Janet Walker from Kinnings, Chittlehamholt at her boarding kennels.

Lynne Fraser, proprietor of the Taw Vale Cattery, Chittlehamholt.

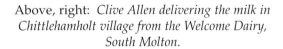

Above: *Glebe Cottage Plants.* Left to right: *Carol Klein (proprietor), Rachel Hill, Sheila May, Barbara Catlin.*

Above, right: *Clive Allen delivering the milk in Chittlehamholt village from the Welcome Dairy, South Molton.*

Right: *Russell Coomber, who delivered the Sunday papers around Chittlehamholt during 2002.*

Apart from the Heards with their steam engines, Tom Stenner from King's Satterleigh had a threshing contracting business and although the Heards were in the centre of Chittlehamholt village, it was the Stenners' steam engine the Pesters used to drive their saw with the help of a belt to cut the wood for their carpentry business and for making the elm coffins. The Stenners later moved to South Molton Road.

Paper Deliveries

Eight years ago Mr Philips from Chittlehampton delivered papers in the parishes. He was followed by Spencer Vivian from the same village. Fred Clarke delivered the *Western Times*. In more recent years I can remember Mr Charlie Guard from Chittlehampton delivering the daily papers in the 1960s, '70s and '80s. He also had a shop and would deliver groceries as well. He was followed by Mr Meredith and then Mr Paddy Steer, all of whom came from the Chittlehampton shop. When Pam and John Lewis opened a shop in Chittlehamholt village, papers were then delivered from there. This is still the case in 2002. On Sundays the paperboy, Russell Coomber, delivers the papers.

Visiting Tradesmen

It is interesting to note how many different visiting tradesmen there have been over the years. Sixty years ago there were two butchers providing a service: Mr Sid Lake from King's Nympton, and Mr Bob Ellicott from High Bickington. More recently, Mr Gordon Burgess from Chittlehampton delivered for many years up until the 1980s.

In the 1970s there were Mr Yeo from the Dartmoor Boot Store in Barnstaple, an 'Easy Cleaning' gentleman, Mother's Pride bakery, and Chanters the bakers.

In 2002 the visiting tradesmen include John Lucas from Chumleigh with his greengrocery business and John Russell with his window-cleaning business.

Milk Deliveries

During the Second World War, the milk in Chittlehamholt was delivered by Jack Congram from Wards Farm and Bill Beer from Pearces. Milk could also be bought from Hills House Farm, known to everyone as 'The Dairy', as well as from Tom Martin at the Exeter Inn.

Jack Congram made a handcart and supplied the school with milk. Mrs Congram had baskets made up for the milk by people called West in Barnstaple High Street, and Jack made a board so that another layer could go on the top. Jack would take the milk up to the school in the morning, and it was the job of Christine, Raymond or Frank Congram to remember to bring back the empty bottles at the end of the day. Of course they didn't always remember to do this!

The bottles were a third of a pint and had a little cardboard disc in the top and a small hole for a straw. When she left school, Christine Congram delivered milk around the village, using a basket on the front of her bike.

When the Congrams gave up the milk round, Albert Ayre took over, supplying milk from Haynetown. Bill Beer continued to supply milk as well. Mr Beer carried on into the 1970s and an early photograph *(below)* shows him with his yoke carrying the milk. On his death, Mr Sandhurst from Spiecott supplied the village and at the time of writing we have deliveries from Welcome Dairy of South Molton. In 2002 we are lucky to still have such services surviving as a lot of people buy their milk from supermarkets. In 1979 we saw the last of the milk-churn lorries coming through the village with the clattering of the churns and the familiar sight of the farmers bringing their churns to the end of their lanes and leaving it on the milk stands. We now see milk tankers which have replaced the milk-churn lorries.

Bill Beer delivering the milk with his yokes in Chittlehamholt village.

Antique Clocks

Ray Carr from Newlands talks about his antique-clock repair business:

I started off in life as an analytical chemist – I really specialised in microanalysis – and in those days it was expected that you could adjust, regulate and clean your own instruments. I spent about 15 years at an aircraft company sorting out any problems that occurred with the aircraft. If an instrument had become contaminated, you had to strip it down, find out what the problem was, analyse it, and if necessary put the instrument back together and make a report of what had happened. Working there, I met some of the finest precision engineers and small-scale engineers you could ever wish to meet, and I learnt an awful lot from them.

When I was made redundant, I thought I should do something useful with my knowledge. Clocks have always held a special interest for me, and I've always been able to strip, clean and repair them, so I started a college course on the restoration of antique clocks. I learnt as much as I could at college, then began repairing clocks at home. Although I do repair modern clocks, it's the old ones which fascinate me, and I've got enough engineering skill and equipment to make parts for really old clocks.

My wife, Brenda, and I regularly go to antique fairs selling the antique clocks we've bought from auctions. At first we only sold clocks from my private collection which I no longer wanted, but gradually we began to advertise the repair business and it grew from there.

Businesses Today

The old trades of yesterday, which were mostly connected with the land, have been replaced by small businesses in the parishes.

In Chittlehamholt we have Janet Walker with her dog-boarding kennels at Kinnings. A few yards up the road at Simmons Farm, Rosalyn Wright breeds King Charles spaniels. Richard May at Farrs Farm runs a carpentry business, while Steve Petherick has an agricultural business and my father Chris Lethbridge also had one until he died in 1991. Heather Hammond works from home as a veterinary surgeon and people can remember Mr Rawle from Chittlehampton trotting out on his pony to see to the animals' needs in the parishes about 80 years ago.

In the tourist and catering trade we have the well-known Highbullen Hotel and the Exeter Inn, plus many bed and breakfasts and Alan and Marilyn Bowen's holiday caravans at Snapdown.

We also have two potters – Eileen Jones in the village makes fine porcelain and stoneware, and just outside the village, Mark Donaldson fires exotic figure-heads and chess pieces.

As a result of an increased interest in plants and

Above: *Stephen Abell at his Higher Watertown nursery.*

gardening, it is not surprising that there are three nurseries in the parishes. Mr and Mrs Maurice Thorne run M & M Plants, Steve Abell has an up-and-coming nursery at Higher Watertown, and at Glebe Cottage is Carol Klein, who occasionally appears in gardening programmes on television.

Hancock's Cider

The well-known name of Hancock's Cider from Clapworthy Mill has been with us for more years than we can remember, but I wonder how many of us know that the Hancock family once lived at King's in Satterleigh and was producing Hancock's Cider there. Norman Hancock now takes up the story of his well-known family:

My great-grandfather came from Middle Blackpool near South Molton and they used to make Hancock's Cider and take it to supply the pubs in Barnstaple on a horse and wagon with four hogsheads onboard. My grand-father, William, ran away to the Boer War and when he returned he went to New Barn near King's Nympton as a tenant under Squire Tanner, and farmed and made cider there. My father, Wilfred, took over and after getting married moved to King's which my mother's uncle – called Bill Luxton – bought for them around 1937. In 1957 Father bought Clapworthy Mill and, although we sold King's in 1957, we had a five-year lease to still make cider there. The first time we pressed cider at Clapworthy Mill was in 1964. As well as making cider, we had a small dairy herd.

We had a small 70-ton press which only pressed out about 2 cwt of apples at a time. In 1948 – about the time I left school – Whiteways were looking for small cider makers to press for them, so Father made it for them and delivered it to Whimple near Exeter. Around the same time he decided to get a bigger 100-ton water hydraulic press from Beers of Newton Abbott, which we've still got and presses 12 cwt at a time.

In 1952 I did my National Service for three years in the Air Force, a short-term regular. When I came out I continued helping make cider and selling to Whiteways. Father managed for the three years I was away. At that time we were pressing 2,000 gallons a day and sending it to Whimple. My job was to fill the barrels and then Parkers Transport used to deliver it. Some years we pressed as much as 60,000 gallons, and I remember at one time there was a shortage of apples and Whiteways had to buy them in from France. One day Pat Tucker and myself unloaded about 50 tons of apples. We used to store cider in barrels at King's and when that fermented Whiteways would send a 2,000-gallon tanker and fetch it that way.

We moved to Clapworthy from King's because of better access – everything at the time had to go up Satterleigh Hill and down again. Often we would come up Satterleigh Hill with our Dodge lorry full of apples and when we got to the level, the manifold would be red hot.

Above: *Norman Hancock, photographed with a cider container that has 'King's Satterleigh' displayed on it. They made Hancock's Cider here in the 1950s.*

Chapter 8
COMMUNICATIONS & AMENITIES

Harold Congram can remember the Chittlehamholt sewer being built, with Welsh miners coming over to do the digging. They lodged with Mrs Tucker at Hills House Farm.

Christine Congram (now Stuckey) can remember the first radio at Wards Farm, during the Second World War. As well as an ordinary battery there was an accumulator attached to it which had to be charged up when it ran down. A man called Manning, from South Molton, would come to collect the accumulator and exchange it for one which had been charged. Christine can remember being ticked off more than once for having the radio on all day when her mother was out because it ran down so quickly. Generally, the family would only listen to the radio for things like the news and weather. After listening to the weather forecast, Christine's father would tap his barometer and say, 'they ain't right you know.'

Christine's husband, George, used to work at Murch Brothers in Umberleigh, which at the time was an accumulator charging agent, and he remembers that they would have a couple of dozen accumulators on charge at once.

Over the years, Florence Congram and later my mother, Diana Lethbridge, have done sterling work in reporting the local news for the *North Devon Journal* and other local papers. In 2002, Jan Sharp is the correspondent and she too continues the marvellous work. Generally, the *Journal* today no longer cuts bits from reports due to lack of space, but allows the correspondent to write as much as possible, which is how it should be. It is important that everything is fully reported for historians in the future. Keep up the good work Jan, you are doing a great job.

John Streetly (British Telecom engineer) talks about the Chittlehamholt telephone exchange:

The Chittlehamholt telephone exchange is a small red-brick building, thought to have been erected in 1940. It sits in a corner of a field at Broadmoor Cross in the parish of Warkleigh – it's not unusual to have an exchange outside the area it's designated to. Before this building was built, it's possible that the exchange was either in someone's house or in the Post Office, like at High Bickington, where the postmistress doubled as a telephonist.

Geographically, Chittlehamholt exchange covers a large area – it's more economical to have one wide-ranging central point than several small exchanges. The exchange covers Chittlehamholt, Warkleigh, Satterleigh, Chittlehampton, the borders of Umberleigh, Bishops Tawton, South Molton and Chulmleigh.

When someone in one of these parishes makes a telephone call, it passes through the network of wires and cables to the Chittlehamholt exchange and depending where it needs to go – whether it be a local or international call – it will get routed through the exchange equipment and then through a network of other larger exchanges. Imagine it to be like a railway station, where there are lots of feeder lines going into the main station – the exchange – and once the call gets there, there are links to, say, Bristol or Exeter, and from there, more links to Cornwall or London, etc., and so on through to the international exchanges. These days all this can be done very fast; gone are the times when you had to ask the operator to connect you manually.

When the exchange was built, the first phone was probably Chittlehamholt 001. I should imagine there are now a couple of thousand lines feeding in and out of the exchange. That may sound a lot, but bear in mind a lot of people have multiple lines these days, so I think British Telecom count the number of lines rather than the amount of addresses. I think you'll always find exchanges like the one at Chittlehamholt. I honestly can't see them being replaced for many years.

There follow some notes on the Chittlehamholt telephone exchange by Doreen Morgan:

When we first came to Whitmore in 1959, to make a trunk call (long distance) you had to contact the operator and give her the name of the exchange and the number. My parents lived in Manchester, and when my mother telephoned she had to spell out 'Chittlehamholt' several times to the astonished operator! In those days, phone lines were in short supply and we shared a line with Mr and Mrs Beer at Pearces (a party line).

Mr Beer milked cows and supplied our milk. He used the old quart bottles. One day we found an earthworm at the bottom of the bottle. We told him and he said, 'Ah, yes, she've [Mrs Beer] bin 'avin' trouble wi' they.' We don't hear the Devonshire talk so much now; it's a pity.

101

The Chittlehamholt telephone exchange at Broadmoor Cross.

Above: *Margaret Hammett from Broadmoor who measures the Warkleigh rainfall.*

Jan Sharp, local correspondent for Chittlehamholt, Warkleigh and Satterleigh, who writes for the North Devon Journal *and the* Tiverton Gazette.
Courtesy of Roland Sharp.

The Village Well

Before mains water, everybody in Chittlehamholt had shallow wells. Our bungalow, Sunnymead – built by Captain Bill Johns, who was also a water diviner – still has the original well.

In dry times there was a need for a village well. This was erected in the 1930s and paid for by the village. It was filled in during the 1970s and today there are no visible signs of the well. It was situated on the corner of Hills House Farm garden wall, but now it has been reclaimed as part of the garden. Captain Johns dug the well with the help of Tom Headon. Tom's son, Aubrey, said that at one stage, Captain Johns only had a short piece of fuse left to blast the rock down below. The Captain was a man who took many risks and Tom was concerned for him, but Captain Johns assured him it would be all right. However, Captain Johns had only just got to the top of the ladder and put one foot on the ground when the fuse went off, sending the ladder sky high. He also dug the well for the Satterleigh council-houses, and Wilson Holland recalls a similar incident with the ladders happening there.

The well was dug to a depth of 30 feet, but they had to go down a further 30 feet before water was found. Around the pump was a small garden with a fence and a gate. George Slee can remember when he and his school mates had to tend to the garden. In latter years, I can remember Mr Cox tending to it.

Harold Congram can remember that John Pester at Fir Cottage had a well which got contaminated with water fleas. Mr and Mrs Holmes, who live there at the time of writing, discovered this well and have now made a feature of it within their conservatory by capping the top with a slab of strong glass which allows you to look down and, if you're brave enough, stand on it as well. Geoff and Shirley Darbyshire at Grange Cottage have also made a feature of theirs, surrounding it with a stone wall. Originally, Frank and Walter Heard, who once lived there, dug the well by hand to a depth of 60 feet.

In 1893 a case came up in the *North Devon Journal* regarding a dispute about the right of way to a well behind the Old Gate House. Mr William Sowden, who was the postmaster next door at the time, rested on the right of way and used it in common with other inhabitants of the village. The field behind the Old Gate House where the well was situated was described as being called Budd's Meadow. Maurice Thorne, who once owned this field, talks of a spring of water that still runs off the land where his cattle once drank. Undoubtedly this must have been the same source of well water the inhabitants were using back in 1893. Another spring on Holtgate Farm was once used by Maurice's grandmother who washed her clothes in it.

When the mains came through in the 1950s, Maurice can remember a lot of Irish workmen who used to come to his mother for eggs and potatoes at Holtgate Farm.

Measuring the Warkleigh Rainfall

Margaret Hammett measures the rainfall for Warkleigh at Broadmoor Farm each month. Margaret's father, Harold Eastman, started doing this in 1974. There follows Margaret's report on rainfall in September 2001:

The average rainfall for September in the parish is 85mm. This year (2001) the month's rains measured 131mm. Last September (2000) was a little wetter with a total of 133mm. Most of the rain this September fell on two days, [the] 1st and 27th of the month, and amounted to almost two-thirds of the total. We also had the wettest day, with 39mm, since August 1997 when 40mm of rain fell and the North Devon Show was cancelled.

Maurice Thorne recalls the Lucas Free Light windmill which stood at Holtgate Farm:

My father had a Lucas Free Light windmill erected at Holtgate and it stood for 14 years. Father bought the windmill from Mr Bendle of Southbray, Chittlehampton, who was an agent for Lucas. It was 40 feet in height and gave us virtually free electricity. Mains electricity came here in 1962 and we were connected in 1963. We had to take the windmill down once a year for greasing, but apart from that it was maintenance-free and served its purpose well. It took three or four men to lower it for maintenance. A pulley was attached to a 15- or 16-foot-high post next to the windmill. Four guide wires had to be released to lower the windmill, then it could be worked on and erected again. It had storage batteries and, believe it or not, the quietest month of the year was November and we sometimes had to have an engine to boost it. Other than that, it was fine – it gave us light, but we obviously had no power sockets. There were occasions when we had to 'furry' it along and bring the tail piece around to stop the propellor because it would overcharge the batteries. We always said that when the windmill was facing over Haynetown it was going to be good weather as the wind was out north or north-west.

Above: *Clyde the cat from the Exeter Inn paying his respects to Percy Johns.*

Right: *Stephen and Mary Jane Clarke from Warkleigh, celebrating their golden wedding anniversary in 1908.*

Below: *The Heard, Beer and Brownstone families, Chittlehamholt village, c.1924. Left to right, back row: Tom Beer, Gladys Brownstone, George Heard, Mable Heard, Jane Heard, Edgar Heard; front row: Reg Heard, Thomas Heard, William Heard; Frank Heard (standing), Walter Heard; sitting in the front: Fred Heard.*

Chapter 9

FAMILIES

Rosalind Reed talks about her grandfather, Captain Bill Johns, and the Johns family:

My mother, Rose (Elizabeth Jane Rosalind Johns), was born in 1899 in Plymouth. When she was a year old, the whole family moved to Deason, Warkleigh, because Grandfather Johns was short of work and he had answered an advert from Squire Moore of Highbullen, Chittlehamholt. Apart from my mother there was also Aunt Lil, Aunt Ivy – who later became a nanny for the Duke and Duchess of Northumberland – Uncle Percy and Uncle Bill. From Deason they moved to Chittlehamholt village, next to the shop. At that time there were two cottages, but now there's just one – September Cottage. My mother was married from this cottage.

Sadly, Uncle Percy died from blood poisoning in 1925 when he was just 11 years old. Frank Heard, who was about the same age, told me [that] when he went home from school one day his mother had told him that my Grandfather had gone into Barnstaple to give a pint of blood to try and save Percy. Uncle Percy had said to Granny, 'if I don't get better soon I shall be in the chapelyard,' so that's where he was buried, although they were really church people. A while ago, Richard Lethbridge took a lovely photograph of the cat from the Exeter Inn sitting right at the head of Percy's grave.

My grandparents then moved from the cottage to Hillbrow, which was built by my grandfather, a mason by trade. He also built Sunnymead.

I remember coming down for summer holidays and I used to go to church with Molly Heard. One day, when we came out, we were told that war had been declared. That year I stayed until Christmas because Father thought London would be bombed. After going home, we then only used to come down periodically.

Grandfather liked Tiverton Ales and when my father came they would go together to Mrs Skinner's at the Exeter Inn and have a 'Tivy', while Granny and my mother would go into Mrs Skinner's sitting-room.

When Granny died, Grandfather sold Hillbrow to Mr and Mrs Thomas of Snydles and he moved to Ivy Cottage. In 1974 Frank, my late husband, and I moved to Chittlehamholt and had a bungalow built. We called it 'Johns' after Grandfather and stayed there until 1987. It has since been renamed 'Roseland'.

Some notes follow on Henry Baker Saunders and his descendants by David Ryall:

Henry Baker Saunders was christened on 12 January 1833 in Chittlehampton, Devon. He died in April 1923 in Chittlehamholt and was buried on 18 April 1923 in Satterleigh, St Peters.

[He was] apprenticed to Thomas Mair of East Street, South Molton, as a boot- and shoemaker. He lived with the family at the time of the 1851 Census (HO/107/1891 f.472) [and] lived at Edgington Cottage, Warkleigh at the time of the 1901 Census. [He] died at Spiecott, Chittlehamholt.

Henry married Jane Squire, daughter of Hugh Ward and Anne Squire, on 16 March 1855 in Satterleigh, Devon. Jane was christened on 7 July 1823 in Satterleigh, Devon. She died in December 1900 and was buried on 2 January 1901 in Satterleigh, St Peters.

It was revealed on Jane's marriage certificate that her father was Hugh Ward.

Henry and Jane had the following children:

Henry Baker Saunders, born about 1857 in Satterleigh, Devon.

Elizabeth Ann Saunders, born about 1859 in Satterleigh, Devon. Elizabeth married William Percy Hanes on 6 August 1881 in Satterleigh, Devon. William was a fishmonger from Islington, son of William Hanes, also a fishmonger (from marriage certificate).

Sarah Ann Saunders. Sarah married William Henry Greep on 6 July 1855 in Satterleigh, Devon. William was a woodman from Buckland Monachorum, son of John Deake Greep, also a woodman (from marriage certificate).

There follows an article on the Bowden family by Steve Martin of Rewe, Exeter:

First of 'The Warkleigh Warriors'

Robert Bowden

Robert Bowden was born in Warkleigh in 1764 (not confirmed). There is not much information about his early life but he must have had a good education to have attained the following:

[He] left the land and joined the Devon Militia in 1782 due to the fear of a French invasion. In 1789, he was promoted to Lieutenant in the 96th Regiment of

Foot to honour the visit of George III with the Queen and three Princesses to Exeter. There were various uprisings in the country due to the bread shortages. Robert Bowden went North for further service with the Liverpool Regiment which he joined in 1793 as Captain. In 1796 he again came south where he transferred to the 54th Regiment of Foot, one of the forerunners of the Devonshire Regiment. In 1796 he was 'sold out', by what means we do not know as this is all that is recorded at the War Office. Perhaps he met a 'woman of means' who desired his company as a civilian! However, he does not appear to have returned to Warkleigh. If he was educated there, it served him well.

Robert Bowden (Nephew of Robert as before)

Son of William and Ann Bowden of the parish of Warkleigh in Devonshire, Robert was born on Sunday May 22 1803 at about seven o'clock in the morning.

Here again, this Warkleigh lad must have had a good education as 'his book' started in 1829 with the note: 'The number of my watch is 17883, maker H. Ellis, Exeter 29th day of April 1829.' Up until this time, Robert must have been apprenticed to a carpenter or a wheel-wright as his tool list comprised 'several saws – chisels – planes etc. – total cost in all on the 11th Oct 1830,

George and Mary Way of Rags Cottage, Warkleigh, now known as Shortridge Cottage.

£5.10s.2d.' He didn't appear to have pursued this line of work as one can see he was involved in other things and appeared to have followed in the line of his 'lost' uncle.

According to family knowledge passed down the line, Robert started in the Army but for some reason was connected with the Civil Service and was for a time a sort of military diplomat and soon became on the staff of Lt Col Sir William Gomm. Robert apparently went on overseas trips with the Lt Col Gomm, but we are not aware of his rank.

His diary of 14th Oct 1832 records [him] having sailed on the steamship Earl of Liverpool (this must

have been in the early days of steam) from London at 7a.m. 'Due to severe wind and badness of the vessel, we did not reach Ostend until one o'clock in the morning of the 13th.' He continues:

... we put up at the Hotel Du Cour – Imperial – a very strongly fortified town with ramparts 30 feet thick, the sea on one side and a great number of common mounted all around the town.

With carriage and horses, he describes each place they stayed the night and the condition of the accommodation – over rivers, up hills, through forest and ending up in Baste, Switzerland. A long way from Warkleigh! He took time out to view the battlefield of Waterloo where a guide showed him the specific sites – needing another few francs to show where Napoleon slept and where the Duke of Wellington stabled his horse. Unfortunately he does not complete his diary with the return visit. That must have been Part II.

It does appear that Robert became an Aide-De-Comp to Sir William as I am aware that he was at a later date (as Lt General)... to forces operating in Canada.

He was married to a wealthy farmer's daughter in Hamp-shire by Henry Bishop of Exeter. They lived for many years in Portland Street, St Mary-le-Bone, London, where they both died without issue in 1860. This is how the Bowden family join mine, as Robert's sister married a Chulmleigh chap!

James Bowden

Born in 1841, James married my grandfather's sister (Uncle Jim). Much the same as before, he left the land and joined the Devonshire Militia. A wonderful marks-man, it was recorded in the family that he more than once put two bullets in one hole while on target practice! A new military rifle which required less time to fire and reload was quickly mastered by James which earned him a place in the Army Marksmen Team of 1863.

In 1866, Private James Bowden (1076), 4th Battalion Rifle Brigade, was sent to Canada to eject the Fenians from Canada. The Fenians were a neo-military Irish political society, the forerunner of Sinn Fein and the IRA. They had many sympathisers in the USA and in 1866 a group of them under Col O'Neal launched a raid on Canada. As there were few British troops in Canada, the Canadian Militia held them back, helped by Naval men from the British Navy from ships in Canadian waters, until the British Army arrived with considerable force. Little did Uncle Jim know that we would be fighting them 150 years on.

Most of the action took place at a small town on the border near Niagara Falls, called Ridgeway. A few Canadian Militiamen were killed and are buried at St James Cemetery, Toronto. The Rifle Brigade were stationed there for some time.

Returning home, James Bowden was once again trained and equipped for further service overseas and by 1875 was en route to Bombay where he took up station in the state of Punjab. Whilst the Indian Military... had been over some 18 years there was still unrest in India which needed the presence of a lot of British troops.

The unrest erupted in Afghanistan so James and his 4th Battalion were sent north where they defeated the Afghans at Charasia and again at Kabul. The Army were under the leadership of General Roberts and continued to engage the Afghans wherever they formed up and by 1880 they had quelled most of these uprisings.

The present day has revealed more of the fighting in Afghanistan. None of this would be new to Uncle Jim.

Uncle Jim was awarded the Afghan Medal for his action at Ali Musjid [in] 1878–80 and the action in Canada at Ridgeway, 1866 – this medal was not issued until some 33 years later. I have Uncle Jim's medals and his watch, all inscribed.

James Bowden left the Army in 1885, having completed 25 years as a soldier. A few years later, he became 'Mine Host' at the Barnstaple Inn at Chulmleigh. He was a founder-member of Chulmleigh Parish Council in 1896 which he served on for several years. He died there in 1913.

These Bowdens were truly remarkable men, much travelled, before the days of steam, and they feared no distance – even on the water. Their record covers well over 100 years for king, queen and country.

The Pester family. Left to right, back row: *Olive, Aubrey, Iva*; front: *Ruth and Vincent.*

The Clarke Family

by Tim Clark

Stephen Clarke and his wife Mary Jane (née Salter) were married in Totnes in 1858 and celebrated their golden wedding anniversary in Barnstaple in 1908. Stephen had seen the world as a sailor, once being shipwrecked in the Bay of Biscay and taking six months to walk home. Stephen and Mary Jane had three of their five children at Warkleigh where they lived at King's Tenement (1873) and at Warkleigh Cottage (1879). Here Stephen worked as a policeman and water bailiff and took part in otter hunting. In 1881 they were at Warkleigh Villa, near the hotel. He lost his sight very suddenly, going to bed one night with a painful leg and finding his sight gone the next morning. After this he earned his living travelling on foot as a salesman for Brook Bond Tea. His son Albert kept his connection with Warkleigh by bringing the workforce of his building business in Weston-super-Mare for a day out each summer.

The Wright family from Simmons Farm, Chittlehamholt. Left to right: *Kathleen, Tom, Beatrice, Sam, Audrey, Olive, Vera, Muriel.*

Above: *Mr and Mrs Congram with their three children at Butlers in 1896. They came to Longwells from Chittlehampton in 1888, and moved to Butlers in 1913, at the time when Butlers was owned with Wards. John (Jack) later farmed Wards. His son Frank lives there at the time of writing, but lets out the ground.* Standing: *daughter Annie Congram, who later married Ernie Jackman and died in childbirth.* Left to right, seated: *William Congram, Henry (Harry) Congram, Mary Congram;* sitting on the floor: *John (Jack) Congram*

Hay harvesting at Simmons Farm, Chittlehamholt, 1996. Left to right: *Matthew Cooke, Sam Wright, Christopher Wright.*

Foot-and-mouth precautions at Simmons Farm, Chittlehamholt, 2001–02.

Right: *At Farrs Farm.* Left to right, back: *Mary and Annie Bater;* front: *Florrie and Sophie Bater.*

Chapter 10

FARMING & FARMING FAMILIES

Farming

Farming in the three parishes continues, but struggles to keep going due to the dramatic decline in the industry. It is increasingly difficult to make a living from farming, with diversification the key to survival; many farmers' wives and husbands have to look for other income to support their farms. So, it's not surprising that these people choose other occupations – in Chittlehamholt, for example, we have a dog breeder, a petrol-pump and shop assistant, two nurses, and a carpenter.

Retiring farmers, or those deliberately coming out of the industry, are not always replaced as people moving on to the land are not always interested in running a working farm, and neighbouring farmers end up renting the land from them. Farms in the parishes which are not farmed in their own right anymore include Fair Oak, Kinnings (now a dog-breeding kennels), Drakes (now a cattery), Higher Beers, Beers, Butlers, Park, Chapples, Mollands, Little Satterleigh, Old Parsonage Farm, Snapdown, Newlands, Hills House Farm, Holtgate and Oldridge. The industry was on its knees in 2001 after the first confirmed case of foot-and-mouth disease in Britain for 20 years. The parishes of Chittlehamholt, Warkleigh and Satterleigh held their breath, waiting to see if the terrible disease would spread to farmers' livestock here. On 24 February, only four days after confirmation of the first case nationally, Devon farmers' worst fears came true when the county's first case was confirmed at Highampton. The disease soon spread into North Devon and the parishes came even closer to being affected as the epidemic swarmed all around us, with nearby Chulmleigh and Burrington having confirmed cases. How the parishes came this close and escaped being infected was a miracle.

The rest of this chapter concentrates on well-established farmers who have been farming on the same farms for generations, along with an update of some of the newer ones. Where possible, a history of the family is recorded, although in some cases this can be somewhat patchy.

In Chittlehamholt, the name of Harris at Presbury goes back a long way, possibly to the 1700s. David Harris runs this farm today.

The name of Wright has been associated with Simmons Farm since 1928 when Tom Wright and his family settled there. In this chapter, much has been recorded by the late Tom Wright's son and daughters and about life at Simmons.

The May family have been at Farrs since 1940. Richard and Michelle now carry on the tradition.

At Wards, the Congrams have been farming since 1912, when William Congram bought Butlers, which came with Wards. Before this the family were at Longwells. A farm sale of 1912 indicates that Longwells was sold along with North and South Hollowmoors, indicating when the farms came together. North and South Hollowmoors no longer exist. The Congrams came from Chittlehampton; the sale of 1912 states that the family had been at Longwells for 24 years. Frank Congram is still at Wards, but now lets out his ground and has more or less retired.

Just a few yards up the road is Featherstones Farm (the Old Vicarage), farmed by Robert Bater with his wife Janet and son Andrew. Bater is a well-established name going back to the 1800s with connections to the manor (see page 79). The original Featherstones Farm was just down the road from Drakes, on the left at the end of the lane. Until recently, some of the farmers came to dip their sheep here.

Richard Hammond has a smallholding at Whitmore Lodge.

Eight years ago Richard Hedges had a pig farm at Fairview Bungalow, but the family has gone and the land is not farmed anymore. Next to the old pig sheds at the time of writing there is a sign with the name of Fairview Barton, and Clive and Alison Kendal from the village have bought part of the land.

At Head Post Cottages, Ken Guard, his wife, Pam, and sons, Derek and Michael, farm nearby Callards Ground. The family previously lived at Longwells and then moved to Headmill. Just down the road from Head Post is Longwells where Felicity Baxter and her daughter Florence have a smallholding. A few yards further down, Ron and Anne Thorne also have a smallholding.

Andrew and Debbie Cook have farmed at Snydles for about nine years under the ownership of the Wildlife Trust.

The Thorne family came from Umberleigh to farm at Holtgate Farm in 1919, where Maurice Thorne still retains the land and now rents it out. Maurice now

Maurice Thorne outside his home at Lloret, Chittlehamholt, on his Massey Ferguson tractor in 2001.

The Govier family at Pearce and Dyers, Satterleigh, who came out of farming in 2002 after 40 years here.

Below: *The Beer family at Deason, c.1900.*

Satterleigh Barton with Michael (left) and David Elworthy in 2002.

Tom Beer and wife Bessie at Higher Ditchaton Water, 1930.

Four generations of the Holland family at Fair Oak, Chittlehamholt, c.1960. Left to right: William, George, Wilson, master Michael Holland.

concentrates his time on his successful nursery business nearby. Maurice Thorne's grandfather was a cobbler as well as a postman at Umberleigh. Maurice's parents married in 1942, with his mother being born at Chapples and then moving to Poole Farm.

Nicholas and Muriel Hill have farmed at Haynetown since 1962.

Snapdown was farmed by Miss Smith from 1942 onwards. She still lives there today at the age of 94. The land is rented out under the watchful eye of Marilyn and Alan Bowen who also have a successful holiday-caravan business there. Miss Smith is a remarkable character and it is not many years since she was regularly seen in the village on her David Brown tractor.

The Govier family, who came out of farming in 2002, have been at Pearce and Dyers for a remarkable 40 years. Some of their land has now been sold off.

The Elworthy family have been farming at Satterleigh Barton since the 1920s.

The name of Beer has been associated with the farming world since the 1800s. In the early 1800s they were living at Shortridge Farm and then some of the family branched out to Park Farm, Rags Cottage and Little Shortridge, before moving on to Deason Farm, which they built, and then to Chittlehamholt village. They

Miss Esther Smith from Snapdown, Warkleigh.

lived in Rattle Street and Beers Farm (which could have been named after them), and Grange Cottage where a Beer married a Heard. They then moved on to Lower and Higher Ditchadon Water with two brothers living side by side before one of them moved to Pearces Farm. From here, Bill Beer did a milk round for 40 years before moving with his family in 1966 to Shortridge Farm, 150 years after the family had left. The Beer brothers, Anthony, Fred and Harold, farm here at the time of writing. Harold Beer is very interested in Massey Ferguson tractors and has recently been voted chairman of the Fergi Club. He has a Ferguson tractor of his father's which was bought in 1949 and is still in working order. A firm recently made a video of the working of the Ferguson tractor which featured Harold taking it through its paces. The video was very popular and won an award for best video, and Harold was presented with a trophy – somewhat of an Oscar for him. Harold is proud to tell people that Sir Frank Whittle, inventor of the jet engine, stayed at the farm in the mid 1930s, as did Harold Bishop, Chairman of the BBC. Harold Beer was badly hurt in around 1990 when a four-inch piece of wire was flung from his tractor while hedge cutting and came to rest near his spine. The wire is still lodged in place, it being thought too dangerous to operate.

The Thorne family have been at Warkleigh Barton since 1970 and in recent years Molly and Jo Thorne's two sons, Christopher and Winston, married two sisters, Deborah and Gaynor, and now live side by side in the farmhouse. Molly and Jo live in a converted barn nearby.

At Pugsley, the Pincombe family carry on the tradition started by Jack Pincombe in 1926.

Nearby, the Eastman family moved to Broadmoor in 1934. When Harold Eastman moved out of Broadmoor his daughter Margaret, who is married to Colin Hammett, carried on the family link with the farm. Hurstone Farm, which Margaret and Colin farmed before moving to Broadmoor, is now run as a smallholding by Jenny and Peter Harvey Bennett.

The Holland family

The Holland family have been farming Hilltown Farm since 1904. Wilson Holland's grandfather was a farm bailiff for Miss Ley of Hilltown for a few years. In 1903, when there was a farm to be let in Chittlehamholt, he thought he should tender for it because he wanted a place of his own. Miss Ley told him that if he stayed for another 12 months he could have Hilltown.

Wilson Holland was born at Pearce and Dyers in 1920. In 1938 the family moved to Hilltown when Wilson's father took over the farm. A year later, they had their first tractor. The family expanded the business during the war, getting two tractors and contracting out. In 1945, Wilson married and moved to Fairoak, Chittlehamholt. He came back to Hilltown ten years later. He handed the farm over to his son Michael in 1990.

The Bowden Family

The Bowden family all became involved in agriculture during their lives after being brought up at Oakford Cottage, Satterleigh, which had 28 acres of land. Oakford was an old thatched house thought to have been two cottages at one time. A photograph shows how the cottage looked 80 years ago. When the Bowdens left the cottage became derelict and more or less crumbled. A modern house was then built on the same site and still goes under the name of Oakford.

Dorothy Bowden (now Ayre) is in her eighties at the time of writing. She was brought up at Oakford with her brothers Reg, Charlie, William (Bill) and Fred. She recalls being told by her father that a Mr and Mrs Boucher brought up nine children in the old cottage. Mr Bowden was a labourer for Mr Elworthy of Satterleigh Barton who owned Oakford, and it was stated in Mr Elworthy's will that no one could rise his rent or turn him out while Mr Bowden was living there. Dorothy recalls that she was nearly three when her mother died and her granny Clatworthy from Lower Watertown came to look after them all.

After leaving school aged 12, Bill went over to Little Satterleigh to work on the Symons farm before moving on to the Hollands at Haynetown. He joined them when they moved to Collacott Farm, Wembworthy, and stayed here until their son Leonard was 16, and then moved on to the Hollands at Hilltown and finally to the Elworthys at Satterleigh Barton. Bill spent over 50 years working there; sadly he died in 2002 in his early nineties.

Charlie went to the Elworthys at Satterleigh Barton when he was ten and stayed until he got married. He then moved to Warkleigh Barton with the Shaplands and worked there until the age of 55 when he suffered a stroke.

Fred went over to the Leys at Broden Hill when he was 14, and then moved to Shilstone, Chittlehampton, and then Dean Farm at Goodleigh.

Reg went to Pilton Dairy when he was 14, and then worked on the timber with Jack Adams. Reg died aged 54.

The Snow Family

An article follows about the Snow family by Ken Snow of The Downs, Chittlehampton:

My great-grandfather, Thomas Snow, and his wife had four daughters and four sons; including my grandfather, John. The second son was Ephraim Howard, who my brother and I got our middle names from – my middle name is Ephraim, and my brother Raymond – who was killed in the Second World War – had Howard as his middle name. The third son was also called John, but was always referred to as Jack. He farmed at Furze, Chittlehampton. The fourth son, Thomas, also farmed at Furze – one farmed North Furze and one South.

Great-grandfather learnt his trade as a carpenter on the Rolle estates in 1799, and became a tenant farmer at Whitstone Barton, Chittlehampton, on the Rolle estate under the Hon. Mark Rolle. Thomas was killed in a water-wheel accident at Whitstone Barton, whilst either repairing it or using it to grind corn. The Hon. Mark Rolle offered Thomas' widow a cottage at Rackmead, Chittlehampton, rent-free for life plus 10s. a week pension. But, as she had such a large family, she asked Mr Rolle if he could let her a small farm. He rang the agent, Palmer, and was informed that Hurstone Farm in Warkleigh was due to be re-let. Mr Rolle told Mrs Snow that if she lived in the old farmhouse while the new one was being built, she could have tenancy of Hurstone Farm at half the rent the outgoing tenant was paying. That was how the Snow family came to Warkleigh from Chittlehampton.

My grandfather, John, was foreman carpenter at the estate yard in Chittlehampton. Hon. Mark Rolle asked him to come to Stevenstone House St Giles to be house

carpenter. My father, John Walter, learnt his trade as a carpenter and wood carver by the Hon. Mark Rolle's wife, Lady Gertrude Rolle – she was a professional wood carver. When my father was 14 he carved some panels from oak from the Stevenstone estate, which he later made into a sideboard and overmantel. I recently thought it would be nice for them to be returned to the place they were made and I contacted the Landmark Trust, who said they would be delighted to receive the sideboard and put it in the library at Stevenstone.

Interestingly, I have a set of chisels (70) which Lady Gertrude Rolle gave to my father, and several other tools including one for cutting wood threads. I also have a grandfather clock which has been in our family for five generations and which has the inscription, 'Made by John Huxtable, Chittlehampton'. It is my wish that the clock will stay in Chittlehampton and I intend to leave it to Chittlehampton Church.

The Hon. Mark Rolle was a good benefactor for all of North Devon and I remember my father saying that he could walk from Head Barton in Chittlehamholt as far as Exmouth – about 80 miles – and still be on his own land. Head Barton has a stone plaque on the wall which reads 'M R 1872' (Mark Rolle's initials). Mark Rolle died without a son so the land fell to his cousin, Lord Clinton.

The stone-built farmhouses, with the red-brick coins and the windows and doors, were all his style and include some of the property in the Warkleigh area. In 1958 the Clinton estate came on the market with 345 lots. It included the following Warkleigh farms: Pugsley, Greendown, Broadmoor, Warkleigh Barton, Hurstone, Pool, Great Shortridge and Park. Presbury Farm, Chittlehamholt, was built by Mark Rolle and sold off in 1914.

I worked for the Clinton estate during the 1950s as a self-employed carpenter. During the Second World War we came down to stay at Hurstone and later lived in Greendown Cottage in the parish of Warkleigh. [See Chapter 4].

David Ryall provides some notes on the Owen family of Watertown:

William Owen came to Watertown at the end of the nineteenth century with his three daughters and three sons; his wife Ellen had died earlier. He had moved from London where he had been a draper. He was originally from Machynlleth in Montgomeryshire, Wales.

He was the youngest of three brothers, whose father had to sell the family lands in 1841 to repay a debt. The three sons, having had an unsettled childhood, all prospered; the eldest, Thomas, founded one of Britain's largest paper-manufacturing companies; the middle son, Owen, did well in business and founded a very successful department store which still bears his name, and William founded a department store in Westbourne Grove, London.

William had married Ellen Sawtell, daughter of Sarah Sawtell, a draper in South Molton. Sarah's maiden name

The Hammett family from Broadmoor. Andrew is in the driving seat with wife Elizabeth in the trailor, and their children James, Jasmin and Stephanie.

Peter and Jenny Harvey Bennett bringing in the hay at Hurstone Farm, Warkleigh, 2001.

Left: *Loading mangolds at Fairoak, Chittlehamholt.* Left to right: *Jim Nation, Wilson Holland and Gordon Snow at the back.*

Bill Bowden (left) and Harold Snow at Satterleigh Barton.

The Clatworthy family at Lower Watertown. Left to right, back: Bert, Fred, William; *front:* Mr Clatworthy, Caroline Lily Clatworthy, Elizabeth Clatworthy.

Ruth Symons on her Massey Ferguson tractor at Little Satterleigh, 1991.

The Adams family at Claytown, Warkleigh, c.1920s. Left to right, back row: Bill, Mary, Ron and John Beers Adams, Annie Adams; *front row:* Hettie, Sarah and Jack Adams.

Mark Rolle inscription on Head Barton.

The Boundy family at the Old Parsonage, c.1900.

Left: *Sidney and Minnie Snow with two of the children, Alma and Ray, c.1900.*

Right: *Left to right: Ervin and Arthur Snow outside Hurstone Farm, c.1900.*

was Huxtable – she was the daughter of Edmund and Sarah, the Chittlehampton clockmaker.

William and Ellen Owen's eldest was William Price Owen. He is remembered in a plaque in Satterleigh Church:

In proud memory of
WILLIAM PRICE OWEN
Private 72nd Seaforth Highlanders of Canada
Eldest son of William Price Owen Esq. of Watertown
and London who laid down his life in the Great War at
the second battle of Ypres April 22nd 1915 Aged 35
years. A Gallant, Brave and Courageous Life
Crowned with a Soldier's death.

The eldest daughter remained unmarried, but lived to over 100 and was a common sight driving to South Molton market on a Thursday.

A descendent of this same family is Miss Smith of Snapdown. Now in her 90s, she is a truly remarkable character who until recently walked to all three churches in the parishes.

John Lowday, whose ancestors farmed at Warkleigh in the 1700s, provides the following information:

Charles Lawdy signed (with his mark) a lease on 17th October 1723 for 99 years with three named lives – three of his sons – Jonathan aged five, John aged 12 and William aged six. The farm was called East Oldridge and was owned by Thomas Jeffrey in the city of Exon [Exeter]. The fee for one lease was £160, followed by annual rental of 9s. per year. Later in 1731, Charles Lawdy took out a second tenancy, this time for Hurstone, a neighbouring farm. Three of his other children were the nominated lives – Charles junr, Anne and Elizabeth. Initially, both Charles senr and junr signed the legal indentures, but later just Charles junr [signed]. It appears that father and son were farming adjacent land in the parish of Warkleigh for several years. There is a bundle of old parchment documents relating to East Oldridge at the North Devon Record Office, Barnstaple, whilst those for Hurstone are held at the County Record Office, Exeter.

Both sets of documents are not easy to read, and even where they have been transcribed they are not easy to understand and interpret. The lawyers were the main beneficiaries I am sure, writing and being paid by the yard for long-winded and hard-to-understand documents. However, it appears that both Charles Lawdy senr and junr used the lease of the farms as security for advances of money. There are also examples of lease and release indentures which were a legal devise invented by lawyers to reduce taxation paid.

The East Oldridge bundle of documents were summarised in 1784 when Grace Saunders purchased the interest in the farm from Henry Crocker of High Bickington. Within this bundle was the will of Charles Lawdy, dated 1760 — a copy of which follows. We are incredibly lucky to have this will, which must have sat on a shelf in a solicitor's office for over a couple of centuries before being deposited in the North Devon Record Office at Barnstaple. Nearly all Devon wills were destroyed in a Luftwaffe raid on Exeter in 1942. The wills were indexed prior to this disaster and I know for a fact that dozens of wills of my Lawday ancestors were destroyed. To my knowledge this is one of the very few that survived.

There was a considerable variation in spelling of the name Lawdy/Lawdey in those days, however, Jonathan Lawdey – Charles' son named in the original 1723 lease and in subsequent documents – could write and sign his name in a style of handwriting not unlike my own.

Jonathan died in 1772 and East Oldridge appears to have been taken over by his widow and her second husband, Michael Dunn. Jonathan farmed in Chittlehampton at Mill Town, and later at South Molton, at Town House (just below the chipboard factory).

All of the Lawday family were baptising children in Warkleigh and Chittlehampton. Charles had several children with his wife Ellen, Eleanor or Helena (surnames were not the only names to be spelt inconsistently!). Jonathan baptised several children in Chittlehampton and later in South Molton.

I believe William, Charles' grandson mentioned in the will of 1760, lived and probably farmed at Chittlehamholt. He and his wife Joan baptised several children, sometimes at Warkleigh, other times at Chittlehampton, and sometimes at both! He was the one that received the clock and case.

I have located just one gravestone of my ancestors in Warkleigh – Charles Lawday junr who died aged 50 in 1755. He married in 1749 and had one daughter, Ann, who later married Henry Crocker of High Bickington, mentioned earlier. The gravestone is one of several used to hold back the soil to the north of Warkleigh Church.

Last will and testament of Charles Lawday of Warkley. Document No. 2309 B/W 146 Barnstaple Records Office In the name of God Amen.

Charles Lawday of Warkley in the County of Devon yeoman being weak in body and sound in mind and per fort in mind and memory Praised be God therefore this second day of February in the year of our Lord God one thousand seven hundred and sixty do make and publish and declare this my last Will and Testament in Manner and Form following. First I commend my soul unto God and my body I commit to the Earth to be decently buried at the discretion of my Executor hereinafter named. And as for that Worldly Estate God hath been pleased to bless me with I give and dispose thereof as followeth.

First I give to my daughter Ann Huxtable one Guinea in gold. Also I give to my son in law Michael Dunn five shillings also I give his late wife my daughter Elizabeth her five children (viz) Mary Turner, Elizabeth Badioke, Eleanor Dunn, Ann Dunn, Michael Dunn, three pounds *a piece to be paid all of them within two years after my decease. Also I give to my Grandson William Lawday four pounds and my clock and case to be paid and delivered him when he shall attain the age of one and twenty years. Also I give to my Grand daughters Mary and Elizabeth Lawday (the Daughters of William Lawday deceased) three pounds a piece to be paid to both of them when they shall attain the age of one and twenty years.*

Also I give to my granddaughter Ann Lawday (daughter of my son Charles Lawday deceased) ten shillings payable when she shall accomplish the age of one and twenty years.

Also I give to my son Jonathan Lawday's two daughters Ann Lawday Susanna Lawday ten pounds a piece to be paid unto each of them as they shall accomplish the age of one and twenty years. Also I give to his son and my grandson John Lawday ten pounds to be paid when he shall attain the age of one and twenty years.

All the rest of my Lands Goods and Chattles I give, devise and bequeath unto my son Jonathan Lawday, his heirs whom I make my whole and Sole Executor of this my last will and testament. In witness whereof I have hereunto set my hand and seal the day and year first above written.

Signed sealed published delivered by the above Charles Lawday As and for his last will and testament in the presence of us who subscribed our names in his presence and at his request.

Nicholas Huxtable	*The mark of Charles*
Robt Stofford	*Charles Lawday*
Jeffrey Harris	*seal*

Details outside of Charles Lawday's will from 1760 state:

William Hole Bachelor of Divinity Archdeacon of Barnstaple lawfully constituted do by those profonts made unto all men that on the fifth day of September in the year of our Lord one thousand seven hundred and sixty at Barnstaple before the Reverend Mr John Hole Clerk our surrogate lawfully appointed the last will and testament of Charles Lawday of Warkley in the County of Devon and Archdeaconry aforesaid yeoman deceased was introduced proved and approved of and that administration of all and singular the goods chattles and proditts of the said deceased was granted and committed unto Jonathan Lawday his Son. Sole Executor in the said will named having first been lawfully sworned well and faithfully to administer the same (saving to everyone his right). In Testimony whereof we have hereunto set our seal of office this day and year above said.

John Dake Deputy Registrar

Muriel Moore (formerly Wright) recalls her memories of early years spent at Chittlehamholt:

I was born at Simmons Farm, Chittlehamholt, on November 12th 1939 – at that time the youngest daughter in a family of five girls. I have often thought that I must have been the biggest disappointment to my parents, as they most certainly would have been hoping for a son at long last, to carry on with the family farm and name.

Simmons back then was a very small two-bedroomed thatched cottage – very primitive with a blue stone slab floor, a large open fireplace with the bread oven in the corner (I can still remember the smell of the roast dinner on Saturdays and the wonderful flavour of the roast potatoes!) and the only water had to be carried from the well a good 100 metres or so away from the house. No doubt these days the Social Services would be called in, if they heard that a couple with five children were living in such primitive and overcrowded conditions!

But we came to no harm, and there was always food to eat – the biggest proportion produced on the farm. There were always plenty of vegetables such as potatoes and swede (I hated it then, but I love it now!), our own pig in the 'salter', hens, eggs and ducks, and when Dad could catch one, a rabbit for a tasty pie! In summer we had great fun going to the orchard to select a nice eating apple (Beauty-of-Bath or a Listener – or was it Glistener?) a choice of juicy plums including greengages and a small pinkish type of plum called a 'Chriseling' (I've never seen this word written down – it could be local dialect). Some of the apples had to be stored for winter use, e.g. Bramleys and one called a 'Cornish Gilliflower' – there was never a large crop of the latter, but they were a delicious flavour.

My earliest recollections are obviously of life during the latter stages of the Second World War – I remember blacked-out windows, having to be very quiet when the news broadcasts were on the 'wireless' and, on one occasion, seeing an enormous amount of aeroplanes flying in formation in the sky – my husband Ken tells me that he remembers seeing them too, and they would have been the ones heading off for the D-Day landings in June 1944.

January 1945 saw me begin my education at Chittlehamholt Village School. The stone-built single-storey building still stands but is now a private dwelling, having closed as a school in 1948. I was one of the six pupils who attended the school at that time – we were then transferred to the Primary School at Chittlehampton.

I remember my first day at school – I walked the two miles with my older sisters, and I sat next to Margaret Heard. She is exactly one week older than me and is the daughter of the late Mr Frank Heard and his wife Irene. Mr Heard was the local 'thrasher' man, whose business was based in the centre of the village. I also remember a boy called Arthur Tucker – I think he lived at Handfords. Later I used to walk home with Robert Bater of Featherstones. Walking to and from school was often an adventure – in summer there were all the different wild flowers to identify – it wasn't considered environmentally unfriendly to pick them in those days, so we could take any unknown ones to school to show our teacher. I could still take you to spots in the road hedges where the wild strawberries grew – but I doubt if they grow there anymore – and there was a patch of whortleberries (we called them worts) that always appeared every year almost opposite Handfords Gate. In the autumn we gathered the 'slipshell' hazel nuts and cracked them with a stone in the road. Often we would meet Mr Cox heading for his run-down premises opposite the school – his comment would usually be the same every time you saw him: 'Make haste home, there are pancakes for tea!'

As well as starting school in January 1945, another big event in our family that month was the arrival on the 25th of Samuel John – the eagerly awaited son for my parents, and a brother for his five sisters. At five years old I think I was a little put out by this new addition to the family – in those days we weren't told about such things in advance, so having been whisked away to spend a snowy day at Farrs Farm without questioning why, it was a bit of a shock to be told later that day that I now had a baby brother! 'But I'm still the baby maid', was my reaction, so I'm told! (We were now a family of eight in a two-bedroomed house!)

I think my first teacher at school was a Miss Lewis, followed by Miss Friday and, in the last 18 months or so at Chittlehamholt, Miss Dorothy Parker. She was an excellent teacher and with so few pupils to cope with she pushed us to far beyond the expected for our age. Unfortunately, when I transferred to Chittlehampton at the age of eight, standards were not as high and progress was limited – fortunately I had learnt enough from Miss Parker to pass my 11-plus in 1951. January 1947 was the time of the big blizzard and the big freeze that followed – an experience of mine while at school with my sister Vera (described on page 68).

*Mr and Mrs Tucker,
Hills House Farm, c.1900.*

Life on the farm was always busy and we were all expected to help out in our holidays and weekends – picking up stones, pulling up 'Lamb's Tongue' in the mangolds, feeding the animals, milking the cows (I was told by my parents that I succeeded in milking one very quiet cow when I was three years old!) and helping to stack the sheaves of corn at harvest time. It was fun when the 'binder' reached the centre of the field and the rabbits bolted! We usually had one day out near the end of the summer holiday and we had to be satisfied with that! Occasionally, when friends or relatives came for the day in summer, a special treat was a picnic by the river – everyone rode on the car pulled by one of Dad's prized cart-horses! Most Saturdays we would walk to the village shop for a few items and we always walked to Sunday school (Mr Constable was the teacher) at the little Plymouth Brethren Chapel on Sundays. So, frequently we walked more than two miles each way, all the days of the week! We didn't need keep-fit lessons, that's for sure! (I used to watch the home games of Chittlehamholt football club at Haynetown some winter Saturday afternoons – it wasn't surprising that they eventually disbanded after losing one match 21-0!)

In 1951 there were big upheavals at Simmons – an extension to the house meant that we had running water indoors for the first time – no more baths in front of the open fire as we now had a bathroom. In the kitchen we had a Rayburn (but the roast potatoes never tasted quite the same!) and we then had four bedrooms – although by this time our oldest sister Audrey had left home to work near Copplestone. 1951 was also the year that I started my senior education at Barnstaple Girls' Grammar School – it was such a big change for me – catching the train from Portsmouth Arms Station on a Monday morning and returning on Friday night – luckily I had my sister Vera to show me the ropes and for company at our lodgings during the week in Landkey Road. I had hardly ever been to Barnstaple before, so it was like a different world to me living in the town – walking to the shops and going to the outdoor swimming pool in Rock Park in the summer – I loved it. No hint of homesickness for me, but of course we were only away for four nights each week – it certainly was the best of both worlds.

At Christmas in 1955 I left school to work on the farm at Simmons – it was very hard for me but I had no choice in the matter because in those days you didn't argue with your parents – they needed help at home and I was the only one left – brother Sam was only 11 at that time. It was one of the biggest disappointments of my life to have to leave when I did – no chance to take any exams or find a job of my choice, but I survived and tried to interest myself in the community by getting involved with the Village Hall and Flower Show, etc. (The Flower Show was always the highlight of the year – Mr Taylor conducting South Molton Town Band and the 'Pillow Fights' are my main memories). Fortunately the Pepper family, who lived at Warkleigh House, had a tennis court in their garden and allowed some local people to form a tennis club there. Tennis had been my passion at school – and still is to this day – so being able to play helped me to adjust to life at home. I used to ride my bicycle – it must have been about four miles each way, but it was well worth the effort!

In 1957 I met a young man called Kenneth Moore who lived near Newton Tracey. He had recently finished his National Service – most of it spent in Celle, West Germany. It was a complete coincidence that four years earlier, while I was at school in Barnstaple, I had acquired a pen-friend called Brigitte who lived in Celle. When Ken and I married in 1961 at Burrington Methodist Church (where our family always attended), part of our honeymoon was spent with Brigitte and her parents, and Ken was able to reminisce and show me familiar places in the town. When we returned we made our home at Lovacott Green Farm, near Newton Tracey where we still live. We have three sons – the eldest is married to a school-friend of my German pen-friend's son – and their wedding in 1997 was in Celle, where Ken had spent most of his National Service days more than 40 years before!

Although I left home in 1961, I was still a frequent visitor to see my parents at Simmons until my father's death in 1992, and still occasionally pass through the village on the way to the indoor tennis court at the Highbullen Hotel. Everything has changed so much in the 40 years since I left – but the old school still looks much the same and I have the photograph that was taken in the classroom in March 1947, of the pony and Miss Parker with her six pupils (see page 69), hanging on my dining-room wall to remind me of my early life spent in the parish of Chittlehamholt!

The following was written in 1985 by Muriel Moore (née Wright) and read on Radio Devon by Douglas Mounce on his show:

Chittlehamholt, the place of my birth.

Dear Mr Mounce I have one plea,
For on your daily show you see
Your comments give me quite a jolt,
Please don't make fun of Chittlehamholt!

It may be off the beaten track,
And public transport it may lack,
But it's really not that bad at all,
With it's quaint old pub and village hall.

At Chittlehamholt my life begun,
And until the age of Twenty-one
When marriage meant I moved away,
It was there I spent my early days.

I was at the school 'til the age of eight,
When lack of pupils sealed it's fate,
It was there I received a boy's first kiss,
At seven years old I was quite a Miss!

I was an ardent fan of the football side,
I watched each game with loyal pride,
One reason they're not playing still,
They lost one fixture, twenty-one nil!

Numerous memories linger on,
Although nigh twenty-four years have gone
Since I left Chittlehamholt to become a wife,
And at Newton Tracey began a new life.

So dear Mr Mounce please listen to me,
Why not travel there for yourself and see
That Chittlehamholt, the place of my birth,
Is not the very last place on earth!

Sam Wright, a local farmer, recalls being brought up at Simmons Farm, Chittlehamholt:

I am a local farmer who has always lived at Chittlehamholt. My parents bought the farm in 1928 when they married. I was born at the farm in 1945, the youngest of six; I have five older sisters.

I can remember the farm from about 1950. There was no intensive farming at that time, so a lot of food was produced and sold from farms such as ours.

The farm had a selection of animals and poultry so as a small boy it was an interesting place to be. My favourite was my small black pony; she was the same age as me and bought when I was six. She used to take me around the farm to look at the sheep because on family farms you were expected to be useful. She was quiet and safe but catching her often took longer than the ride.

In a 1952 diary I found some prices of animals and produce grown and sold from the farm, and animals bought.

Piglets were sold for £5. A calf was bought from a market for £4 (some calves can be bought for the same price now). Breeding ewes were bought at a market for just over £6. The horse was shod for approx £1. Four dozen eggs were £1. Six rabbits were £1.

The rabbits were wild and caught in gin traps which were legal at that time. As a boy I sometimes set the traps. They had a very strong spring and I had to stand on it to set it. Surprisingly my fingers are all undamaged. The rabbits needed to be controlled as eight rabbits ate as much as one sheep.

There was nothing at that time to prevent children from riding or driving farm machinery. Driving a tractor at about eight or nine was quite common. The most fascinating machine to me was the binder, which was pulled by the tractor to cut the corn. I often used to ride on it, even though it had a knife to cut the corn, a reel to pull the corn in and revolving parts and chains, all unguarded.

Bird nesting was also permitted but I only took one egg and it was usually a blackbird's. I remember at senior school there were boys who brought in trays of eggs all neatly labelled and priced. There was no hint of disapproval from the teacher.

I left school at 15. By that time it was just my father and me, all my sisters were married and gone. I married in 1968 and we now have 3 children, none of whom have remained on the farm.

In the second half of my farming career, farm commodities have increased and profits decreased. Now my wife and I run a smaller farming enterprise with two rather more profitable sidelines.

Taken from the *Western Times*, the excerpt below reveals how two brothers won the county championship cup for ploughing:

3rd May 1918

Devon's Champion Ploughman – Mr Wm Medland, of Chittlehamholt – who has just relinquished work on the land to join the Army, the efforts of the Food Production Department to retain his services for ploughing having proved unavailing. Medland and his brother, who has *also joined up, have played a great part in North Devon's splendid achievement of having won the County Championship Cup on two successive occasions, and occupying a leading position in the All England list. They christened their tractor 'Flying Molly', and the amount of work that it has accomplished in their hands is astonishing. Both brothers have taken a personal interest in their work, and have laboured early and late to plough as much as possible, and their loss to the Food Production Department will, no doubt, be considerably felt. For the past seven weeks the two brothers working the same tractor, one as driver and the other as plough-man, have ploughed an average of 18 acres per week. Their best achievement was for the week ending March 15th, when they ploughed 30 acres, while another of their best records was 22½ acres during the week ending March 22nd. And this has been accomplished on land that does not permit the best results being achieved. North Devon's record is undoubtedly a most excellent one and Mr H.J. Butler, the divisional tractor represent-ative, and the men of his department (among whom he has infused a commendable enthusiasm) are naturally proud of what has been achieved. And justly may they be, and congratulations have been bestowed on them upon it.*

Ian Tucker talked about his time at Warkleigh Barton:

Our family moved from Lapford to Warkleigh Barton at the beginning of the Second World War. It was a big day for all of us, we were to become tenants of the Clinton Estate of Merton, as were all of our neighbours, and most of them were there to help us move in. I was leaving Lapford School as a nine-year-old and the prospect of making new friends did not appeal to me, but those of us who were new to Warkleigh School were introduced to the rest of the children by the head teacher, Miss Harding. There was also a local lady teacher, Miss Molly Heard, who lived at Chittlehamholt. I settled in very quickly and, like most kids, we didn't realise how good an upbringing we were having; friends made at the school have remained life-long friends.

As the war was on, most of us had evacuees from London to stay. We were lucky enough to have a com-plete family. For them the freedom of movement was something to get used to, but they soon became part of the family. I think that the numbers at the school were anything between 30 and 70 with the influx of children.

As our enemy commanded the coastline and sank our imports, the farmers were working almost around the clock to feed the country. Rabbits were in great demand and a very good meal too. The ministry controlled the amount of meat we could kill on the farm, and as long as we let them think they were in control, we did as we wished. I never remember meeting an official who would refuse a leg of lamb or a loin of pork. We killed double our quota and delivered the meat to the parishioners who had helped us with the harvest.

With regards to our enemy, we were taught that the

Germans were 'no good', but it wasn't long before we had prisoners working on the farm, and as a schoolboy I had a culture shock. We had two lads from the Brayford camp; Ronald, the son of a factory owner, who had been taken out of university and put into the Navy, and was very much a gentleman. Francis was a farmer's son from the north, so he was in his element on the farm. He was as strong as a donkey and so that was what we christened him. At Christmas they were allowed to stay all day with us. They made us all presents from wood and gave them to us personally after we had eaten our Christmas lunch. The Germans were a very gifted nation, who I feel were let down by a dictator.

Because we had double British Summertime – two extra hours of light meant that twilight wasn't until about 11.30 – it was a very long day for both farm and factory workers. Looking back, I really quite enjoyed my war years, but mustn't forget my friends who went to war and never returned.

Mr Bill Lewis, whose family once lived at Satterleigh Barton and Lower Ditachdon Water, Chittlehamholt, writes about his family:

I have been told that I must be Welsh because Lewis is a familiar name in the principality, and also because of my musical leanings! I reply that there is a Scottish island of Lewis (with Harris) and a Sussex town spelt with an 'e'. Until the reign of King Athelstan (925–40), Cornwall and Devon were known as West Wales, so perhaps my paternal ancestors were in this area then, when the total population of the whole country num-bered less than one million. My primary-school teacher told me I must have Saxon blood because my hair then was almost white.

Be that as it may, the family could have crossed the Bristol Channel to Ilfracombe, as one researcher consid-ers that a John Lewis, born there in 1691, and his wife Sarah, had a son called William. Born in 1724 and later of Swimbridge, William married Sarah Baker at Chittlehampton in 1747. The Swimbridge Registers show two families running almost side by side, spelt with an 'i' and an 'e' respectively. What is absolutely certain is that my late father's great-grandfather John Lewis was born in 1761 and later married Elizabeth Rowe of Satterley at Chittlehampton's St Hieritha Church when they were both 20. This was before Chittlehamholt's St John's Church was built. John was probably employed by his farmer father because, when he died in 1835, he was described as a Yeoman at 'Janes'. He left a will and after his widow died in 1840 a beautiful tombstone was erected to their memory.

Their sons, John and William, both rented land at Chittlehamholt from John Brown, one of the largest landowners in the district. William also owned land. John married Jane Kingsland at Chittlehampton in 1841, and they lived in a Chittlehamholt farmhouse named Featherstones. John was clearly musical as he played the violin, amongst other instruments, in church. Henry, my

Paul Wingrove, agricultural contractor from Satterleigh, 2002.

George Slee, now retired, seen here at Farrs Farm in 1960.

Right: *Harold Beer from Shortridge Farm, Warkleigh, sits on his Massey Ferguson tractor which has been in the family since 1949. He proudly shows, with his wife Eileen, a trophy he won through a video on Fergie tractors that was taken on his farm in 2002.*

Below: John and Elizabeth Pester outside Fir Cottage, Chittlehamholt, c.1900.

Chittlehamholt and Warkleigh Young Farmers' calf judging, 1950. Left to right: Mr Purchase, Ella Ley, John Murch, David Harris, Mr Eggerton.

William and Louisa Ann Webber at Easton Barton, Morchard Bishop, c.1900, but formerly of Satterleigh Barton.

Reg Pincombe from Pugsley Farm, Warkleigh, holding his grandson Benjamin Tranckle alongside Reg's son Michael Pincombe, 2002.

father, told me that his mother, Martha, a Cornish woman, had been told to be careful of the low ceilings and replied that she wouldn't worry as long as she was wearing her hat! Unfortunately the farmhouse later burnt down and was uninsured. Two items of furniture at least were saved as Dad kindly handed them on to me. John and Jane then moved to Wards Farm some distance below, where Dad's father John William was born in 1847. His sister Mary Jane died in 1869 of appendicitis when only 25. (My appendix was removed when I was 25, such have been medical advances.) Her poignant epitaph reads, 'Short was my journey here on earth, My soul hath took its flight. It's done a journey much more worth, To meet the Lord of Light.' In that same year, John L. Brown of the Manor House died at only 40.

In 1838, Chittlehamholt had a population of 400 inhabitants and needed its own church. John Brown of Sandford gave the site and the Chapel of St John (which St John is in some doubt) was built at a cost of £1,000, being consecrated by the Bishop of Exeter on 30 October 1838. The same year a barrel organ in the west gallery was built by John Heard (whose tombstone is near the church entrance), being later replaced by a harmonium and this in turn by a two-manual pipe organ. A handsome set of church plates was given by Lord and Lady Rolle (among the largest landowners in Devon). Marriages here did not take place until 1863. Baptisms and burials at Chittlehamholt were recorded in the Chittlehampton Registers until 1843.

John Lewis and Jane died in 1874 and 1884 respectively, and when their tombstone deteriorated, Dad had cast an exact replica replacement including 'Their End Was Peace'.

The aforementioned fire must have been a financial disaster as John William and Martha moved down to a smallholding, an idyllic situation on the banks of the River Taw, named Lower Ditchadon Water at Chittlehamholt. Their family consisted of four sons and four daughters. Dad's sister, Thomazine told me a few years ago that a man from Twitchen described their father as 'the nicest man I ever met'. Martha took fruit and vegetables by pony and trap to the still-existing South Molton market, as well as produce to Exeter Cathedral, presumably by train from Portsmouth Arms Station with the help of her husband. All the children attended the Church school at Chittlehamholt, also Church and Sunday school at St John's. A glance through Dad's exercise books shows it was an excellent school and he once quoted a phrase from Tennyson about not looking back mournfully at the past. Our friendly editor, Richard Lethbridge, will no doubt be publishing some information I gained about school life there.

Another disaster struck the family – John William had appendicitis. In 1902, King Edward VII recovered from appendicitis after his Coronation had been postponed. In 1906, however, there was to be no successful outcome for John William. A doctor was urgently summoned to Lower Ditchadon Water and he attempted an emergency operation on the kitchen table, but John William died.

Dad was only 12. His mother, Martha, was faced with an uncertain future and some of the offspring went to live with William, brother to John William, a building contractor. My father and Thomazine lived with Martha in West Street, South Molton. Dad attended the nearby school for about two years, playing for the football team before joining his brothers. Martha became a midwife and attended the Congregational Church, which in recent times has been converted to living accommodation. I was the last person to play its organ. She was the only grandparent to know of my existence, holding me in her arms during 1924, the year of my birth, and sadly dying the following year. Chittlehamholt became a place of pilgrimage and I took several members there over the years, including two of Dad's brothers from Australia, John and James. Dad's love was strongest and he built a retirement bungalow called Silver Birch near his former school. One of his memories remains unchanged – the narrow lanes with hedges full of primroses in springtime. His support for the church has been entrusted with me.

We are, all of us, descended in a direct line from numerous families. In Georgian times, the total population of the whole country was only in the region of seven million people, whereas today it numbers something like 60 million. My late mother's family were much more extensive and more well-to-do than my late father's. Offspring from the farming community would quite often marry into families from surrounding farms.

From my research I find that Robert Hacche and Lewis Hacche were buried at 'Saterley' in 1625 and 1637 respectively, and that prior to William Hatch of Aller, his son Thomas Hatch (previous spelling) bought 'Saterleigh' (now The Barton and much altered) in 1553, also that a descendent, Robert Hatch Gent's tombstone outside the church, bears the demi-lions of Hatch. In 1680 the last Robert Hatch purchased the Manor of Chittlehamholt. The Hacche family is also notable in King's Nympton parish.

I am directly descended from Mary Hacche who married Christopher Shopland (1746–1802) in 1773 at George Nympton. Mary had at least two sons, James and Christopher. James married Elizabeth Elworthy in 1817 and lived at the particularly fine house of Snerridge on the outskirts of South Molton. Christopher Shapland (change of spelling), the other son, was born in 1781 at Sampson Farm, George Nympton. He and his wife had a son John (1812–75) who married Jane Louisa, farmed at South Bray in the parish of Satterleigh, and had a daughter, Louisa Ann, who was my mother's mother. Her brother George, on the death of his father John, then farmed South Bray, and Mum remembers playing croquet on the lawn there with her cousins. Louisa Ann married William Webber (1850–1906) who was born at Cadbury Barton, Chulmleigh. They had four daughters and three sons, all born at The Barton and baptised in Satterleigh Church. I do not know how many attended Warkleigh School, but Mum had to walk there and back in all weathers (no tarmacadam roads!) and later *attended Edgehill College, Bideford. The Webber family moved to Easton Barton, Morchard Bishop, and Louisa Ann died in 1915.*

William Thorold (1841–88) was Rector of Satterleigh, as was his son, John Leofric de Buckenhold Thorold (1891–1907) (dates of their ministries), [and] William and his three daughters Godiva, Salome and Eleanor were buried in the churchyard there. My mother and her sisters and brothers always had a deep affection for Satterleigh. Her brother Richard had his house at Whimple (built by Dad's firm) named Satterleigh. They said that John Leofric was a wonderful preacher. He was a patron of the church as late as 1933.

My wife (Nancy) and myself visited Lower Ditchadon Water in 1970 to find just a doorway and an open fireplace with its beam and bread oven and iron door surviving. Two of our children, Rachel and Rosalind, played on a pebble beach by the Taw and I had a swim there. I was devestated to lose my parents, with whom I had lived for 42 years, within 16 months of each other, and both are buried at St John's churchyard (which Richard Lethbridge keeps so beautifully) and [I] had Mum's tombstone inscribed 'Shall the righteous shine forth' (she was never self-righteous), and on Dad's, 'In my Father's House are many mansions' (Christ's description of Heaven).

I am distantly related to the Elworthys of Honiton Barton, South Molton.

John Webber and James Webber were churchwardens at Satterleigh in 1779–97 and 1815–17 respectively.

Among the tombstones in the churchyard are: Joan Webber, who died 17 September 1835 aged 62 years, and James Webber (her husband), who died August 1854, aged 82 years.

There is an older Webber tombstone against the south wall of the church [Grace Webber died in 1801 aged 63 and John Webber died in 1823 aged 85].

Since the Webbers left The Barton, the Elworthys have been farming there and caring for the church. They are probably distantly related to me. Mrs Pauline Elworthy certainly is as my great-grandfather Richard Webber of Cadbury Barton was her great-great-grandfather. Her mother's great-grandmother Mary (Pollie) married Thomas Baker (she being the sister of William).

The Chittlehamholt, Warkleigh & District Young Farmers' Club

At one time, Chittlehamholt, Warkleigh and District had a Young Farmers' Club which ran from 1944–55 and took over from the Chittlehamholt Youth Club. The Young Farmers' Club died out because big farming families weren't around anymore. Back then you had to be a young farmer to join, but today anyone can join. It was a very strong group and had several members.

Jim Thomas instigated the club, Alfie Gay was the first club leader, and Christine Congram – now Stuckey – was the first secretary. (She was also the first secretary of the South Molton group.) Christine recalls cycling into South Molton on her own to the Young Farmers' Club there, and when fiancé George thought it was time for her to come out of the meeting, he would cycle in from Umberleigh and see her home.

Marilyn Baghurst – now Bowen – became secretary for a while. After leaving school in around 1948 she left Wales and came to Snapdown to help Miss Smith on the farm. She remembers joining the Young Farmers' right away and, as at that time there were fewer outsiders coming to live in the parish than today, she was something of a novelty. Marilyn recalls the Young Farmers' Club having an open day in the village, including tractor and trailer backing, and can still picture Leslie Pincombe backing his trailer. The Young Farmers used to have Christmas parties, and Marilyn and fiancé Alan Bowen would often go to other Young Farmers' parties, coming back from the Chulmleigh district at one o'clock in the morning on Alan's motor bike, singing at the top of their voices, sometimes in thick mist with frost settling in, and with no crash helmets.

Before meeting Alan, Marilyn used to go to the Young Farmers' Club dances with Olive Vine from Newlands, the adjoining farm. Mr Vine used to drive sometimes, but he would never come and pick Marilyn up so she had to walk across the fields to Newlands in the dark, wearing her dancing dress and her wellington boots, and carrying her shoes. One night, coming home, it was misty and she lost her bearings and ended up in the wrong field; suddenly a white image appeared and terrified her. It turned out to be a pony.

From the minute book for the year 1947, the membership grew to 39. A very interesting summer programme was made up from the meeting on 9 April 1947, which included sheep shearing, an outing, show stock judging, rope and spar making, and thatching which was to be held on the same day. It was decided to start the sheep-shearing classes on 24 May at Mr Thomas' of Snydles. The second class was on 26 May at Mr Gay's at West Hele, the third was on 29 May at Mr Tucker's at Warkleigh Barton, the fourth was on 31 May at Mr Thorne's at Halswell, the fifth on 3 June at Mr Pincombe's at Pugsley, the sixth on 5 June at Mr Holland's at Hilltown, and the final competition on 10 June was held at Mr Ley's at Broden Hill.

In 1952 quotations were received for the club outing from Messrs Terraneaus of South Molton and Turners of Chulmleigh. It was proposed, seconded and carried that Mr Terraneaus should provide the buses for the outing which was to be to Weston-super-Mare via the Exe Valley, Dunster, Brendon Hill, Bridgwater and Burnham, on 19 July at the cost of 12s.6d. per head. The secretary was to write to the Warkleigh vicar to ask him to draw up an agreement as to how much the club should pay for each meeting held in Warkleigh School. As a result, the charge was 3s. for meetings and 15s. for parties. It was decided to hold a dance at Chittlehamholt on 16 July with the Skylarks dance band being engaged and Les Gale to be the second band.

Also in 1952 the president, Mr J. Thomas of Snydles, gave a silver cup to be awarded to the Young Farmer who collected the most points. For each meeting attended, two points were awarded – providing members were present by 8.30p.m. For any prizes won through entry in YFC competitions points were awarded – three points for first prize, two points for second prize, and one point for third prize. Three points were awarded for a special prize. Any member representing the club in a quiz team was awarded two points, win or lose. Any member representing the club in a Brains Trust competition or public-speaking competition was awarded two points.

In 1954 the YFC club name was changed to the Chittlehamholt Young Farmers.

The excerpts below, taken from the *Western Times*, reveal just a few of the other things the Young Farmers used to get up to:

January 12th 1945
A successful social took place in the village hall. The profits, over £8, are for the Club funds. Mr Harold Congram was MC and Mr Brend door steward.

March 16th 1945
The Young Farmers' Club meeting at the village hall was a Brains Trust and was well attended. The members were Mr A.G. Beynon, MRCVS, DVSM (Divisional Inspector, Ministry of Agriculture and Fisheries, Lime Dept); Mr G.H. Murrin, DWAEC, Farms Dept; Mr D.K. Strutt, Area Officer, Barnstaple; and Mr A. Porter, County Sec., NFU, made the 'perfect' question master. They were warmly thanked by Mr Harold Congram.

**CHITTLEHAMHOLT, WARKLEIGH AND
DISTRICT YOUNG FARMERS' CLUB
A TRACTOR-PLOUGHING COMPETITION
will be held at
WARKLEIGH BARTON
*on Saturday, October 6th 1945.***

Competitors praised at Chittlehamholt
The first tractor-ploughing competition organised by Chittlehamholt, Warkleigh and District Young Farmers' Club was held at Warkleigh Barton by invitation of Mr E. Tucker, on Saturday.

The advisory Committee, with Mr J. Thomas (chairman), Mr J.C. Ley (vice-chairman), Mr J. Congram (secretary) and Mr G. Holland (treasurer), made the arrangements. Mr Beele (county machinery instructor) and Mr Sampson were judges. The prizes were presented by Mrs Tucker.

The awards were: Young Farmers' Club – 1. J. Pincombe; 2. R. Holland; 3. R. Ayre. Local – G. Thomas, W. Holland, R. Snow. Open – Mr Down, Mr L. Holland, Mr Chapple. Special – J. Pincombe. Mr C.

Thomas (Umberleigh) spoke of the excellent work done by the competitors. Mr Beele congratulated them on doing some of the best work he had judged in Devon. Mr Harold Congram (club leader) thanked all for the interest in the event, the donors of prizes, Mr Tucker for the loan of the field, the Advisory Committee and the ladies committee for the refreshments and all who had worked to make the event such a success. Mr R. Ayre (joint club leader) seconded.

Chittlehamholt, Warkleigh and District Y.F.C.
A Tractor Ploughing Match and exhibition of sheep, roots and corn in sheaf. Produce exhibition for girl Y.F.C. members will be held at Warkleigh Barton (by kind permission of Mr E. Tucker, President) on Sat., Oct. 5th 1946 commencing at 10.30a.m. Entries close Saturday Sept 21st. Schedules and entry forms obtainable from J. Congram (Secretary), Wards, Chittlehamholt, to whom entries and fees must be sent. Admission 1s.0d.; Car Park 1s.0d.

June 20th 1947
YFC prowess, Chittlehamholt And Warkleigh
In connection with Chittlehamholt and Warkleigh Young Farmers' Club, classes in sheep-shearing have been held at the farms of Mr Thomas (Snydles), Mr Gay (West Hele), Mr Tucker (Warkleigh Barton), Mr R. Thorne (Allswell), Mr Holland (Hilltown), and Mr Pincombe (Pugsley).

The classes were well attended and excellent instruction was given by Mr H. Balment (West Buckland) and Mr G. Friend (Umberleigh).

The competition was held at Mr Ley's (Broden Hill), the judges being Mr Loosemoore (Atherington) and Mr Parkhouse (Shirwell) who expressed appreciation of the splendid work done by the members.

The prizes, presented by Mrs Ley, were won by: – 21 years and over: J. Pincombe, R. Holland, R. Westacott. 20 years and under: D. Herniman, F. Congram, J. Thomas. 16 years and under: I. Tucker, J. Murch, W. Westacott. Open class: W. Bowden, J. Fewings, A. Ley. Special prize: R. Holland.

Mr Gay (club leader) thanked Mr and Mrs Ley for their hospitality, the judges and instructors. Mr J. Murch voiced the club's thanks to all the farmers who had loaned sheep for shearing and had provided refreshments.

May 25th 1948
Chittlehamholt and Warkleigh Young Farmers' Club
Sheep-clipping competition will be held at Warkleigh Barton by kind permission of Mr Tucker on Tuesday, May 25th. Open classes commence 6.30p.m. Prizes for open clipping £3, £2 and £1. Entries taken on the field.

Chittlehamholt, Warkleigh & Dist Y.F.C., 1949
Show & Competitions in a Field adjoining the village hall, Chittlehamholt (by kind permission of H. Congram Esq.), Saturday Oct 2nd. Open at 1.30p.m. Adm 1s.6d.

Sheep, Roots, Corn, Cattle Judging, Rope and Spar-making, Tractor Backing, Weight Judging, Clay-Pigeon Shoot, Ladies' Classes of Produce in the village hall. Schedules and Entry Forms obtained from the Secretary G. Friend Overweir, Umberleigh, to whom all entries must be sent in by Sept 27th. Dance, village hall. B & M Dance Band 8 to 12.

Adm. 2s.6d.

Refreshments at Moderate Prices.

May 4th 1950

At the April meeting of the Chittlehamholt and Warkleigh Young Farmers, a summer programme was drawn up, which included poultry trussing, rope and spar-making, thatching classes, a sheep-shearing competition and an outing to Paignton with a trip on the River Dart. Entries were received at the Devon County Show at Barnstaple.

January 8th 1951

About 100 people attended a party held by Chittlehamholt and Warkleigh Young Farmers' Club in the village hall on Wednesday. The programme included dancing, games, and competition prize-winners being Miss O. Wright, D. Herniman, O. Westacott, Miss J. Fewings, Mr E. Fewings, Miss D. Dicker, L. Pincombe, Miss M. Baghurst, and Miss A. Brooks. Mr J. Murch and Mr R. Holland were MCs. Mrs J.S. Thomas gave a birthday cake with six candles, and on cutting it, she wished the branch well.

Oct 19th 1951

Chittlehamholt & District Y.F.C.
Grand Dance
Chittlehamholt Village Hall
on Friday October 19th, 8p.m.–1a.m.
Music by Ray Carter and his Rhythmets.
Admission: 3s.6d.
Refreshments at moderate charges.

March 14th 1952

Chittlehamholt & Warkleigh Y.F.C
Whist Drive
to be held at Warkleigh schoolroom
on March 14th, at 8p.m.
Good Prizes (including Poultry)
Admission 2s.0d.

The Chittlehampton & Warkleigh Ploughing Match

At one time Chittlehampton and Warkleigh had ploughing matches. An account below from the

War Agriculture Executive Committee certificate awarded to John Fewings in 1945.

North Devon Journal of December 1839 describes part of the day's proceedings at Higher Biddacott Farm, Chittlehampton.

December 12th 1839

Chittlehampton and first Warkleigh Ploughing Match.

The Journal *of December 12th 1839 states that it reported the first ploughing match at Swimbridge a fortnight since. Since then it was the subject of much conversation in the adjoining parish of Chittlehampton and Warkleigh. It was quickly decided to form a match of their own headed with a munificent contribution of £5 and it was scarcely set on foot before £25 was raised and an advertisement issued, announcing the match for Tuesday last. It stated that the parishes of Chittlehampton and Warkleigh offered a favourable field for the successful cultivation of an agricultural society, comprising together an acreage of upwards of 10,000 a very considerable portion of which was tillage land. The Match was held in three fields of Mr Webbers on Higher Biddacott Farm, at a given signal 28 ploughs were put in active motion. To the agriculturist it was interesting to witness so large a company of ploughs, the elite of the two parishes. At three o'clock, a party comprising about 60 people of the principal inhabitants of the two parishes sat down to a substantial old English fare in the schoolroom. The ploughmen of Warkleigh parish that were awarded prizes included the following:*

Premiums for Ploughmen: Fourth prize 7s.6d. to Abraham Manaton, servant to Mr T. Burgess of Edgington, Warkleigh. Class 2 – boys under 18 – First prize, H. John Beer, son of farmer Beer of Shortridge, Warkleigh. Third prize, 10s., Thomas Huxtable, son of the late farmer Huxtable, Chittlehamholt.

Premiums for Agricultural Labourers, Servants and Apprentices: Class 1 – Labourers who have brought up the largest families with the least parochial assistance, – First prize 10s., Edward Fairchild of Warkleigh who had brought up 12 children with very little assistance from the parish. Class 2 – Agricultural Labourers who have worked the longest with the master or on one farm – First prize, 15s., Thomas Shaddick, who had worked 52 years on Warkleigh Barton, now farmed by Mr Mortimer. Second Prize, 10s., William Skinner, who had worked 50 years on the same farm in the family of Mr Burgess of Warkleigh. Class 3 – Servants who had lived the longest with one master or on one farm – Second Prize, 10s., William Joslin, 12 years servant to Mr Darch of Warkleigh.

Chapter 11

THE POST OFFICE & ROYAL MAIL

Chittlehamholt Post Office

The 1893 *Kelly's Directory* states that William Sowden was postmaster and shopkeeper. A postcard dated 1912 with a Warkleigh date stamp shows a lovely old photograph taken in the Square, where the Post Office used to be situated. It was to stay here for the next 67 years. In 2002 the same building is in the occupation of Collette Potter and family, and is appropriately named the Old Post Office. I remember previous owners, a retired vicar, Revd Paine, and his wife, called it Robin's Nest.

The photograph of the Post Office with the two people standing outside *(below)* shows who we believe to be William Sowden and his wife. You will notice there are two boards on the building saying 'Chittlehamholt Post Office'. Also included in the photograph of The Old Gate House is tailor Hammett with his wife and daughter. By 1914 William Sowden's daughter (Ellen May) was postmistress and another photograph taken outside shows a lady thought to be her.

Searles as seen when it used to be a Post Office before the Second World War.

An old photograph of Chittlehamholt Post Office. This is thought to be the Sowden family outside, with the Hammetts outside The Old Gate House.

The old Chittlehamholt Post Office. The lady is
thought to be Miss Sowden, early 1900s.

The old Chittlehamholt Post Office, now a private
dwelling called September Cottage. The Post Office
was moved to Grange Cottage in 1986.

Chittlehamholt Post Office, 2001.

Postmaster David Moseley with his wife
Adrienne at Chittlehamholt Post Office, 2001.

Right: *Ruby Kingdon from Warkleigh did the
afternoon Chittlehamholt collection in the 1990s.*

Far right: *Postman Richard Lethbridge, 1982.*

Below, right: *Postman Barry Clemens with
Douglas Grose in Chittlehamholt village.*

Below: *Postman Charley Smith handing over
the mail to Mrs Ford outside the Exeter Inn.*

By 1939 Louisa and William Heard were at the Post Office. They ran it for a few years next door at Searles before reverting back to the old Post Office. It is not known for certain in which order they did this, whether they were at Searles first or not.

In 1954 Joan and Cecil Dockings took on the Post Office. A later photograph shows that a telephone box has been added outside. It was certainly there when I was growing up in the 1960s and '70s. Mr and Mrs Dockings retired in 1968 and Charles and Valerie Stewart, who were running the main shop known at the time of writing as September Cottage, took on and ran the Post Office alongside their shop, bringing many of the fixtures and fittings from the old Post Office. At the same time the telephone box was moved to its present site. Charlie Stewart was quite a character and whenever I went into the Post Office and stores, he always said 'Good Morning, vicar'.

In 1984 Mr and Mrs Stewart gave up the Post Office and Patrick Padfield and his wife ran it. They left in 1986 and Don and Eva Jeffs, who were living at Grange Cottage at the time, ran it from their premises. Yet another change took place in 1988 when Don and Eva moved and bought part of Northview Bungalow from John and Pam Lewis and ran the Post Office from there. The bungalow at the time was split and sold as two properties. Don and Eva called their property Uplands; the other half of the bungalow was bought by Neil and Patricia Dyke, who called theirs Ravello. Today it is known as Foxes Walk.

In 1996 Don and Eva left and David and Adrienne Mosley now run the Post Office.

The Royal Mail

The 1883 *Kelly's Directory* tells us that the mail was dispatched to Chittlehamholt by main cart from Chulmleigh. Molly Wilkey (née Heard), now 88, remembers this from when she was a young girl and recalls that the postman who drove the pony and cart from Chulmleigh was known as Postman Joint.

In the 1930s, Fred Clarke and William Heard delivered the mail around the village with it being dispatched from Umberleigh then. In the 1950s and '60s, Charley Smith and Cecil Dockings were postmen, followed by Charley Stewart and Peggy Carpenter. Diana Lethbridge used to stand in for Peggy while she was on holiday and I can remember helping her on Saturdays. This was in the 1970s before the concrete road leading into Mollands and Chappels was laid in the 1980s, and so we had to walk from Spiecott across the fields to see Miss Bird at Chappels, and then down the main track to Mollands to see Mr Cooper. He lived a reclusive existence with the buildings falling down around him – he went around on a bicycle wearing a black beret and would often be seen cycling to Exeter. I found it very spooky walking down to see him.

My mother took over from Mrs Carpenter when she retired. I can remember the three postmen who dispatched the mail from Umberleigh to Chittlehamholt in the 1970s – Harold Rice, Frank Hookway and Gerald Snell. They used to drive Morris Minor mail vans and would rotate the round – one week they came up with mail to the village, the second week they would deliver to High Bickington and the third week they would do part of Warkleigh and all of Satterleigh. This last route was a bicycle round but sometimes they did it in their own vehicles as a mail van was not provided. This route took in the long pull up Rags Hill and I did this when I joined the Post Office in 1981, before they motorised the round. I used to enjoy cycling the round then and calling in on Fred Brend and his wife at the Old Parsonage for a welcome cup of tea before peddling on again and eventually reaching the enjoyable ride down Dorridge Hill and back to Umberleigh.

Since 1984 the Chittlehamholt, Warkleigh and Satterleigh round has been delivered by the mail van from Umberleigh with Barry Clemens and Doone Baker sharing these rounds between them. The other postmen stationed at Umberleigh include Julie Woolacott who does part of the Umberleigh round, Gordon Webber doing Burrington, Paul Ayres on Chittlehampton, and Wendy Loosemore doing Atherington. I do the High Bickington round. Brian Harper stands in on our day off as we have a five-day week established here at Umberleigh and Sue Hayes provides holiday cover.

Until recently, an annual competition was held to find the Postie of the Year. A postman or woman could only win if someone wrote in and nominated them, and in 1992 I was nominated for Postie of the South West by customer Rita Morgan. I won and it was a very proud moment for me, earning myself the South West regional title of Postie of the Year and then going to London with ten other finalists from all over the country to find out the overall winner. This article is not intended to blow my own trumpet, but to share a moment of fame which does not come along often in one's lifetime. There were many postmen who equally deserved to win this award. Below, a Janet Leatham describes my moment of fame.

South West Postman of the Year
Richard Lethbridge
In case anyone missed all the media coverage last month, our very own postman, Richard Lethbridge, was nominated South West Postman of the Year in the annual competition run by the Royal Mail and Radio 2.

Customers were encouraged to write if their postman was special. Mrs Rita Morgan of Umberleigh nominated Richard, earning him the South West regional title and £500 in travel vouchers. Overnight, Richard became a celebrity with photographers, Radio Devon and an invitation onto the Post Office stand at the Devon County Show with buffet lunch afterwards. If John and Jill Snell of Newnham Barton wondered what Richard was doing up there raising his glass to them – this was the reason! A few days later Richard was interviewed live by phone on Radio 2.

Then, on June 2nd, Richard and Rita went to London along with ten other finalists for the national competition of Postie of the Year, the winner to receive a further £1,000 in travel vouchers. Richard's mother and aunt also went as their guests for an all-expenses-paid overnight stay at the luxurious St George's Hotel, Langham Place, W1.

'As we travelled up to London, my nerves followed me.' Richard was not looking forward to the live interview that evening but on meeting the other contestants soon started to enjoy himself, although his nerves returned on the way to Broadcasting House. Richard was third and admits it wasn't too bad as by then he had an idea of the questions Ken Bruce would ask.

'I got off to a fairly good start but had to pause at one question as my mind became a blank and when that happens there's nothing you can do about it', said Richard. The winner was Judy Cross of Norfolk. Richard received a framed certificate from Debbie Greenwood, of which he is justifiably proud, and goodies including an umbrella, watch and pen and £500 vouchers. Rita received a years' supply of letters, envelopes and stamps. A celebration reception followed and [there was] a press photo-call outside Broadcasting House the next morning.

Richard admits that it was a wonderful occasion which he will remember for a very long time.

Postman Richard Lethbridge, 1992, South West Postie of the Year, seen here collecting his award from Radio 2 presenter Ken Bruce at Broadcasting House, London.

I was little prepared for what was to come ten years later when, on 15 June 2002, I was presented with the MBE in the Queen's birthday honours list for services

to the Royal Mail and the community. I have to thank the people of High Bickington where I am the resident postman for putting my name forward to the Prime Minister. He in turn submitted my name to the Queen with a recommendation that Her Majesty graciously approve that I should become a Member of the British Empire.

Warkleigh Post Office & The Royal Mail

At one time Warkleigh had a Post Office. *Kelly's Directory* of 1890 states that Mr James Somerville was postmaster at the Post Office, then situated at the Old Parsonage. By 1893 Sarah Somerville was postmistress, followed by Miss Charlotte S. Somerville in 1914. By 1930 Thomas Sanders was postmaster, and finally Herbert Jones took over.

We are lucky to have a Warkleigh date stamp from a Chittlehamholt postcard of 1912.

From *Kelly's Directory* we learn that from 1866 onwards mail was dispatched to Warkleigh and Satterleigh from South Molton. Dot Ayre (née Bowden), now in her eighties, remembers as a child seeing postman Bodley walking from South Molton each day to deliver the mail to Warkleigh and Satterleigh. On the way he would deliver mail to Kingsland and Blackpool, etc. Between Trevor Snow's house (The Nook) and Alex Hill's (Little Satterleigh), there used to be a postman's hut in the dip of the hill and this is where postman Bodley would rest his weary legs during the day, spending the time here before clearing the mail box in Warkleigh at 4 o'clock and then making a special journey up to Warkleigh House for any outgoing mail before going on to Meethe Gate to clear that box, George Nymton to clear the Post Office, and then back to South Molton.

Vera Pearse, whose father, Denis Brooks, was a postman at South Molton, enlightens us more on the postman's hut:

Between the two wars – about 1930 – the GPO here in South Molton had three or four postman's huts erected in the villages of Warkleigh, Satterleigh, Mariansleigh and Meshaw for the benefit of villagers to take their mail to send back to South Molton. Postage stamps were also available from the huts. My late father, Denis Brooks, a long-time postman, was one of the employees who had to spend the day at one or other of these huts, and the villagers used to call in during the time he was there. They were very cosy, being equipped with a fire and chimney and facilities for making tea, etc. At about four o'clock each afternoon, my Dad would blow a whistle to enable people to come with last-minute mail. Me and my sister and brothers spent many a happy day during school holidays with my Dad in the huts and we used to play in the nearby fields, or if wet in the hut. It was great fun, and we all walked or cycled there. Happy days!

Chapter 12

ORGANISATIONS & EVENTS, PAST & PRESENT

The Parish Council & Politics

Parish Councils were established in the rural parishes of England and Wales in 1894. The reason for their formation was to divest the established church of various powers which it had acquired over the years. These had reached the point where, regardless of one's spiritual leaning, one was obliged to contribute to the church by the payment of tithes, and to accept the authority of the church in the running of the parish. When the Parish Council Act was made law, it established a parish meeting, and a Parish Council in every rural parish with a population of 300 or more people. Where a rural parish had a population under 300 but exceeded 100, it could, if the parish meeting so resolved, apply to the County Council for an order establishing a Parish Council. If it did not apply, or if it had a population under 100, it would be governed by a parish meeting. Parish meetings were not to begin before 6p.m., and one such meeting had to be held in every year.

The following gentlemen were appointed Deputy Returning Officers and Poll Clerks at the election for District and Parish Councillors in the South Molton District in 1894 by the Returning Officer, Mr R.L. Riccard. The first named in each parish was the Presiding and Deputy Returning Officer, the others being Poll Clerks. Appointed for Satterleigh and Warkleigh were Messrs J. Smith and C.J. Robinson. The Parish Councils were divided in different unions and Chittlehamholt came under the South Molton Union and granted a parish meeting, together with Charles, Creacombe, East Anstey, East Buckland, Filleigh, George Nymton, Marriansleigh, Meshaw, Rackenford, Romansleigh, Twitchen and West Anstey.

In the 30 years preceeding 1961, Satterleigh and Warkleigh were without a Parish Council. The newspaper at the time said that:

... the first Parish Council meeting for about 30 years for Satterleigh and Warkleigh was recently held. The parish representative on the South Molton Rural Council, Mr W. Hancock, said there had been a lot of controversy about their election and the press had tried to make out the Council was void, the clerk to the Rural District Council, Mr C.N.B. Willey, had told him that it was quite in order. Satterleigh and Warkleigh had

had a Parish Council in 1927 and 1930 when there had been a letter from the Council complaining about the surface of a road. The man who tapped the poll, Mr Wilson Holland, was elected chairman, and Major H.L. Owen was elected clerk.

In 1976 Warkleigh and Satterleigh agreed in principle to the parish being grouped under a common Parish Council with the parish of Chittlehamholt. Under the Local Government Act of 1972, District of North Devon:

The parishes of Chittlehamholt, Warkleigh and Satterleigh shall be grouped under a common Parish Council, the group shall be named the Chittlehamholt and Satterleigh and Warkleigh group and the common parish council shall be named the parish council of Chittlehamholt, Warkleigh and Satterleigh (herein after referred to as the Parish Council).

The first Parish Council meeting under the new group was held on 30 November 1977 with Mrs Lennard as chairman, Mr Brend as vice-chairman and Frank Reed as Parish Clerk.

An article by Mrs R.M. Wright, Chairman of the Parish Council, follows:

The Parish Council, I feel, has changed quite substantially over the years. We are still a joint council known as 'The Chittlehamholt, Warkleigh and Satterleigh Parish Council', and we are required to have ten councillors, five representing Warkleigh and Satterleigh, and five representing Chittlehamholt. All councillors must either live in their represented parish or have permanent employment in the parish or reside within three miles thereof. We have elections every four years when anyone can put up for office provided they meet with the legal requirements. If a councillor resigns within the four years, a by-election can be called, or the Parish Council can co-opt a new councillor. The legal structure has changed this year with the introduction of the new 'Model Code of Conduct' which was laid out by The Standards Board of England and passed by the government. We are each expected to declare our Assets, Businesses and even gifts of over £25 in value. Unfortunately we lost one councillor, Mr Chris Thorne of Warkleigh Barton, because he felt he couldn't agree, [although] *the remaining councillors duly signed even though some didn't agree entirely. We have an audit every year, with the County Council auditor. All monies must match with the banking and minute-books down to the last penny. We are under the instruction of the North Devon District Council where we can obtain help when required. We hold meetings once a month and an annual parish meeting in May. In the year 2001, because of the foot-and-mouth outbreak, we abandoned all meetings from March until July and we held our annual meeting in September. Our views on planning applications in the three parishes are sought from the NDDC – we don't always agree but do in general. We attend meetings such as the South Molton Area Committee where planning applications are discussed and decisions are made, we also attend meetings of Molton 2000, a committee concerned with reshaping South Molton and adjoining parishes, we attend DAPC (Devon Association of Parish Councils) meetings where we are told the latest information and what we can and cannot do. There are many other meetings we attend.*

The Parish Council purchased the field now known as 'Launds Playing-Field' in 1977 and it is for the use of the three parishes although it is situated in Chittlehamholt. It is generally run by a separate committee under the umbrella of the Parish Council, but at this moment in time, because of differences of opinion, the committee have all resigned. The play equipment has been removed because it didn't meet with the safety requirements, we are now considering replacing the equipment at an estimated cost of £30,000 plus. We have a working foot-path team known as P3 (Parish Paths Partnership). They keep the footpaths and bridle-ways free from becoming overgrown in the summer and maintain the stiles and do other maintenance work during the winter. P3 organised a footbridge to be built over the stream at Cleave Copse and had involvement with the footbridge at Watertown over the River Mole. Councillor Alex Hill is the co-ordinator. We also have a TPO (Tree Preservation Order) officer, Mr Robert Bater of Featherstones. As far as I'm aware, the only trees in the parishes with TPOs are the the Scots Pines in the playing-field. We also have the Neighbourhood Watch Scheme under the leadership of Mrs Frankie Sheath. There are several people involved from all three parishes, who attend meetings and are on call at any time. The Parish Council is responsible for reporting to the NDDC any problems with roads, fly tipping, hedgerows and flooding, etc.

We receive letters of approval and letters of disapproval. I suppose we should accept these because we are in the public eye and always open to criticism. Being a parish councillor is not easy; it is very time consuming and unpaid, but at the end of the day, it is quite rewarding to see some plan or discussion come to fruition.

Parish councillors at the time of writing representing Warkleigh and Satterleigh are Mrs Anne Hamilton-Clark, Mr David Buckle, Mr Mark Donaldson, and our vice-chairman, Mr Alex Hill. Representing Chittlehamholt are Mr William Congram, Mr John Robinson and our chairman, Mrs Rosalyn Wright. We are three parish councillors short at this time. The chairman, who has been acting clerk with the help of her computer for nearly a year, is the longest-serving councillor at present and was elected when Mr W. Holland was still on the Parish Council.

Politics

There was once a Liberal party for Warkleigh, Satterleigh and Chittlehamholt. It was formed in 1959 after a meeting held at Holtgate, at the time the home of Mr and Mrs Thorne. Mr A.E. Cook, divisional vice-chairman, presided and Mrs Prowse, divisional organiser, attended. Plans were made for a membership drive and future social activities. A Liberal Fête was held in 1960 at Chittlehamholt Manor where Miss Pat Lock was crowned as Liberal Queen; her attendants were Marian Tucker and Joyce Pimm, and the crown bearer was Margaret Adams. Mrs Leonard from the manor was presented with a bouquet by Marian Adams and Sheila Tapp gave Jeremy Thorpe, MP for North Devon, a buttonhole.

Today there is a Chittlehamholt, Satterleigh and Warkleigh branch of the North Conservative Association.

The Alphabet Parishes Passport Scheme

In 1994 the Parish Councils of England celebrated their centenary, and in conjunction with this a unique project aimed at putting communities on the map was launched by Danny Hughes of the Beaford Centre. The project fell within the framework of the Local Distinctiveness Programme which set out to enable local people to promote what is distinctive about their neighbourhood, and to help celebrate the Parish Council's centenary year. Communities in the Torridge and North Devon district were invited to apply for a letter of the alphabet and become one of the Alphabet Parishes. Chittlehamholt, Warkleigh and Satterleigh went for the letter 'H' for 'Holt'.

The idea for the Alphabet Parishes arose directly out of an archaeological dig which took place as part of the Torrington Commons Project. During the excavations, shards of sgraffito pottery were found which clearly showed designs characteristic of North Devon. In choosing a letter each community focused on a special aspect of the parish – such as a myth, personality or unusual building – and a plaque was then made by local potter Harry Juniper in the sgraffito style, applying a technique used in North Devon since the sixteenth century. The Chittlehamholt, Warkleigh and Satterleigh plaque is sited on the wall of the Exeter Inn.

Some of the smaller parishes could not contribute the £100 originally requested to pay for the plaques, but as Torridge and North Devon District Councils and South West Arts made financial contributions

Harry Juniper designing the Chittlehamholt, Warkleigh and Satterleigh plaque in 1994.

Chittlehamholt was runner-up in the 'Best Kept Village Competition' in 2000. Rosalyn Wright, Chairman of the Parish Council, receives a certificate from Sir Ian Amory.

verges had been kept both tidy and friendly to wildlife. The chapel yard was neat, but the grass cut too low for wild flowers. The condition of the commercial properties is an asset to the village. We would like to see a new village map, brought up to date to show the golf course, etc. In summary, a very good entry to the Best Kept Village competition.

Historical Pageant

There follows an interesting story which appeared in the local paper and relates to the photograph of the Historical Pageant overleaf, held at Warkleigh House, in June 1956, then the home of Mr and Mrs Frank Pepper.

to the scheme, it became possible to reduce the minimum cost to £50.

A total of 29 parishes are now part of the individual plaques scheme and holiday-makers and locals alike are given a 'passport book' and are invited to go around to all the parishes and get them hand stamped at each control.

Best Kept Village Competition

Every year, Chittlehamholt enters the Best Kept Village Competition and in 2000 it came runner-up. Rosalyn Wright, the chairman of the Parish Council, went to accept the award at Atherington Church Hall – their village had won the competition that year. Below are the comments made by the judges on the state of Chittlehamholt village on the day of judging:

We visited Chittlehamholt on 6th June 2000, a sunny afternoon after morning rain, and were impressed by this attractive village which, in spite of its small size, has many amenities and evidence of an active community. The roads through the village and the car park were completely free from litter, although there were two drinks cartons in the children's play area. Private properties were well cared for but there was an occasional unsightly growth of coarse grass at the bottom of walls. The parish hall was in good condition, the telephone kiosk and the area around the recycling pavilion clean and tidy. We found the footpaths to be well maintained and were especially pleased with the way the hedges and

Mr Reg Thorne of Halswell Farm, Chittlehampton, who was not in the photograph, was in the role of an ancient rustic, with cowherd's smock and red neckerchief. When he paused during a conversation piece to light his clay pipe, spectators surrounding the open air lawn theatre were astonished to see Mr Thorne's false beard and wig – made out of jute from old packing material – burst into flames. As the Pageant producer, Mrs J. Dockings dashed to the rescue, Mr Thorne whipped off the burning disguise and flung it to the ground, not before he had slightly singed the back of his neck. Unperturbed, Mr Thorne carried on with his act, and Major H.L. Owen, who was playing the part of a dandy, departed from his script to comment, 'No wonder we've had so many heath fires lately.'

Intrigued by the unrehearsed incident were two Oriental visitors to the garden party; Chinese amahs to a British household in Hong Kong who were staying in the country. They were in native dress and, with jet-black hair, their appearance contrasted sharply with the summer frocks of the other visitors and with the medieval dress of the players.

Dresses for the Pageant, which depicted scenes from early English rural life, were made by Mrs Jean Sheldon

131

of Watertown, who organised the garden party. The script was by Mr K. Evans, a Master at South Molton Secondary Modern School, and those participating in the Pageant were children of Chittlehamholt, Warkleigh and Satterleigh. The opener of the Pageant was Mr J.A.P. Martin.

Bands in the Parishes

Over the years the parishes have had a number of bands. The earliest was in the 1920s–'30s when Reg Heard, Frank Heard, Eddy Kingdon and Ruth Pester provided entertainment in Chittlehamholt. After the Second World War a band in Chittlehamholt, consisting of Claude Eastmond from Stonehayes, Mr and Mrs Jack Thorne and Peter Bater, played to the crowds and went as far afield as Chittlehampton and Umberleigh. Later, Claude Eastmond played on his own and then in 1972 started a trio band consisting of Ronnie Wallace, himself and Des Leat, calling themselves 'Cy Eastmond and His Band'. Sometimes they needed an extra player and they would call on Bill Tuner. Claude, who is 79 at the time of writing, still plays at the odd tea dance, sometimes with the help of another player. He has been providing music for over 50 years.

In the 1950s, Alan Bowen from Snapdown, Warkleigh, was a drummer, not in a Chittlehamholt band, but in one formed by Sam Wilsby from Lapford called 'The Beverley Quartet' which also included two lads from North Tawton. Claude Eastmond joined them occasionally.

In 1959 another Chittlehamholt band emerged in the shape of Bill Hammett's Ferguson Trio. Who would have thought a band named after a tractor would have survived for almost 30 years? The Ferguson Trio Band, formed in 1959 by the late Bill Hammett of Fair Oak Farm, Chittlehamholt, did just that. Here, Jim Moore, one of the original players talks about this unique band:

In 1959, while I was a representative for an agricultural firm – Gliddon and Squires – in Barnstaple, I sold a tractor to Bill Hammett, and in time we discovered that we had something in common – we both played the piano accordion. Six weeks later, Bill got in touch with me and asked if I'd like to play with him at a Conservative 'any questions', followed by a social at Chittlehamholt: our first booking. We didn't rehearse for that night, but everything came together. We didn't have any music stands so we stuck our music onto the backs of chairs.

Historical Pageant at Warkleigh House, June 1956. Beside the children stand two Chinese amahs who served a British household in Hong Kong. Left to right, top row: Christine Jewell, Mary Salter, Jean Baker, Elizabeth Clarke, Eileen Carpenter; middle row: Michael Holland, Ken Carpenter, Gerald Harris, Jennifer Heard, Maurice Thorne, Elizabeth Moore, David Elworthy, Michael Clarke; front row: David Heard, Pauline Sowden, Christine Sowden, Maureen Thorne, Norman Holland.

Another booking – at the Flower Show – came soon after, and as time went on many more enquiries came along. At one time we were playing three nights a week and were in demand throughout North and Mid Devon; we played in almost every village and town in the area. The band survived throughout years when there was a lot of competition for gigs; the Skylarks, the Hotspots,

The Ferguson Trio, seen here playing at Dolton in 1969. Left to right: *Pam and Bill Hammett with Jim Moore.*

Chittlehamholt band in the 1930s, taken outside Grange Cottage. Left to right: *Reg Heard, Walter Heard, Eddy Kingdon and Ruth Pester.*

Claude Eastmond, who still entertains after playing for 50 years. For many years he played in the Chittlehamholt, Warkleigh and Satterleigh Village Hall.

Roy and his Blue Stars, and Graham and his Green Echoes were all around at the same time.

At the beginning, as well as Bill Hammett and myself, there was Mo Beeson on drums. Sadly Mo died, and then Bill's wife Pam took over. In the winter of 1963, Bill taught himself the guitar; he borrowed one from his brother, Colin. Eventually he bought a second-hand compact organ which folded up like a suitcase. The first owner of the organ was Roy Davey of Roy and his Blue Stars. I used to play the organ and alternate with the accordion while Bill sang in the style of Jim Reeves.

At one point Bill thought we ought to have a uniform, so we got these blue shirts with a red bowtie with black and white spots. One night at the New Inn at Bideford, where we became a sort of resident band, someone was laughing at us saying we reminded him of Pinky and Perky.

When we were first asked what the band was called, Bill, on the spur of the moment, thought about the Ferguson tractor I sold him and said 'The Ferguson Three'. This soon got changed to The Ferguson Trio.

We started off playing mostly socials and parties; our first real dance was at Chulmleigh Week Hall. While we were setting up, the stage started to give way and we found ourselves searching in the adjoining field for some oil drums to prop it up. There was no electricity in the hall; a torch lit up the exit signs and a Calor Gas boiler was used to make the teas. Running Bear was top of the hit parade at that time, and, with a full hall, it was a good gig. As time went on, we needed some amplification and so I bought an ex-government amplifier – 12 volts or mains, and one of my old teachers from Barnstaple let me have a speaker. Of course, when we went to Chulmleigh Week there was no electricity so we took the battery out of Bill's Dexta tractor and plugged into that and played from the 12-volt system. There was no parking at Chulmleigh Week either, so people parked in the middle of the road.

We didn't make much money out of the band – I can remember getting four guineas for five hours at a Liberal dance at Burrington – but we had a lot of laughs.

I gave up in 1970 because I was busy doing other things and I also wanted to give Bill and Pam's daughter Pauline the chance to play. She was a teenager at the time, and it didn't seem right leaving her at home on her own when she could play better than me and Bill could ever hope to; we were good entertainers but not good musicians. When I left the band, Pauline, Bill and Pam played with some of the other bands at large barn dances held at Parsonage Farm, Chulmleigh, the home of Bill and Margaret Crowcombe. In the 11 years that I was with Bill, we never once had an argument or disagreement; we thought and played as one, and both knew what was going to happen before it happened. I could read Bill like a book, and vice versa. If it wasn't for Bill, I don't suppose I would have gone out playing. In latter years, Bill played with Ron Cooke until ill health prevented him carrying on and he sadly died in 1993.

Above: *A children's party in the Village Hall, c.1954. Included in the photograph are: Brian Kelly, Anthony Beer, Mervyn Harris, Maurice Thorne, Tony Hancock, Arthur Adams, Gerald Harris, Sam Wright, Phylis Adams, David Peters, Margaret Adams, Harold Beer, Alan Ayres, David Heard, Michael Holland, Michael Clarke, David Elworthy, John Adams, Pat Bonfield, Janet Eastman, Pamela Bonfield, Marian Adams, Anne Thompson, Pat Lock, Norman Holland, Donald Moore, Rosy Penfold, Barbara Williams, Maureen Thorne, Colin Ayre, Elizabeth Clarke, Winnie Harris, Margaret Adams.*

Opposite page: *Children's Christmas party in the Village Hall, c.1950.* Included in the picture are: *Mrs Beer, Mrs Skinner, Joan Skinner, Bessie Skinner, Joyce Heard, Mabel Holland, Mrs Baker, Spencer Vivian, Mrs Passmore, May Herniman, Mrs Scott, Janet Judd, Ruby Herniman, Norah Herniman, Mrs Mackenzie, Mrs Seage, Gerald Harris, Mrs Harris, Mrs Wardrop, Mrs Salter, Mrs Holland, Mervyn Harris, Vera Wright, Norah Moore, Norman Bowden, Reg Pincombe, Adrian Balman, Dennis Turner, Sybil Judd, Margaret Guard, Joyce Sanders, Maurice Thorne, Robert Bater, ? Pike, Sam Wright, Muriel Wright, Dorothy Bater, Jean Baker, Florence Pike, Margaret Heard, Margaret Adams, Elizabeth Clarke, Barbara Williams, Anne Thompson, Jennifer Heard, Mary Slater, David Heard, Sally Hatwell, Anthony Beer, Harold Beer, Fred Beer, Judith Hatwell.*

Pantomime

Each year the Really Useless Theatre Company at Umberleigh puts on a pantomime. In 2002 the panto had a Warkleigh theme – *Sherlock Holmes and the Wolf of Warkleigh*. The story revolved around Holmes and Watson coming down to Warkleigh Hall to investigate the sudden death of Sir Charles Warkleigh, he being the last in the Warkleigh family line.

The Launds & The Launds Playing-Field

The Launds, or Lands, is the ground within the circular road which starts and ends in the village. Many village inhabitants use this road to get to church, or simply as a favourite walk. The route is referred to by many different names by members of the village – I call it 'walking around the block', while many of the older residents call it 'walking the entrance' (the crossroads known as Entrance Cross is featured on the route). The road past the council-houses is also known to the older residents as Land Lane. The Launds is mentioned in the book written by the late Revd Andrews of Chittlehampton, published in 1961. Over more recent years, the name has been kept alive in the Launds Playing-Field, and a bungalow called the Launds owned by Willie and

135

Chittlehamholt, Warkleigh and Satterleigh WI, c.1959, in the Village Hall.
Left to right, back row: Ella Thorne, Mabel Holland, Diana Lethbridge, Evelyn Holland; third row:
Irene Heard, Ida Pearce, Mrs Heard, ?, Winnie Harris, Lily Johns, Marilyn Baghurst, Mary Martin,
Daphne Vasey, Phylis Carter; second row: Lily Malcolm, Jenny Skinner, Lucy Carter, Mrs Salter,
Mrs Turner, Mrs Holland, Mrs Seage, ?, Mrs Lennard, Mrs Owen; front row: Mrs Scott, Norah Moore,
Mrs Cleavely, Miss Binnie, Mrs Congram, Mrs Passmore, Mrs Baker, Ruth Buckingham.

Guests at the Chittlehamholt, Warkleigh and Satterleigh WI party in the Village Hall, 1952.
Left to right, back row: Alan Bowen, Mr Sing, Fred Brend, D. Turner, Mr Street, Mr Seage, Alfie Gay;
third row: G. Holland, A. Baker, C. Eastmond, F. Heard, W. Johns junr, Fred Moore; second row:
W. Johns senr, Edward Dicker, Mr Lewis, Revd Cleavely, Duncan Mackenzie, H. Owen, G. Martin;
front row: Maurice Thorne, Mervyn Harris, Mervyn Gay, Gerald Harris.

Marion Sanders. Bill Congram, who used to farm Butlers, recalls that the fields within the Butlers lands are known by the following names: Cook's Lands, which Paul Wingrove now owns; the fields that occupy the golf course are 'Greater Butlers Lands'; the field directly below Hillbrow and the one next to it are called 'Lesser Butlers Lands'; and the field opposite the church is 'Bricklands', where they used to dig clay to make building bricks.

In notices of sale in 1799 and 1810, Lands is called the Launds, and in a conveyance of 1808, it appears as tenement or overland called the Launds, together with a cottage. It totalled 86 acres, but there was no farmhouse. 'Overland' was probably a term applied to a form of land tenure, but was also used for any place of land left without farmhouse or buildings. 'Laund' is a word akin to 'Lawn', meaning an open space among woods – a glade. It is a Shakespearean word – 'under this thick grown brake we'll shroud ourselves, for through this laund anon the deer will come.' (Henry VI)

The Playing-Field

The playing-field on the land that was once known as the Launds was bought by the Parish Council for the community in 1978 for £2,000 from Mr J.H. Davies; it was known as Vicarage Field. In 1979, it was officially opened by the late Mrs Joan Lennard of The Manor.

Heather Petherick's remembers:

When Frank Reed suggested we bought a playing-field for the village, once again the village pulled together. Funds were raised and I remember one hot Sunday afternoon me, my husband and children – John, six and Annie, three – along with half the village, turned up to pick up stones from the field after it had been ploughed and before the grass seed was tilled. Richard Lethbridge was there with his cine camera to film the occasion for posterity.

The number of children in the village had increased tremendously and gradually we raised funds for swings, a roundabout and a see-saw, but it was a while before we reached the dizzy heights of a slide! It took a lot of fund-raising, but when the slide arrived the children were thrilled; it was a beauty.

I personally found it a wonderful asset, and cries of 'why don't we go and play on the playing-field' echoed from many a house.

The Women's Institute

The Chittlehamholt, Warkleigh and Satterleigh WI was disbanded in 1971 after 40 years. The following articles, along with photographs opposite, show what they used to get up to. A few years later, in 1973, a Mothers' Union was inaugurated, but this was also disbanded.

May 14th 1937
The monthly meeting of the Women's Institute was presided over by Mrs Beaumont (vice-president), in the unavoidable absence of the president. An excellent talk on 'The Queens of England' was given by Mrs Over of Saunton. The competition tulips grown from bulbs purchased at the WI were judged by Mrs Over who gave the awards to: 1, Mrs Baker; 2, Miss Evelyn Holland. A display of brass, brought by the members, was greatly admired. Mrs J. Congram was tea hostess.

July 30th 1937
The garden meeting of the Chittlehamholt, Warkleigh and Satterleigh Women's Institute was held at Edginton, at the invitation of Mrs Beaumont (vice-president). Owing to unsettled weather conditions, the meeting was held indoors. Mrs Carter (president) who presided, gave a report of her visit to the Barnardo Home at Exeter, where she saw the 'silver' cot, which had been bought with tinfoil, which the Institute members generously helped to contribute. Mrs Simmons, who attended the summer meeting at Exeter as delegate, gave an interesting account of the proceedings. Tea was served, and there was a lovely birthday cake, it being the 21st anniversary of the Women's Institute movement. The members adjourned to the lawn, where they listened to Lady Denman's broadcast speech. Games and competitions were enjoyed, for which prizes were given by the hostess. A doll, given and attractively dressed by Mrs W. Pester, realised over 13s. Its correct name (Barbara) was guessed by Mrs Owen. Mrs Warren proposed a hearty vote of thanks to Mrs Beaumont for her kindness in providing such a pleasant afternoon. The competition, 'Wild flowers, pressed, dried and named', was judged by Mrs Morrell, who awarded the prizes: 1, Mrs M. Hopper; 2, Mrs J. Congram.

April 22nd 1938
The monthly meeting of the Women's Institute was well attended, over 40 members being present. Mrs Carter (president) was in the chair. A demonstration on dyeing and dry-cleaning was given by Miss Adam. The competition, 'Six best eggs', was won by: Equal 1, Mrs J. Medland and Miss Ella Turner; equal 2, Mrs F. Clarke and Mrs Tucker; 3, Mrs Turner. Miss Adam was the judge. A tea given by Mrs Baker was enjoyed, and a hearty vote of thanks was accorded her. Mrs W. Skinner has given some Jerusalem leaflets and Mrs Scott some plates for the use of WI. A collection of eggs on behalf of the North Devon Infirmary met with an excellent response.

At the recent Taw Valley group exhibition held at Chawleigh, the Institute gained fourth place.

A successful social in aid of the village hall funds has recently taken place in the hall.

October 21, 1938
The monthly meeting of the Women's Institute was held in the village hall. Mrs Carter (president) being in the chair. An excellent demonstration was given by Miss Milner on 'Poultry trussing'. She trussed a chicken, step

The Flower Show

The bicycle race at the Flower Show, July 2001.
Left to right: *Tim Nicholas, Nicholas Gillanders,
Charlotte Moseley, Siobhan Smith.*

Organisers of the sports at the Flower Show,
July 2001. Left to right: *John Petherick,
Eileen Scoins, Marion Sanders.*

Runners-up at the Flower Show five-a-side football
in 2001 were the Chittlehamholt All Stars.
Left to right, back row: *Tom Bowman,
Cliff Stapleton, Colin Jennerson;* front row:
Tim Nicholas, David Page, Sam Bowman.

The wheel-and-barrow race at the Flower Show, 2001.
Left to right: *Willie Sanders guiding Derek Guard,
Marcus Keenor guiding Carol Sanders.*

Fred Herniman the starter with Christopher and
Debbie Thorne in the three-legged race, July 2001.

Derek Northcott, who has been coming to the
Flower Show for the last 30 years with his
public-address system in July 2001.

by step, and kept her audience interested in the process. She was heartily thanked on the proposition of Mrs J. Congram. The competition, 'The tidiest parcel made with a coat hanger and shoes', was judged by Mrs J. Symons, who awarded first prize to Mrs Salter and second to Miss L. Skinner. The co-operative tea was managed by Mrs Dicker. Miss Carter was warmly congratulated on passing her knitting test. A spelling bee closed an enjoyable afternoon. A good number of members visited the produce exhibition at Exeter and won 29 awards, among which was a star, awarded Mrs J. Congram.

Other prizes were awarded for a variety of produce, including: eggs, mint jelly, grapefruit marmalade, bacon, cream, biscuits, lemon curd, bread, cake, bramble jelly, raspberry jam, pears, butter, Cornish pasties, apple jelly and blackcurrant jam.

November 23, 1945

Chittlehamholt, Warkleigh and Satterleigh – The November meeting on November 15th was presided over by Mrs Wardrop (president), who was re-elected. Mrs Thomas and Mrs Passmore were re-elected vice-presidents, Mrs Skinner secretary, Mrs J. Congram treasurer, Mrs Carter for war savings, Mrs Mackenzie and Mrs W. Holland entertainment, Mrs G. Holland 'home and country', Mrs Dicker trading stall, and Mrs Seage competitions. Mrs Salter and Mrs T. Turner, Mrs Worthington and Capt. Wardrop were tellers and were thanked by Mrs Mackenzie. Competitions resulted: Prettiest button, Mrs Carter; feather hat mount, Mrs Mackenzie. Mrs Thomas judged. 'Sing, say or 2d. pay' brought in help to the funds. Mrs M. Congram generously gave a sumptuous tea. It was decided to have a Christmas party, and later an outing to the pantomime.

August 5th 1954

The July meeting of the WI was held in the village hall, Mrs J. Thomas presiding. A cooking demonstration on savoury snacks was given by Mrs Westacott of Hatherleigh. Mrs G. Holland proposed a vote of thanks. The competition, a bouquet of vegetables, was judged by the demonstrators, their awards being, 1, Mrs L. Baker, 2, Miss T. Turner, 3, equal, Mrs Dicker and Mrs Smith. The summer outing was to Lynton and Lynmouth and Ilfracombe.

February 3rd 1955

In the village hall, decorated with evergreens, festoons and artificial flowers, the combined Christmas and Birthday party of Chittlehamholt and Warkleigh WI took place. Members of Chulmleigh WI accepted the invitation and each member invited a guest, members' children also attended. They were welcomed by Mrs Thomas. Dances and tea games were organised by the Bandit Band. There was an interval for refreshments given by the members. Then followed the cutting of the birthday cake, given and cut by the president. It was decorated with 24 candles, and guests joined in singing

'Happy Birthday' to the Institute. The awards to those who had gained highest marks in the year's competitions were presented by Mrs Thomas as follows; 1), Mrs Baker, 2), Mrs T. Turner, 3), Mrs Dicker. A large cracker in WI colours, made and given by Mrs Mackenzie, was pulled by Mrs F. Heard (secretary) and Mrs Pearce (assistant secretary), and from it all the guests, over 100, received a gift. Mrs Turner, on behalf of the Chulmleigh Institute, thanked the host Institute.

December 20th 1966

In celebration of its 35th anniversary, the WI held a dinner, followed by a social at a South Molton hotel. The table was decorated in WI colours. A cake was given by Mrs R. Thorne (president) which was cut by her assistant Mrs J. Congram (vice-president). Mrs Buckingham was the pianist.

December 24th 1969

At Chittlehamholt, Warkleigh and Satterleigh WI, Mrs Dampier-Bennett presided. A competition was organised by Mrs R. Thorne. The year's competition prizes were won by Mrs R. Thorne, Mrs Turner, Mrs J. Congram. Hostesses were Mrs Brend and Mrs W. Holland.

December 4th 1971

The closure meeting of Chittlehamholt WI took place at the Warkleigh Social Centre, Mrs Bennett presiding in the chair and Mrs Tilson, county secretary, explained the rules appertaining to the closure. A gift token from the members was presented to Mrs W. Holland in recognition of her work as treasurer for many years. A presentation of a golden jubilee goblet by Mrs Tilson was made to Mrs J. Congram for 40 years as a committee member. Prizes for the year's competitions were awarded to Mrs J. Congram, Mrs W. Holland and Mrs Turner.

August 16th 1973

A full branch of the Mother's Union was inaugurated for the parishes of Chittlehamholt, Warkleigh and Satterleigh on Sunday. The enrolling member, Mrs Dampier-Bennett, presented the members, and the rector, the Revd G.R. Dampier-Bennett, conducted the admission procedure. Lessons were read by Mrs Bennett and Mr B. Scrivener and the organist was Miss D. Scrivener. The deanery presiding member, Mrs C.E. Hutchings, Mrs M. Oliver, with members of St Mary Magdelene branch of the Mother's Union at South Molton, also took part in the service. A message was read from the Exeter Diocesan President, Mrs Puddicombe. Mother's Union members from Bishop's Nympton and Chittlehamholt took part.

The Chittlehamholt, Warkleigh & Satterleigh Flower Show

The Chittlehamholt, Warkleigh and Satterleigh Flower Show has a long history and in 2002 is in its 78th year.

It is an annual event which attracts crowds from both the village and outside, with people coming together year after year to show their produce and handicraft and meet up with people they perhaps haven't seen all year. Some visitors even plan their holiday to coincide with the sports so the families can take part. The show is officially opened each year by a local celebrity or sometimes a person who has moved away from the village.

The children all look forward to competing in the races with their mums and dads cheering them on. Fred Herniman starts the races, calling in his broad Devonshire dialect, 'are y' ready? [clap of hands] Go!' Fred was brought up at Deason and is a familiar figure on the field. He looks forward to the sports as much as the children do, and has been involved with the event for many years. Heather Petherick introduces the races – having first paid a quick visit to the hall to see if her home-made wine has won a prize. 'Oh, the power you can yield with that micro-phone,' she says, 'welcoming children and adults onto the field from 50 yards away to join in the racing.' Heather's son, John, takes a turn on the microphone if he's at home, and they both bring their own sense of humour which adds to the enjoyment of the day. Alongside Heather or John is Marion Sanders in charge of scoring, and Eileen Scoins with the prize money. Carol Griffiths (among others) is on the finishing line while Jim Page and Linda Leach prepare the races. As well as the races, a five-a-side football competition is ably run by referees Mark Craze and Steve Tranckle. Not an official football team, but some of the local lads who have a kick-about after school, take part in this competition, calling themselves the Chittlehamholt All Stars. In 2001 they were runners-up and the year before they won the cup. The combination of the two sports results in an afternoon filled with cheering and laughter.

Suitable musical melodies are provided by Derek Northcott, who has been coming to the show for 30 years. The chiming of the melodies puts an extra spring in your step, giving you that feel-good factor and adding to the atmosphere of the day. Refreshments are provided on the field by the Warkleigh Church ladies: hot dogs, cornets, etc., and Jenny Kelley runs the bottle stall.

Back in the hall, people admire the exhibits and the secretary, Heather Page, prepares herself, getting the prize money ready. The rest of the committee are kept busy selling draw tickets and manning the food department from the kitchen hatch.

George Martin proudly displays the Waldrop Challenge Bowl Cup he won three years in succession in 1948, '49 and '50 at the Chittlehamholt, Warkleigh and Satterleigh Flower Show.

With the afternoon nearly over, the children get ready for the last race – the bicycle race – and then it's back to the hall at 5.30p.m. for the prize-giving and awards to finish the day's proceedings. Challenge cups given by families in memory of loved ones include the Acty Cup in memory of James Acty, a one-time head gardener at Highbullen.

With the exhibits in the Village Hall and the sports on the playing-field, the show has a permanent site, whereas in the early days it was held at different venues including Holtgate, Haynetown, and just down the road from Holtgate in a field known as Broadley. Back then, it was a different type of show than the one we know today. Stafford Constable can remember horse-racing – one lap around the field walking, second lap trotting and the third at full gallop – and Tom Martin always won. Other activities included swinging boats and motor bike races – the sons of Tom Stenner (Fred and Harold) were enthusiasts and were usually first and second.

Opposite Haynetown Lane there used to be a big red shed where the Flower-Show equipment was stored, and Maurice Thorne and his father used to bring it out in a horse and butt. Before the new hall was built, there wasn't enough room for all the exhibits so two marquees were put up in the field next to the Village Hall, and this is where the main sports were held before the playing-field was opened. As kids, we used to watch the firm of Braunds of Braunton erect the marquees.

There was one year – 1964 – when a show didn't take place because there was very little support which made it impossible to form a full committee.

There follows a report of one of the shows.

Chittlehamholt, Warkleigh and Satterleigh Flower Show
August 9th 1928
Favoured with glorious weather, Chittlehamholt, Warkleigh and Satterleigh Flower Show, of which Mr H. Bryant is president, was a great success. Mr W. Johns was the energetic Hon. Secretary. The show was held in a field lent by Mr C. Holland of Haynetown. The proceedings commenced with a luncheon ably catered for by Mrs C. Holland. The Torrington Band rendered selections. There was a large attendance, the pourers were Mrs James, Miss Beaumont, Mrs Webber, Mrs Eastmond and Mrs Thorne, while Mrs French, Mrs Warren and Mrs Baker assisted. Messrs Vickery and Mears were the judges. The horse races had fewer entries. [North Devon Journal]

The Chittlehamholt football team in the 1950s. Left to right, back row: *Percy Wheaton, Arthur Parkhouse, Raymond Skinner, Herbert Tancock, Desmond Peters, Michael Caws;* front row: *Victor Hulland, Gordon Parkhouse, Bob Brock, George Hakin, Alfie Gay.*

The Wine Circle

Heather Petherick recalls that the wine circle was a monthly evening of great fun and entertainment:

Frank and Rosalind Reed initially started the group. I remember that there was a bucket placed in the middle of the room – not for the 50p donation to charity, but to pour the wine you didn't like into it. As the wine was all home-made, there was the occasional disaster. Desmond and Fred had the most rejects, although we all had our share. Many jokes were made and great laughter had over our local elderflower, parsnip, rose petal and blackberry wines. Sadly the wine circle now consumes mainly commercial wines, the country wines have gone – along with most of the wine makers.

The Chittlehamholt Revel, 1978

The first and only revel day held at Chittlehamholt in 50 years took place in 1978. The centre of the village was the setting for the sports and side-shows, a gymkhana and a clay-pigeon shoot. The main attractions were a helicopter fly-past by Flt Lieut Jeff Whitehead and his crew from RAF Chivenor, and a chance for two people to fly in a hot-air balloon on the day, with Tracie Bennett and Kelly Hearn being the lucky – or not so lucky – girls who won the flight. However, when the pilot Mr James Joiner carried out a partial inflation of the balloon, it was too gusty to hold the balloon safely and it swung across the ground towards the crowd. The flight had to be abandoned.

Chittlehamholt Football Team

The football team was first mentioned in 1928 when the *Western Times* reported a friendly return match at King's Nympton between King's Nympton Harriers and Chittlehamholt Rovers. The previous match, played on the visitors' ground, resulted in a win for them of 3-1. On this occasion the Rovers played a strong team which included their reserves, and it was at first thought that the Harriers would be hard-pushed to secure even a draw. Within the first ten minutes, the Harriers' captain (Wise) had his team well in hand, he himself quickly shot a goal and

141

before his opponents could realise it had repeated the trick. In the second half, Pester, the captain of the Rovers, secured their only goal. No one remembers the Chittlehamholt Rovers team, but there are plenty of memories from the 1950s when Chittlehamholt had a football team instigated by Albert Ayre, Alfie Gay and Frank Heard. Mr Ayre was the manager and their home games were played in one of his fields at Haynetown, before playing opposite the Village Hall. Frank Congram, one of the players, remembers that the team changed behind the Exeter Inn as well as in Frank Heard's house. For home matches, a tea was provided in the Village Hall. For away matches, for those who didn't go in their own vehicles, transport was provided by Albert Ayre from Haynetown and Bill Skinner from the Exeter Inn.

The team were in the third division of the North Devon league and attracted players not only from the village itself, but also from Burrington, Chittlehampton and Umberleigh, who were unable to get into their home teams which were strong at the time. The club became known as the Football Club of All Nations.

Some of the teams Chittlehamholt played against included Barnstaple Colts, Filleigh, Chittlehampton, Kentisbury, Bratton Fleming, Brayford, North Molton, Winkleigh and Landkey. Raymond Ayre, another of the players, says the team were usually bottom of the division, but according to newspaper reports, they won a few games as well:

Dec 9th 1952
Fourth Defeat for North Molton Chittlehamholt win
North Molton, for whom little seems to be going right this season, received their fourth successive North Devon league third division defeat on Saturday, losing 2-1 at home to Chittlehamholt, hard hit by injuries. To begin with North Molton had to start their programme with three tough matches against Umberleigh, Barnstaple Town Colts, and Chittlehampton, so that their youngsters have had little chance to gain from their experience. They are still without several regulars and on Saturday Chittlehamholt gained a 2-0 interval lead through Claude Eastmond and Bob Brock before Vodden replied in the second half. North Molton did a great deal of the attacking, but missed a number of gilt edged chances. In addition Parkhouse (centre half), Wheaton (left back) and Skinner (goalkeeper) played very well in a much improved Chittlehamholt team.

1st Oct 1953
New men score for Chittlehamholt
Chittlehamholt gained a 3-1 victory in a friendly match at High Bickington where the home club fielded a mix-ture of new men and last season's regulars. Hilton Webber and Norman Bowden, two newcomers, were among Chittlehamholt's scorers, the third goal coming from Herbie Tancock. The scoring was completed before the interval, and although High Bickington pressed in

the second half, the visiting defence held out.

19 Nov 1953
Chittlehamholt secured their first point and were unlucky not to take two from Filleigh with whom they drew 1-1. Filleigh faded out after taking the lead in the first half hour and the home keeper Skinner rarely touched the ball in the second period. Bob Brock who scored the equaliser hit the upright once and a visiting defender kicked the ball off the line twice. Filleigh also had to thank a fine performance by goalkeeper Seatherton.

The Queen's Golden Jubilee, 2002

In 2002 the nation celebrated the golden jubilee of Her Majesty Queen Elizabeth II. Before we see how the parishes celebrated, let's look back at past coronations and jubilees.

According to a newspaper report, the coronation of Edward VII in 1902 was celebrated:

... with great enthusiasm in Chittlehamholt, and will be long remembered. There was a service in the church at 2.15p.m. which was very well attended. On its conclu-sion, the congregation, headed by an excellent band, marched to a field kindly lent by Mr Bater of the Manor House where a dinner was provided for all parishioners, the catering being excellently carried out by Mr W. Clarke. The chairman proposed the health of the king which was received with ringing cheers. The rest of the afternoon was spent in sports and dancing until 9p.m. when the prizes for the sports were presented to the win-ners by Mr Bater of the Manor House, and 'God Save the King' was sung to the accompaniment of the band. Mr G. Pope kindly gave a gramophone entertainment in the school until 10.30p.m. when the company dispersed, all having thoroughly enjoyed a day that had been most successful in every way.

George VI and Queen Elizabeth's coronation in 1937 was marked in Chittlehamholt when:

... an enjoyable afternoon was spent with a coronation programme by a number of parents and children in the schoolroom. The children sang patriotic songs, recited, danced some pretty country dances and acted Shakespeare's Merchant of Venice *in a creditable manner. The boys' woodwork of the coronation coach horses, etc., called for much admiration as did the win-dows, which were prettily decorated in red, white and blue flowers by the girls. Mrs Pollard proposed a hearty vote of thanks to Miss Cable.*

The school log-book states that in the afternoon the children visited South Molton cinema to see the coro-nation film. The celebrations for the silver jubilee of Her Majesty Queen Elizabeth II in 1977 began with sports followed by a tea in the Village Hall, where children were presented with jubilee crowns by

Mrs J. Lennard and Mr F. Brend. The programme continued with skittles, a clay-pigeon shoot, and a bonfire and barbecue at Beers Farm by invitation of Mrs R. Hall. Celebrations ended with a family social and dance run by Mr and Mrs W. Hammett.

Coming now to Her Majesty Elizabeth II's golden jubilee, the parishes of Chittlehamholt, Warkleigh and Satterleigh celebrated on Saturday 1 June with a barbecue and disco in the Exeter Inn car park, hosted by landlord David Glenister and his wife Debbie. The following day a commemorative service in St John's Church was conducted by Revd Rob Simpson (a vicar within the South Molton team of parishes) – at the time of the jubilee, Chittlehamholt, Warkleigh and Satterleigh were without a vicar after Revd John Bell left in September 2001. The service included participation from members of all three Parish Churches. Lunch followed in the Village Hall for the more senior members of the community. Heather and Steve Petherick generously provided a three-course lunch for about 30 people. Well-known songs were played on the piano by Rosalind Newton of South Molton. On behalf of everyone present, Ron Thorne thanked Steve and Heather for the lovely lunch and glasses were raised to the Queen. The nation had two days' holiday and on Monday 3 June a good crowd gathered on the Launds Playing-Field. On the cold and windy afternoon, children ranging from toddlers to teenagers enjoyed a variety of races including dressing up, as well as sack and wheelbarrow events, with tea following. The balloon race took place during the afternoon, the wind taking them up and eastwards at great speed. During the afternoon, Michelle May brought her pony and trap to give rides around the village; these were very popular. Commemorative mugs were presented to the children of the three parishes by Rosalyn Wright, chairman of the Parish Council, alongside Alex and Georgina Hill. There was a last-minute change to the plan for the evening arrangements. As the weather had been so wet it was not possible to cut the grass on Firebeacon Field, Warkleigh, so it could not be used. Word was quickly passed around and a beacon was lit on the playing-field. A large barbecue was going all evening for everyone to use. While the fire was burning, other beacons could be seen across to Atherington and High Bickington. 'Rule Britannia' and 'God Save The Queen' were played over the public-address system with much participation.

Marion Congram seen here at the Chittlehamholt Gymkhana with her daughter Carol.

Chittlehamholt Gymkhana

Many years ago Chittlehamholt had a gymkhana. It lapsed, but was revived in 1978 following the Chittlehamholt Revel, and became a regular and very popular show. In the late 1980s the gymkhana came to an end, although a mini-gymkhana takes place at Swinggate Cross, where Cheryl Gordon has a riding school. Below are results from a show in 1990:

The Queen's golden jubilee celebrations on the Launds Playing-Field. Alex Hill is seen here handing over Elsie Payne's jubilee mug.

Swinggate Gymkhana Results
On 1st September we held our annual gymkhana. 15 children competed in the individual races and 15 competed in the teams.
Team results:
1st, Lucy Leatham, Sharon Tucker and Georgina Smoldon.
2nd, Emma Gale, Eleanor Lunn and Sarah Crabb.
3rd, Claire Sexon, Charlotte C. Williams and Josie Gordon.
Altogether, £125 was donated to Riding for the Disabled.
The afternoon finished off with a musical ride display of 12 horses and riders performing to 'Mambo No. 5', 'Love Shack' and the James Bond theme.

The Rational Sick & Burial Association

Although no longer in existence, Chittlehamholt, like many parishes, once had a Rational Sick and Burial Association; a kind of insurance company. Many of these societies were stopped during the war, but Chawleigh is thought to have one of only two remaining in the country.

Members were required to pay 2s.6d. per quarter on the first Monday after quarter day. They would then receive 8s. a week sick pay if confined to bed, 4s. a week if incapable of labour, and £5 towards a burial, thus escaping the stigma of a pauper's funeral (members' wives would get £2.50). The Association had a club day each year, and below are details from the journals of 1890 and 1892, giving accounts of its annual meeting and meal which was accompanied by a procession through the village:

June 5th 1890
The members of the Chittlehamholt branch of the Rational Sick and Burial Association held their annual festival on Wednesday. The members headed by the Chulmleigh Volunteer Band proceeded to Whitmore, the residence of Mr W.J. Hadden, and from thence to Highbullen, the residence of W.R. Moore, where a capital address was delivered by Mr W.R. Moore junr. The village having again been reached, the members proceeded to the church, where a very suitable sermon was preached by the Revd W.B. Gascoigne. After [the] service, a call was made at the Manor House, the residence of Mr Bater. A good dinner was served up by host Jenkins. During the afternoon, dancing and a series of athletic sports were indulged in.

June 2nd 1892
The Chittlehamholt branch (476) of the Rational Sick and Burial Association held its annual fête last week. At 10 o'clock, the members assembled in good number at the Exeter Inn, where the roll was called by the secretary, Mr Thomas Heard junior, headed by the Chulmleigh Volunteer Band. They proceeded to the vicarage to call the vicar, the Revd M.T. Loveband, from thence to the church, where divine service was held. The lesson was read by the Revd M.D. Buckingham, vicar of Burrington, who also preached a very appropriate sermon. After the service, the procession reformed, and after calls made at Manor House, the residence of Mr T. Bater, and Whitmore, the residence of Mr W.J. Hadden, a return was made to the village to a capital dinner, served by host Clarke. The following presided at the tables. Revd M.T. Loveband (vicar), the Revd M.D. Buckingham (Burrington), Mr L. Thorold (Warkleigh), and Dr Tucker, Chulmleigh. The usual toasts were duly honoured. The 'visitors' was proposed and responded to by the Revd M.D. Buckingham, L. Thorold, Dr Tucker and Alderman Mortimer, Mr Thomas Heard read the annual report, which showed the branch to be in a flourishing condition. A vote of thanks was accorded to the vicar for the loan of the schoolroom. An adjournment was made to a field near the Inn, where a series of athletic sports were gone through. Dancing was freely indulged in to the strains of the band.

Chapter 13

HUNTING, SHOOTING, FISHING, RIVERS & WILDLIFE

Like all rural areas, field sports have played their role in Chittlehamholt, Warkleigh and Satterleigh over the years. Hunting with hounds has been a sport that I have had a passion for from an early age, so much so that in 2000 I wrote a book on the Tiverton Staghounds. The two packs of hounds that hunt through Chittlehamholt, Warkleigh and Satterleigh today are the Tiverton Staghounds and the Eggesford Foxhounds. The Tiverton Staghounds were established in 1896 by Sir John Amory of Knightshayes Court, Tiverton, becoming known as the Tiverton Staghounds in 1919. The Eggesford hounds were established by the Hon. Newton Fellowes in about 1800. In the 1930s, a second pack was formed to hunt the Chittlehamholt side. Mrs Beaumont of Edgington House, Warkleigh, who had close connections with these hounds, became the Master for the few years during which they operated, and the pack was known as the Eggesford Foxhounds (North). This pack operated in the 1950s and '60s, when the Torrington Farmers Hunt hunted through Chittlehamholt, Warkleigh and Satterleigh. At the same time, Mrs Beaumont was also Master of the Cheriton Otterhounds whose country included the Taw and Mole Rivers which sweep around the boundaries of Chittlehamholt, Warkleigh and Satterleigh. Mr Mackenzie from Cleave Copse, Warkleigh, was hon. secretary and treasurer.

Otter hunting stopped in 1978 when numbers crashed due to pesticide pollution. The decline was so severe that, before long, hunts voluntarily ceased hunting otters altogether, selecting only mink. At the time, the introduced American mink had become widely established and was starting to earn a reputation as a ruthless destroyer of Britain's wildlife. It was logical that otter hunts should switch to controlling mink numbers. The effect of mink on wildlife has been catastrophic – water voles are now extinct in

Meet of the Eggesford Foxhounds (North) at Edgington House in 1934. Left to right: *Arthur Ford (groom shofer and whipper-in) riding Sprig, Tom Allison (huntsman), Mrs Sybil Beaumont riding Sheila, Mrs Bryant from Highbullen and Ken Dart.*

most areas, coastal seabird colonies have been decimated, and coots and moorhens are under threat. Mink also kill whole broods of chickens and pheasant poults. They are extremely agile and they climb, run and swim with ease, so their prey have nowhere to hide. The hounds could catch anywhere up to 50 or 60 mink in a good season, but now the numbers have decreased. After the reintroduction of otters into the rivers ten years ago, they have steadily increased in numbers, and it's not surprising to get on to the scent of an otter on a mink hunt. At the time of writing, the Culmstock Mink Hounds and the Devon and Cornwall Mink Hounds hunt close to the parishes, on the upper Taw.

Hare hunting no longer takes place in the parishes. The brown hare population in Britain has fallen by more than 80 per cent in recent years and much of its decline has been attributed to changes in modern farming methods, which have reduced the diversity of habitats. The South Molton Harriers once hunted the hare in the area. They were formed in 1882 and disbanded after the First World War. In 1962, Graham Heal became Master of his own pack of foot beagles, known as the Torrington Foot Beagles, and they also hunted the hare. They met regularly at Hilltown Cross, Warkleigh, and hunted in the Warkleigh area until the hunt was disbanded in the mid 1970s. In 2002 the Taw Vale Beagles hunt in the King's Nympton area, with a few enthusiastic supporters in Chittlehamholt holding functions in the Village Hall for them.

The foot-and-mouth outbreak of 2001 prevented any hunting for a year. Not only did it knock the farming community for six, but also the finances of the hunts. At the beginning of 2002, hunting was slowly allowed to return again but under restrictions.

I found the following letter in an 1875 copy of the *Daily Western Times*. It explains the meaning of the world 'holt' – as in Chittleham<u>holt</u> – and its connections with hunting:

To the editor of the Daily Western Times, *June 1875.*

Sir – In the graphic account given by my respected sporting townsman of the spirited pursuit and capture of two otters in the River Mole and its tributary, the Bray, by Mr Cheriton's hounds, among other technical words employed in describing the hunt there occurs the word 'holt', the meaning of which, as there used, is the hiding place of the otter. The word is British, and originally signified a wood, but some writers in the seventeenth century employ it to denote a mound or hill. Now, as the woods were the only safe hiding places during the incursions of the Danes and other marauders who infested this country in the early part of our history, it will easily be seen how the term became extended to any hiding place. The word has long been obsolete in literary composition, but is used by the common people in this part of the country in its original and legitimate sense. For example, a woman who has a husband drinking in a public house; *she becomes cognizant of the fact, routs him out, and induces him to go home. As soon as the good wife's vigilant eye is withdrawn from him, he escapes from the house, and then, as soon as she has missed him she exclaims, 'I'll warrant that he's gone to the old holt.' The word is also a corruption of hold. Among wrestlers it means the grip, or any portion of the jacket that the hand has fast holt of. It also means stop! and in this sense – it is narrated – it was used by his Satanic Majesty himself. Being on business at a farmhouse near Chittlehamholt hamlet, a few miles from this town, I asked the worthy farmer if he knew the etymology of his residence. To this he replied in the affirmative, and told me the following anecdote:*

A party of bacchanals were carousing at Chittlehampton, when the devil joined their company in the garb, shape, and form of a respectable farmer. After having drunk their fill, and midnight fast approaching, they left to go home; and as the devil had been such a sociable companion, they endeavoured to induce him to go home with them and finish up the bout with cider. This proposition was peremptorily declined. The party then said that if he would not go voluntarily they would take him by force, which they did, each one taking it by turns to carry their new acquaintance pick-a-back. In this primitive locomotive fashion, he was conveyed near to where the Toll-bar now stands in Chittlehamholt. He had been remonstrating with the party for his abduction all the way along to no purpose, when he assumed his normal shape – horns, hoofs and tail, and vomiting out a sulphurous flame, thundered out 'Holt!'

Of course, he was suddenly dropped in the road, and the party decamped in all directions, so that no record was left of the way which the ghostly personage took – whether he remained where he was set down, went back to Chittlehampton, or took the road to South Molton. My informant was inclined to think that he took the latter course.

I remain, Mr Editor, yours truly,
JOHN MILLS
South Molton, June 25th, 1875.

There follow accounts from newspapers of runs in the parishes:

<u>A meet of the Eggesford at Meeth Gate, November 1879</u>
After drawing Oldridge Plantation and its furze brake, where foxes in old days loved to dwell, we found a cub in Satterleigh Wood, that kept ringing round and round that covert until every yard of it must have been foiled, and even Littleworth's patience exhausted. A fox had gone away at the western end, almost at the first whimper of hounds; and, in hope of getting on his line, the pack was taken first to Snapdown, and thence to Edgington Wood. Here a line was hit off, and hounds ran it merrily for some time; but the scent was cold, and

they were trotted on to Little Shortridge. The coverts here lie in a deep hollow, and stretch far away, broken by many little glens, so that a fox and a pack too much addicted to silence might slip away without anybody being the wiser. These hounds, however, have not this fault. The Eggesford kennels have ever been famous for music – a quality of the highest importance where hunting has to be carried down for the most part in vast woodlands. Listen when a fox is found. It is not a whimper, but a deep-tongue challenge like the first swing of a tenor-bell, and a moment after it is followed by a clanging peal. As they go from one side of the covert to another, you can follow almost every yard of the fox's track by the music of his pursuers. One ring round; a momentary check, where Reynard has attempted to break, but headed short back; another flood of melody streaming through the covert; and then they are away. Nobody has viewed the fox, but their merry tongues are enough to guide us, though they are racing at a pace that keeps us galloping hard to catch them. Through a covert below Cleave Farm, then on by Warkleigh Church they swing; thence to within a field or two of Hudscott, and back to the ridge above Clapworthy Mill without a check. Over the cold fallows here they are at fault for a moment, but, hitting off the line again, they hunt it well to a brook backed by a bullfinch, where the cleverness of a hunter is tested; up through Oldridge Brake, and on where sheep have foiled the scent, across grass fields and turnips to Satterleigh Wood. To get to hounds as they push him through the covert, a bit of awkward timber on the river bank has to be negotiated. The Revd Mr Blathwayte, of whose resolute riding I remember to have written last year, gives a lead, and, breaking the top rail, lets those who come after him easily over. Breaking at the top of the wood, hounds run on over a few fields, and thence down to Hele Wood, where two or three foxes are on foot, and they divide. Our hunted one, however, crosses the river once more, and gets into Edgington, where they hunt him patiently, with little chance of doing more. The cream of a good hunting run is over, and, as twilight begins to fall, most of us turn our horses' heads homewards.

South Molton Harriers at Warkleigh, 19th November 1914
The Master (Mr Hamlet B. Rather) was numerously supported at the meet of the South Molton Harriers at Warkleigh. There were four excellent runs, resulting in four hares being killed. Mr and Mrs Tucker of Deason Farm kindly entertained the field and Mr Dick Townsend noted as honorary whip. So far this means South Molton Harriers have accounted for more hares, hunting one day a week, than when they were out twice each week.

November 10th 1933, A New Pack – Mrs Beaumont's Hounds Hunt in Conjunction with Eggesford
Mrs Beaumont, who has undertaken to hunt part of the Eggesford Hunt country this season and has established a new pack for the purpose, held her opening meet at Edgington House, Warkleigh, on Tuesday, and there was a large gathering in the picturesque grounds. The weather was excellent, as are also the prospects for the season's hunting.

Mrs Beaumont is joint Master of the Cheriton Otterhounds with Mr A.J. Heaman, and Tom Allison is huntsman of the new pack as well as of the Cheritons. Major and Mrs Beaumont cordially greeted the field and generously provided refreshments, which were partaken of before the move off was made with 14½ couples of hounds looking well.

The first draw was the old stronghold, Shortridge Wood, where there were four or five foxes waiting for the chase. Two went down Oldridge Bottom and two others broke cover out over Oldridge and onto Pool. The main pack went down Oldridge after the first brace and on to Clayton Wood, through Crickety Cleave and on to Strawberry Cleave, where scent failed, and then the Master gave orders for Slew Wood. Here they found a fine old dog fox, which gave a grand run, first calling at Slew Brake on to Oldridge Bottoms, then turning left hand on the Claytown Wood, turning left to Vanstone Cleave and passed close to Claytown House on through Little Shortridge land to Warkleigh Barton, down over these large fields and on to Broadmoor bottom, climbing the other side, and on reaching the top road turned left, right on Hillton bottom. Here he left the bottom and turned rights and on to Eastacott fields, where hounds had a slight check owing to a flock of sheep crossing the line. It was quite fast enough, for the Huntsman and his grey mare were glad of a breather. Tom made a cast or two and got on the line again up over Southcott on through Brightly Barton; turning left on the top brought us to Brightly Wood, where it came to an end, hearing Tom giving the note from his horn the end was come, and the time about one hour and twenty minutes after the hounds had their feed, which they had well earned. They were coming down over Eastwood Close, when we were glad to hear that good sportsman's voice, Mr Heaman, tallying a fox away from the corner of Brightly Wood, crossing the road on to the marshes, running up some distance and, turning left, crossed the road in Courage Copse right up through Great Shortridge to the end of Claytown Lane, where we had a check. The last who saw her here was Mrs Heaman, but, however, Tom made a cast or two and made things right again, on through Little Shortridge fields to Claytown through Vanstone Cleave, down through Claytown bottom, Claytown Wood, turning left took us right up across Oldridge and into our old stronghold, Shortridge Wood. After driving her around a time or two, she waded into a rabbit's earth, where she met her doom.

A presentation to Mrs Beaumont of Edgington House, Warkleigh, after retiring from the Mastership of the Cheriton Otter-hounds in 1938
The Chairman, on behalf of the Hunt, made a presentation of a clock, surmounted with a beautiful

representation of an otter, and accompanied by a framed list of subscribers to Mrs Beaumont. Mr Rogers said Mrs Beaumont had given them most extraordinary sport during her Mastership, and had done it for the love of hunting, and because she was fond of the hounds.

Mrs Beaumont said the clock would always remind her of many happy days spent hunting with the Cheriton Otter-hounds, and hoped that the Hunt would continue for many years longer.

August 13th 1954 – Chittlehamholt to send £300 to hunt contribution

The North Side of Torrington Farmers' Hunt decided at their annual meeting at Chittlehamholt on Monday, to stand by their decision to contribute £300 towards the hunt this year. Subject to the approval of the annual meeting, it had been agreed at a meeting with a deputation from the hunt that the contribution by the North Side should be £300, the chairman, Mr J. Thorne explained. In a review of the season, the chairman said they had had 16 meets and had killed 13½ brace of foxes. 'Everything has gone with a swing. We have had some happy days and I hope we shall continue,' he said. The Treasurer, Mrs R. Lake, said receipts had totalled £360.17s.6d. They had made a contribution last year to the hunt of £200 and there was a balance of £150.18s.3d.

January 6th 1966 – Hunt turns out to greet the bride at Warkleigh

Huntsmen with white carnations in the lapels of their bottle-green jackets, took a pack of beagles to Warkleigh Parish Church on Saturday, to greet the bride. The wedding was at the 700-year-old church of St John, where Miss Margaret Cole married Mr Herbert Carpenter, who works in agriculture and keeps his own flock of sheep. He is the eldest son of Mr and Mrs P.B. Carpenter of Dawn Cottage, King's Nympton. Miss Cole is the only daughter of a prominent North Devon farmer and South Molton rural councillor, the late Mr John Cole and the late Mrs Cole. She lives at Sunnydene, Chittlehamholt. It was the first time that the 4-year-old Torrington Foot Beagle pack, led by 19-year-old hunt master Graham Heal, had held a good-luck meeting for a bride. The hare hunt which followed the wedding was not started until the youngest supporter of the hounds, 6-year-old Andrew Sing, had walked through a crowd of spectators over 100 strong, standing in thick mud outside the church's lych-gate, to present a pouffe to the couple. Mr Carpenter has hunted on foot with the beagles ever since it was formed. There was a congregation of 120 at the wedding ceremony conducted by the Revd Tim Jones. A surpliced choir, of which the bride is a member, led the singing, and peals before and after the ceremony were rung by the King's Nympton ringers. Miss Cole wore a dress of crisscross taffeta, in biscuit shade and cut on classical lines. She wore a French navy feathered hat, with toning accessories. An orchid was attached to her handbag. She was given

away by Mr R.J. Williams. Mr Carpenter's niece and god-child, Miss Diane Carpenter, was the only bridesmaid. She wore a pink dress under a white nylon fur-fabric coat, and carried chrysanthemums. Huntmaster Mr Heal and 1st whip Mr Harold Sing, father of Andrew, led 15½ couples of hounds over neighbouring land after the wedding, but no hares were caught.

A Meet of the Tiverton Staghounds – March 27th 1982

With the beautiful weather still holding, the Exeter Inn, Chittlehamholt, was the scene of the meet on March 27th, and a stirrup cup was generously provided by the landlords, Norman and Margaret Glenister, to whom our thanks are due. Drawing Satterleigh Wood, the tufters were away at once towards Chittlehampton, crossing the Umberleigh road by Winson and going down into Cleave. Running round the back of Chittlehampton – where the pack was laid on – they went to Stowford, and then up the valley under Furze to Cawsey Barton Plantation and down the Bray Valley to cross the South Molton road above Clapworthy Mill. From here they went out over the top towards George Nympton, but keeping right-handed, came down the Mole Valley past Cawsey Meethe and so back to Satterleigh Wood. Away again after some delay, they ran high down the valley to Edington, only to [be] held up again on fresh deer. Put right, they ran their stag down to the Mole, where he was taken at about 3.30p.m. Scent good while they were on terms; weather warm and sunny; river cold and wet!

Today, farmers in the parishes shoot like they have done for many centuries, keeping down the vermin. There are many commercial pheasant-shooting syndicates in neighbouring parishes, but not here.

The Rivers & Fishing

Chittlehamholt, Warkleigh and Satterleigh rise up from the Rivers Taw and Mole which make a wide berth around them and partially, but not completely, surround them. At Satterleigh, below the old Meeth Chapel, the Rivers Bray and Mole meet. The combined river then drifts on downstream through King's Nympton estate where it meets the Taw at Junction Pool. Risdon says of this:

The Bray meeteth with the river Moule, which strengthened with her stream, fleeteth with a full current, to pay tribute to the Taw, and giveth it a great push over against.

The Taw then glides downstream to Watergate in the parish of Warkleigh, where it changes direction, heads for Umberleigh, and then on to Barnstaple and the open sea. In total the two rivers follow the boundaries of the parishes for some ten miles.

I have conversed with Roger Bickley, who has for

Junction Pool where the Mole meets the Taw.

19 years been a bailiff and fisheries officer on the two rivers and is now the environment protection officer. His comments gave a useful insight:

The Rivers Taw and Mole are still well fished and popular, but have declined as have many rivers from their heyday in the earlier part of the twentieth century. The stretch of river from Junction Pool downwards on the Taw is the most prolific for salmon and sea trout and very sought after. Fishing beats have exchanged hands for in excess of £300,000 in recent years.

The Highbullen Hotel lease some excellent beats from the Wildfowl Trust as well as owning a stretch themselves. This, together with their golfing facilities, allows them to offer a high-class sporting image, which in turn is good for the local economy and employment.

The lower Mole, in King's Nympton park estate, and the Taw have one of the highest concentrations of otters in the West Country, with many major holts in the lower reaches. When night fishing for sea trout it is not uncommon to see one or two otters come into the pool. Often a splash at the end of the pool will indicate a fish rising but instead an otter appears, circles you and snorts, as if to say 'clear off, this is my territory!' If anyone wishes to see an otter, I usually direct them to Junction Pool which is featured in Henry Williamson's book Tarka the Otter. *You may have to wait some time, but the reward is great if you are lucky enough to observe the spectacle of an otter capturing and dispatching a sea trout or large eel on the pebble bank.*

The population of the otter in this area remains high, but due to the river running closely to both road and rail, sadly we may lose as many as 20 to 30 per year in accidents.

Poaching on the two rivers has been pretty rife over the years, especially with professional gangs. The main exponents were known as the Bridport gang who operated throughout the 1980s and '90s, and to a certain extent are still active today. Bridport is where the traditional net-making industry is, and so a cottage industry grew up in this area. However, they had been known to travel up as far as Wales and Scotland to poach. The Taw remained one of their favorite targets

and their knowledge of the river was as good as the bailiffs. Their favorite pools were Little Silver (named so because it is directly below Little Silver House in High Bickington), Long Pool (which is the big pool below Western Ground House, adjacent to Farrs Farm, Chittlehamholt), the Pott (below Chittlehamholt Manor), and of course Junction Pool, which is probably one of the most poached pools in the South West.

Cars belonging to the poachers were often parked a mile or so away from the river and hidden in fields that had been recently cut in an attempt to disguise any tyre tracks. As a bailiff one of my jobs was to combat this menace, which often resulted in long nights of surveillance, chases across fields in the dark and scuffles with poachers. Police back-up was regularly called for, arrests made and vehicles seized.

When salmon farming became popular thousands of tonnes were produced and obviously the value of salmon dropped. However, this did not deter the professional gangs and they found a niche market in London, selling wild salmon for events such as Wimbledon or Ascot. Wild salmon have always been valued as a specialty by some chefs and restaurants, who claim that it has a superior taste (I agree).

Salmon enter the river from February onwards, staying in the lower reaches where the pools are deeper, until they get the urge to spawn around November or December. They then move upstream to gravels on the higher reaches of the river to deposit their eggs in pits or redds usually excavated by the female. The eggs hatch after approximately 60 days and grow in the river for approximately two years before returning to the sea to start the cycle over again.

Head Mill Trout Farm

Head Mill in the parish of Chittlehamholt has been turned into a successful trout farm which was founded in 1980 by Robin Boa. It utilises one of the West Country's most famous fishing rivers to rear trout for the table. Since the whole emphasis of the farm is on providing the best-tasting trout, all rearing tanks and ponds have a solid base, which means the fish never

Robin Boa, proprietor of Head Mill Trout Farm, Chittlehamholt.

come into contact with mud and never have that earthy taste which can be such an unpleasant feature of farmed trout.

Over the past few years, Head Mill has been perfecting a way of smoking trout the old-fashioned way. After brining, the trout are immersed in oak smoke for several hours, during which time the temperature is slowly raised and the fish are gently cooked, retaining their subtle flavour, mixed with a hint of wood fires and traditional chimney smoke. As the popularity of smoked foods has grown, so Head Mill has gained a reputation as a skilled smokery producing delicacies that fill the demand for easy-to-prepare yet naturally made meals. Head Mill smoked and fresh trout are served in many hotels and restaurants in the South West.

The Guard family were the last people to use Head Mill as a working mill. In 1978, *Tarka the Otter* was partly filmed there as it is close to Junction Pool, which author Henry Williamson mentions in his book. In the film, set in the 1930s, Tarka is pursued by the otter-hounds and takes sanctuary at Head Mill, hiding in one of the runners of the mill as it goes around, which gives the impression that the mill was still in operation. The film features the Guard family themselves.

A newspaper cutting from 3 September 1896 shows that at the Chulmleigh Brewster sessions, George Pope, proprietor of Head Mill, was charged with setting his mill to work on Sunday 16 August for the purpose of grinding corn. The defendant said he had done nothing more than was usual in time of drought. The bench dismissed the case, but cautioned the defendant not to resort to the plan again.

Donn's map of 1765 shows the old Head Mill which was then sited on the River Taw about half a mile below its junction with the Mole, where there are still the remains of a mill and a leat. When the Guard family were at Head Mill they used to deliver the meal in a horse butt to the farmers. Ken Guard remembers Harry Congram at Butlers and Jack Congram at Wards each having a sackful of flour with which to make their own bread. They also used to supply a teacher at Wooda Cottage, King's Nympton, who requested brown flour. During hard winters, the mill-wheel would freeze right up with icicles forming which, in the night, would fall and kick the boards. Sometimes in the summer there wouldn't be enough water to drive the wheel, and then the farmers started to complain.

Plants & Wildlife

Father and son, Cyril and David Morgan, talk about the plants and wildlife at Whitmore and around Chittlehamholt:

If you're going to talk about wildlife you've got to start with plants because they're the basis of everything.

If there weren't any plants, there wouldn't be any animals. When we first came to Whitmore in 1959 the place was fairly bare and basic, the major plants that were here were ferns, and some of those had been planted in Victorian times when they were a craze. There's a special fern, which we've still got, which is the Royal Fern [Osmunda] and that's down by the pond. It was probably dug up in Victorian times and brought in as a garden plant. It might have come from Hartland as they grow naturally there. There is a fern which grows along the front of the house – the Lady Fern – and when it comes up from spores we get all sorts of crested and unusual forms. I'm sure that's to do with the fact that they were grown here in Victorian times. We have a reasonably rare primitive fern called Adder's Tongue, which is found in the rides of our woods. We didn't spot it when we first came here, as the rides were overgrown, and not open as they are now. When you open up a ride through a wood, you allow more light to come in and, because it's not treated, you get old-fashioned plants growing there.

Where the Chittlehamholt playing-field is, there was a row of 100-year-old Scots Pines growing. Two of these remained until 1993, but one was felled because it was thought to be too dangerous. The Parish Council and the Playing Field Committee have had the good sense to plant more of them on the same site so that they will preserve that tradition. I think that's lovely because I'm all for preserving traditions.

Staying with trees, at Whitmore, we have a rare one, only found growing in North Devon, called **Sorbus devoniensis** *(French Hales). This also grows all over the parish near old holdings and used to be sold for fruit in Barnstaple Market. Doreen and I planted one each for the millennium at Whitmore. They're only three or four feet high and we won't see them at their best. We grew these trees from seed – we collected some fruit from a tree that's growing near High Bullen [sic] on the edge of Muxsey [sic] Lane. The seeds need to be frosted for them to come up, so I frosted them one winter, and the next winter they came up, producing six or eight seedlings.*

Coming on to wild flowers, my favourite is a funny little plant called the Town Hall Clock. This has a flower just like the town-hall clock in Barnstaple – it has a spike sticking up and a flower on each face as if it was on the face of a town-hall clock. It's only three inches high so you've got to get down on your knees to look at it. It's a little beauty when you get close. Another of my favourites are the Early Purple Orchids, and we've got a nice lot of those flowering up in the wood and down the drive. You don't find them everywhere, but there are plenty around here in Chittlehamholt. Down by our ash tree there's a plant which I think probably is a Southern Marsh Orchid, but I'm not absolutely sure. It has increased in size since we've been here – sometimes it has 16 separate flower spikes – and it's a big clump now. Down in the orchard we have a little area where about 40 or 50 rare orchids called the Common Twayblade grow. Even rarer, up in the wood, is the

Bird's Nest Orchid, so called because the root of it looks like a bird's nest. It doesn't have any leaves at all. Most plants need leaves to make food, but this particular plant gets its food by living on dead plants, and it puts up a flower that is as brown as a sheet of brown paper. You can never tell where it will come up next, there wouldn't be more than half a dozen in any one year but they are dotted about all over the wood. Even rarer than that is an orchid called the Violet Helleborine. Several of them came up here, but I didn't see it again for another ten years. If it's a poor year it doesn't come up at all, and another year it might come up and have leaves but no flowers, and then suddenly, when conditions are right, up it comes and flowers.

I used to teach at Torrington school, and one morning I was passing Collins' cottage when a bird flew up from the road in front of me and was flying a bit like a butterfly with the wings coming up over its back — most birds fly from horizontal — and it landed on the road and I recognised it as a hoopoe – a very rare visitor. I watched it for a time, and then had to move it out of the way so I could go to work. When I got to Torrington, I rang my wife, Doreen, and told her what I had seen. Later on that day she went up to the Post Office (which at the time was in the village square) and told Mr Dockings, who was in charge, that I had seen a hoopoe, and as Mrs Dockings wasn't there to look after the place, he closed the Post Office, got on his bike, rode down to Collins', and spent all morning looking for that bird.

Recently I saw 24 red deer in our field, and another 18 across the valley in Hele Wood. Years ago we only saw them when they were being hunted. In the early 1970s we saw the first roe deer, and now they come into the garden, eating the roses.

There used to be glow-worms on the grass up the drive, but you never see them now. The lawn used to be covered with grasshoppers, but now there are very few of them. Not so many butterflies either.

Sometimes we get a rare hummingbird hawk moth, and you see it hovering in front of a flower and it looks just like a hummingbird. I caught a bee fly once and there are only about 12 different ones in the country, some of them so rare they haven't been seen for ten years, but this one was called Bombylius Major. That was a rarity never seen before or since at Whitmore.

In May and June we used to get these big brown beetles (cockchafers) smashing against the windows at night. When you went downstairs in the morning they would be lying on the windowsills, on their backs with their legs in the air, and sometimes still struggling. You used to get half a dozen to a dozen, but now, some years you might see one, and some years none at all.

David Morgan also talks about the wildlife at Whitmore and around Chittlehamholt:

Looking through my list here I see I've recorded about 90 different species of birds seen around the area over the years. Some of them only seen once like the hoopoe, and some of them old friends like the robins and blackbirds, but over the years there have been a few changes. Curlews used to nest below Hillbrow in the field when it was all rushes and you could hear them coming over Whitmore 'crying' (a nice sound), but they've gone now the land has been drained, but other things have arrived, like the collared doves which started off in

David Morgan, a keen ornithologist, checking his jackdaws at Whitmore, Chittlehamholt.

Turkey and spread across Europe after the war. They came to Britain in the early 1960s, and in 1976 the first nest in Chittlehamholt was found in Mr Baker's barn at Hills House Farm. We get them down here occasionally, but mostly you find them in the village.

The other species which has arrived is the pied flycatcher. The first one arrived at Whitmore in 1978, and he didn't find a mate for a while, then three years later the first ones started breeding. Since then they've been breeding in our nest boxes every year. They spend the winter in West Africa, and I catch the birds and ring them every year. I get some that have come home and found their way back to the same nest box. I catch a few birds that have been ringed by other people in different parts including Okehampton and Torrington, and have come to nest here later on. From other ringing I've done, you get an idea where some of our birds come from. I caught a few starlings on the apples one autumn and one of them was later shot in Holland during the breeding season. All the big flocks of starlings you see in the winter are not our birds, so to speak, they're visitors for the winter coming after the apples. I've caught a great tit which was ringed in Combwich near the Hinckley Point power station, and six months later it was down at Whitmore. I put nets up under a government licence and you get the odd surprise. One day I went down and found a Firecrest in my net, quite an unusual bird.

There are quite a few bats around here, and I think I've recorded six different species in Chittlehamholt so far.

In the Wild Fowl Trust magazine I read an article about a family of otters who were seen at the bottom of Headwood, so they do breed in the parish, but you need to know where to look.

We get buzzards, kestrels, and sparrowhawks as well as the more unusual birds of prey like peregrines, and a red kite was spotted here in January 1988.

One species we've got more of is jackdaws; one of our garages is virtually falling down and it provides lots of spots for jackdaws to nest in. We have a long job in the spring keeping them off the house and stopping them going down the chimney. Every year I ring the baby jackdaws but so far I've not been lucky enough to have one found away from here. They stay in the nest for three weeks, but they don't all survive; it has to be a good year for the parents to rear them all.

Sometimes when the rivers are very high we've had kingfishers up at the pond here. They get driven up the little stream and we've had them up here a couple of times now.

There follows an article from the *North Devon Journal* of 25 July 1878, regarding an abundance of honey at West Satterleigh:

SATTERLEIGH

A Prolific Beehive – A circumstance of great rarity in the production of the honey bee has occurred at West Satterleigh, at the residence of Mr H.B. Saunders, shoe-maker, who is proficient in the rearing of bees. The hive in question is a new one. The bees were hived on the 22nd day of June last on the new system. On the top of the hive was placed a bell glass, which they soon filled, as well as the hive. The glass was removed on July 10th, and found to contain over seven pounds of honey of the most delicious kind, which found a purchaser in Mrs Thorold, of Warkleigh. This was accomplished without the destruction of a single bee, and they are fast filling

the second glass. The bee-house contains seven swarms, and eight new swarms have been successfully hived this season. The owner would be glad to show the house to anyone who delights in bees.

Revd Jones made some notes on the wildlife around the Warkleigh Rectory in 1963. Some extracts follow:

During the last few days, we have seen in the garden, a dunnock, a nuthatch, a tree creeper and a black redstart. The latter is rarely seen around here, but can sometimes be seen as a winter visitor in North and East Devon.

Since we enlarged our family by three muscovy ducks, I have enjoyed dreams of stocking the rectory lake with exotic waterfowl. As I have gazed from my study window, I have seen quite clearly in my mind's eye, gorgeously coloured birds preening their feathers, flying around the rhododendrons and landing spectac-ularly on the water. Today, however, I received a price list from the Wildfowl Trust at Slimbridge, and my vision has dulled a little. Black-necked swans are £60 a pair; ring-tailed swans, £25; Argentine red shoveller, £25; Mandarin ducks £12.

One begins to feel that spring is almost here; flocks of curlew are back and beginning to call. Major Owen's garden at Watertown House has been visited by mistle thrush and nuthatch, and there is an abundance of tits and finches of all types. The green woodpecker has reappeared in the rectory garden.

Chapter 14
REPORTING PARISH FIRES

May 10th 1894
WARKLEIGH

On Thursday last at Oldridge, in this parish, the house in the occupation of Mr J. Clatworthy was accidentally destroyed by fire. The master being at market, the house was left in the charge of some children, through whom, it was supposed, that the fire originated. The neighbours kindly rendered every assistance possible, but owing to the rapidity of the fire, but little of the furniture was saved – a recently killed pig was among the salvage. Great sympathy is felt for the suffering family and financial help is being rendered to them in their great loss. PC Legg of Chittlehampton kindly gave the homeless ones 5s. from his own means, and the neighbours promptly gave them the necessary shelter. The young squire of Manor House worked heartily in the good cause, and rendered himself temporarily penniless in efforts to alleviate their sufferings. A subscription is being made in this and the neighbouring parishes for their permanent relief.

April 28th 1898
FIRE NEAR CHITTLEHAMPTON

A fire occurred at Pugsley Farm, occupied by Mr Henry Tucker, on the afternoon of Thursday, resulting in the total destruction of the barn, cart shed, and some of the other outbuildings, with their contents. The origin of the fire remains somewhat of a mystery. Mr and Mrs Tucker were from home at the time, having gone to Southmolton in the forenoon, leaving the premises in charge of two servant lads. Shortly after dinner the workmen on a neighbouring farm saw smoke issuing from the barn, and at once gave an alarm and ran to the spot, but before they had time to remove any of the machinery, save a mowing machine, the roof fell in, the fire having originated inside. A messenger was dispatched to Chittlehampton for the fire engine, which was soon on the spot, and although the supply of water was limited the brigade succeeded, with the aid of willing helpers, in preventing the fire from igniting adjacent buildings, which were also thatch covered. The property is owned by the Hon. Mark Rolle. Mr Tucker, who is uninsured, has sustained a great loss, the whole of his machinery (except the mowing machine) being totally destroyed, together with a waggon, lotts and carts, a quantity of artificial manure, two calves and a quantity of other articles that were stood in the burnt

buildings. The rapid spread of the fire in the thatch of the roofs, and no grown-up person being on the spot at the outbreak, account for so little of the tenants property being saved. But for the prompt arrival of the fire brigade, the whole of the buildings, together with the dwelling house, would have been destroyed. The Southmolton Town Council fire engine came on the scene, but on account of the scarcity of water did not connect as the Chittlehampton engine had the fire well under control. Much sympathy is felt for Mr Tucker in his great loss.

5th May 1898
FIRE

Snapdown Farmhouse, Warkleigh, the property of the Southmolton Town Council and the Municipal Charity Trustees, was burned down early on Friday morning. On November 2nd last the outbuildings belonging to the same estate were burnt. The owners were insured in the Liverpool, London and Globe office, and the furniture of the tenant in the Queen. The furniture was almost entirely consumed, only a table being saved. Two Town Council and Charity Trustees were making joint arrangements for the erection of a new house and outbuildings.

There was another fire at Snapdown two years later:

April 14th 1900
SOUTHMOLTON COUNTY COURT
THURSDAY — Before His Honour Judge Beresford
FIRE INSURANCE CLAIM

A claim for insurance occupied nearly the whole of sitting (which lasted over five hours) in which William Henry Manning, a farmer, formerly occupying Snapdown in the parish of Warkleigh, claimed of the Royal Insurance Company the sum of £2,510 value of goods alleged to have been destroyed in a fire which took place on February 6th 1899. Mr Pridham Wippell (instructed by Messrs Shapland and Son, of Southmolton) represented the plaintiff, and Mr Pearce, of Plymouth (Messrs Bond and Pearce), appeared for the Insurance Company. The jury consisted of Messrs G.W. Shapland, R. Arnold, S. Brown, J. Squire and W.A. Madge. The policy had been issued by Messrs Sanders and Mountjoy the local agents at Southmolton, and was for £150. The Claimant (W.H. Manning)... farmed Snapdown as a tenant under the Corporation of Southmolton, and at the time of the fire he was riding at Little Satterleigh. He last saw Snapdown on the Sunday night about 9.30p.m., when he went to see his sheep. He left the lantern in the bottom between Little Satterleigh and Snapdown. The next morning he was awakened by a man named Heard, of Chittlehamholt, about 6a.m., who said his shippen was on fire. He hurried to the spot, and saw that the roof had fallen in. On the Thursday after he wrote out the claim and took it to the agent; and after much correspondence the Company refused to pay. This was on July 17th. He also claimed for soroe sacks valued at £1.2s.6d. which Messrs Sanders and Mountjoy afterwards claimed from him at the price of £1.17s.6d. He went over the scene of the fire with the Company's Inspector, who asked him how he accounted for the fire, and who said he could not have the claim if he could not say who did it. He thought it was not an exorbitant claim. Cross examination elicited that he had previously suffered from fires. The corn which was in the house was distributed about the floor to avoid damage by rats. Mrs E. Manning, wife of the claimant, gave corroborative evidence as to the fire. David Slader, formerly landlord of the Hare and Hounds, Southmolton, gave evidence as to seeing ten or 15 sacks of corn in the granary on the first of February. George Ford, labourer, of Southmolton, said he remembered the corn being threshed in the previous October. Sarah Slader, wife of David Slader, corroborated her husband's evidence. For the defence, Mr Courtney Edmonds, Insurance Inspector, of Exeter, said there was no trace of any corn in the place on his visit of inspection. The only thing bearing any resemblance to it was burnt thatch. Evidence was given as to the fire by George Jackman and William Heard, living at Chittlehamholt, and by James and William Hulland, formerly in the employ of Mr Manning. PS Leyman, Devon Constabulary, went to the scene of the fire. He found no trace of any burnt corn in the place. Superintendent Pelly corroborated the evidence of Mr Edmonds and PS Leyman. He had had previous experience of similar occurrences. Mr James Sanders, one of the local agents, said he visited the farm (being then Mayor of Southmolton) in company with the Borough Surveyor and formed the same opinion as that given by previous witnesses. Mr Pridham Wippell, in his concluding remarks, said the plaintiff had been tried at Exeter on a charge of arson, and had been honourably acquitted. There had been an analysis of the debris and the evidence given for the defence was only a matter of opinion. His Honour, in summing up, recapitulated the principal points in the evidence. The claim had been reduced to £12.1s.6d., and it was for them to say if the things claimed for were in the place at the time of the fire. Retiring for a short time, the jury returned a verdict for defendant with costs.

There were no other cases of public interest.

July 28th 1921
FIRE AT CHITTLEHAMHOLT
About 5 o'clock on Thursday evening, a disastrous fire occurred at Snydles Farm, Chittlehamholt, the house and most of the buildings being gutted. Willing workers were quickly on the spot, and Southmolton Fire Brigade were summoned, thanks to the kindness of Mrs Munro of Whitmore, who drove to Southmolton for the purpose. Eight members of the brigade under Captain J.E. Bulled, were prompt in answering the call. Owing, however, to the extraordinary dry state of the buildings, and the fact that they were mostly thatched, the fire swept the buildings within a short time of the outbreak. Though handicapped by shortness of water, the brigade prevented the fire from spreading to the stable and cart linhay. After spending the night on the scene, the brigade were able to return home about ten in the morning. The greatest sympathy is felt for the occupiers, Mr and Mrs Thomas, who, in addition to losing their home, have lost heavily, as they were only partially insured. The premises were insured.

Stafford Constable remembers the following fire well. As he was going home during the school dinner hour, he saw South View Cottages were burning. He lived next door at Edgington Cottage, now called Spring Cottage, which went with Edgington House where Stafford's father was the gardener. Stafford particularly remembers Mrs Skinner's burnt Christmas puddings which were put out into the garden. At the time of writing two houses remain on the original site of the four cottages and still go under the name of South View. The firemen came to Stafford's house to draw water from the well. He recalls Mr Helstone lived in the first cottage, then Mr and Mrs Skinner, Mr Gulley, and Mrs and Miss Manaton. Stafford's mother and father took Mrs and Miss Manaton in until they could get rehoused. Mr and Mrs Skinner moved to Ilfracombe.

December 23rd 1927
CHITTLEHAMHOLT FIRE, FOUR FAMILIES HOMELESS.
Four families were rendered homeless last week by the destruction of four cottages by fire at Chittlehamholt, three of the occupants being over 80 years of age. The outbreak was discovered by Miss Helstone, daughter of the owner, who gave the alarm. A band of helpers assisted in removing the furniture, practically the whole of which was saved. The South Molton Fire Brigade on arrival were handicapped through lack of water, the only two wells available being quickly pumped dry. The fire, fanned by a strong easterly wind, spread rapidly, and it was apparent the property was doomed. The cottages which had thatched roofs belonged to Mr J. Helstone (owner), Mr W. Helstone, Mr Skinner, and Miss Manning. PS Morrish (Chulmleigh) rendered valuable assistance. A telephone message was sent to the South Molton Police Station and in response to a maroon, the Captain of the Fire Brigade, Mr J.H. Bulled and a number of firemen were quickly at the fire station. It so happened that the driver and deputy driver were

out of town and there was a delay of several minutes in finding a substitute. Owing to the frozen state of the ground a great deal of trouble was experienced in obtaining an adequate water supply. It was a long time since the brigade worked under such bad weather conditions. The couplings of the hose frequently froze, and the men were practically covered with frozen spray.

5th June 1941

<u>A SATTERLEIGH FIRE</u>

A large pond in the farmyard of Satterleigh Barton,

Satterleigh, in the occupation of Mrs M. Elworthy, enabled Southmolton Rural Fire Brigade to save a large quantity of corn and other produce when fire was discovered in a Dutch barn on Saturday.

When the brigade arrived they found the barn, containing 500 nitches of reed, well alight. Within 100 feet was a barn containing wheat in sacks, the produce of threshing of two days previous and very close was a large rick of dredge corn. The brigade succeeded in saving the wheat and the corn rick, and Capt. Hawkes, chief officer, said this was possible only through the plentiful supply of water close at hand.

Fire at the Mole Cottage Pottery, 1950s.

The Heard family outside the house now known as Grange Cottage.

The Green Family at Whitmore, c.1900.

Chapter 15

SUPERSTITIONS & FOLKLORE

It is good to keep alive old superstitions and stories which have been handed down through the generations. Stafford Constable has relayed a few of these stories to me.

For example, he was told that in the bit of plantation behind the Warkleigh War Memorial at Cockram Butts Cross, there is a man with a glass wheelbarrow. The late Mr Beer from Deason told Stafford that when he was going home from courting one night, he approached the memorial and, remembering the tale, looked down at his feet and suddenly saw a growling white dog.

To the right of Edgington drive there was a barn which was reputed to have a headless man inside. Lower Ditchaton Water, which no longer exists, was thought to be haunted. In more recent times, the Beast of Exmoor was spotted by a very reliable person on Snapdown Drive.

The Congram family at Butlers. Bill Congram (now in his eighties) is the young boy at the front of the picture.

A popular present from Chittlehamholt.

Working at Warkleigh Barton, c.1900.

SUBSCRIBERS

Tracy Ashford, Burrington, Devon

Mrs D. Ayre, Kingsnympton, Devon

Dorothy E. Ayre (née Bowden), formerly of Satterleigh, Devon

Mr Des Ayto, Spiecott, Chittlehamholt, Devon

L. and J. Baker, Raleigh Close, South Molton, Devon

D.E. and L.A. Ball, Chittlehamholt, Devon

Mr and Mrs Barrett, Warkleigh, Devon

Sue Batt, Chittlehamholt, Devon

Rachel Beckett (née Lewis), Aylesbury, Buckinghamshire

William H. Beer, Lapford, Devon

Noel Beer, Rayleigh, Essex

Revd John and Dr Hazel M. Bell, Stoke Fleming, Devon

Mr and Mrs L. Birch, Harwell

Dixie Blunt, Chittlehamholt, Devon

Dick Blunt, Chittlehamholt, Devon

Eric and Margaret Bolt and family

Alan and Marilyn Bowen, Warkleigh, Devon

A.E. and B.J. Brant, Russons Farm, Chittlehamholt, Devon

Gary Buckingham, Chulmleigh, Devon

Wendy and David Buckle, Oldridge, Warkleigh, Devon

K.J. Burrow, Bucks Cross, Devon

Sheila J. Caws, Barnstaple, Devon

Mr and Mrs Chapman, Southsea

Timothy M. Clark, Earley, Reading, Berkshire

Michael Clarke, Exeter, Devon

Lilian Clements, Woolsery, Devon

Harold Congram, Chittlehamholt, Devon

Frank Congram, Chittlehamholt, Devon

Rosemarie Cooke, Umberleigh

F.W.J. and A. Crabtree, Todmorden, Lancashire

Dr and Mrs S. Ellis, Leeds

David and Pauline Elworthy, Satterleigh Barton

Caroline and Michael Elworthy, Satterleigh Barton

Mrs Patricia Eva (née Medland), East Anstey

Bernard and Christine Fyson, Barnstaple, Devon

Mrs Vera Geatches, St Dominick, Cornwall

Elizabeth Gibson, Alresford, Hampshire

Elizabeth Gibson, Hampshire

David E. Gillanders and family, Warkleigh, Devon

Margaret I. Gordon-Lee, Chittlehamholt, Devon

The Gordon-Lee family, Chappels and Mollands, Chittlehamholt, Devon

Neil Govier, Exeter, Devon

Elizabeth Grant, Plymouth

Novello M.P. Gregory, South Molton, Devon

Captain P.R. and Mrs J.A. Griffin, Chittlehamholt, Devon

Carol and Michael Griffiths, Whitmore Cottage, Chittlehamholt, Devon

Jean Grose, Chittlehamholt, Devon

Willian Hopton Hadley, ex 'Farriers'

George Hakin, Croyde, North Devon

Colin and Margaret Hammett, Broadview, Warkleigh, Devon

Anthony Hancock, South Molton, Devon

Sue Hancocks, Heanton Punchardon, Devon

Gerald Harris, Snap Dragon Antiques, South Molton, Devon

Wendy Harris (née Cooke), Alverdiscott

Sarah J. Hicks, Warkleigh, Devon

Nicholas and Muriel Hill

Paul Hill, Southleigh, Devon

Peter, Sara, Daniel and Amy Holland, Clapworthy Mill, Devon

Mike and Jenny Holland, Warkleigh, Devon

Roy and Joan Hooper, Chittlehamholt, Devon

Brian, Rauchele, William and Daniel Huxtable, Umberleigh, North Devon

Ivan, Edna and Paul Huxtable, Umberleigh, North Devon

S. Huxtable-Selly, Cobbaton, Devon

Eileen Jones, Chittlehamholt, Devon

Janet Judd, Warkleigh, Devon

Jennifer Kelley and S.R. Priddle, Chittlehamholt, Devon

Richard Lethbridge, Chittlehamholt, Devon

May Lethbridge, Chittlehampton, Devon

Rosalind Lewis, Poole, Dorset

Edward Lewis, Leicester

William H. Lewis, Rose Ash, Devon

Joanna Lewis, Ascot, Berkshire

Kevin P. Lynch, Barnstaple, Devon

Elizabeth A. Machin, Torrington, Devon

Stephen Martin, Rewe, Exeter, Devon

Richard and Michele May, Chittlehamholt, Devon

Stan Medland, Eastacombe, Nr Barnstaple, Devon

R.G. Medland, Parkfield, East Anstey, Devon

Muriel J. Moore (née Wright), Newton Tracey, Devon

Mr and Mrs M.H.F. Morgan, Newport

Mr and Mrs D.H.W. Morgan, Brussels

Mr and Mrs C.W. Morgan, Chittlehamholt, Devon

A.M. Morrish, Chittlehamholt, Devon

Daphne P. Munday, Sandford, Devon

The Neil family, Chittlehamholt, Devon

Evelyn F. Newton, Tiverton, Devon

Mr Peter E. Nicholls, Upminster, Essex

The North Devon Athenaeum

Valerie Partridge, Woolsery, Devon

Hugh and Dorothea Pattison

Bryan, Jo, Chris and Richard Pearson, Pearces Farm, Chittlehamholt, Devon

Mrs Margaret Pepper, Bath

David Pepper, Marwood, Barnstaple, Devon

Mr and Mrs J. Petherick, London

Annie Petherick, Wales

Mr and Mrs Petherick, Chittlehamholt, Devon

Reg and Rosemary Pincombe, Warkleigh, Devon

Michael and Lisa Pincombe, Warkleigh, Devon

Marjorie Pincombe, Warkleigh, Devon

The Pokoj family, formerly of Cleave Copse, Umberleigh, Devon

Major J.E. Pollard, Lyndhurst, Hampshire

Glyn and Mary Anne Pope, Chittlehamholt, Devon

Mr J. Prowse, Barnstaple, Devon

David L. Purnell, Warkleigh, Devon

Paul Reed, New South Wales, Australia

Robert Reed, Ludlow, Shropshire

Mrs Rosalind Reed (née Pam Murkitt), Wells, Somerset

Harry Richardson, Chittlehampton, Devon

Joan and John Robinson, Hills House Farm, Chittlehamholt, Devon

Mr John Russell, Highwinds, Chittlehamholt, Devon

Gary and Jackie Russell, Chittlehampton, Devon

W.J. and M.J. Sanders, Chittlehamholt, Devon

W.J. Seage

Mr Terry Sedwell, Warkleigh, Devon

Sybil Slee (née Judd), Warkleigh, Devon

Kenneth E. Snow, Chittlehampton, Devon

Linda J. Snow, Chittlehamholt, Devon

Ken Stenner, Eggesford, formerly Satterleigh

Ken Stinton, High Bickington, Devon

Christine Stuckey, Homelea, Eastacombe, Barnstaple, Devon

Mike Thorne, Pool, Warkleigh

Ron and Anne Thorne, Higher Ditchaton Water, Chittlehamholt, Devon

Maurice and Margaret Thorne, Chittlehamholt, Devon

Mr Ian Tucker, Umberleigh, Devon/formerly of Warkleigh

Mr Stephen Tucker, Fremington, Barnstaple, Devon/formerly of Warkleigh

Mrs Shirley Tucker, Chittlehampton, Devon

Jeremy Turner, Kings Nympton, Devon

Jill O. Vernon, Warkleigh, Devon

John F.W. Walling, Newton Abbot, Devon

Mr Nicholas R. Way, Burrington, Devon

Leonora (Mollie) Wilkey, Barnstaple, Devon

Dr R. Trevor and Mrs Mary P. Wilson, Umberleigh, Devon

John Haydn Wood, Mortimer West End, Berkshire

Titles from the Series

The Book of Addiscombe • Various
The Book of Addiscombe, Vol. II • Various
The Book of Bampton • Caroline Seward
The Book of Barnstaple • Avril Stone
Book of Bickington • Stuart Hands
Blandford Forum: A Millennium Portrait • Various
The Book of Bridestowe • R. Cann
The Book of Brixham • Frank Pearce
The Book of Buckland Monachorum & Yelverton • Hemery
The Book of Carshalton • Stella Wilks
The Parish Book of Cerne Abbas • Vale & Vale
The Book of Chagford • Ian Rice
The Book of Chittlehamholt with
Warkleigh & Satterleigh • Richard Lethbridge
The Book of Chittlehampton • Various
The Book of Colney Heath • Bryan Lilley
The Book of Constantine • Moore & Trethowan
The Book of Cornwood & Lutton • Various
The Book of Creech St Michael • June Small
The Book of Cullompton • Various
The Book of Dawlish • Frank Pearce
The Book of Dulverton, Brushford,
Bury & Exebridge • Various
The Book of Dunster • Hilary Binding
The Ellacombe Book • Sydney R. Langmead
The Book of Exmouth • W.H. Pascoe
The Book of Grampound with Creed • Bane & Oliver
The Book of Hayling Island & Langstone • Rogers
The Book of Helston • Jenkin with Carter
The Book of Hemyock • Clist & Dracott
The Book of Hethersett • Various
The Book of High Bickington • Avril Stone
The Book of Ilsington • Dick Wills
The Book of Lamerton • Ann Cole & Friends
Lanner, A Cornish Mining Parish • Scharron Schwartz &
Roger Parker
The Book of Leigh & Bransford • Various
The Book of Litcham with Lexham & Mileham • Various
The Book of Loddiswell • Various
The Book of Lulworth • Rodney Legg
The Book of Lustleigh • Joe Crowdy
The Book of Manaton • Various
The Book of Markyate • Various
The Book of Mawnan • Various
The Book of Meavy • Pauline Hemery
The Book of Minehead with Alcombe • Binding & Stevens
The Book of Morchard Bishop • Jeff Kingaby
The Book of Newdigate • John Callcut
The Book of Northlew with Ashbury • Various
The Book of North Newton • Robins & Robins
The Book of North Tawton • Various
The Book of Okehampton • Radford & Radford
The Book of Paignton • Frank Pearce
The Book of Penge, Anerley & Crystal Palace • Various
The Book of Peter Tavy with Cudlipptown • Various
The Book of Pimperne • Jean Coull
The Book of Plymtree • Tony Eames
The Book of Porlock • Denis Corner
Postbridge – The Heart of Dartmoor • Reg Bellamy
The Book of Priddy • Various
The Book of Rattery • Various
The Book of Silverton • Various

The Book of South Molton • Various
The Book of South Stoke • Various
South Tawton & South Zeal with Sticklepath • Radfords
The Book of Sparkwell with Hemerdon & Lee Mill • Pam James
The Book of Staverton • Pete Lavis
The Book of Stithians • Various
The Book of Studland • Rodney Legg
The Book of Swanage • Rodney Legg
The Book of Torbay • Frank Pearce
Uncle Tom Cobley & All: Widecombe-in-the-Moor • Stephen
Woods
The Book of Watchet • Compiled by David Banks
The Book of West Huntspill • Various
Widecombe-in-the-Moor • Stephen Woods
The Book of Williton • Michael Williams
Woodbury: The Twentieth Century Revisited • Roger Stokes
The Book of Woolmer Green • Various

Forthcoming

The Book of Bakewell • Various
The Book of Barnstaple, Vol. II • Avril Stone
The Book of Brampford • Various
The Book of Breage & Gurmoe • Stephen Polglase
The Book of the Bedwyns • Various
The Book of Bideford • Peter Christie
The Book of Bridport • Rodney Legg
The Book of Buckfastleigh • Sandra Coleman
The Book of Carharrack • Various
The Book of Castleton • Geoff Hill
The Book of Edale • Gordon Miller
The Book of Kingskerswell • Various
The Book of Lostwithiel • Barbara Frasier
The Book of Lydford • Barbara Weeks
The Book of Lyme Regis • Rodney Legg
The Book of Nether Stowey • Various
The Book of Nynehead • Various
The Book of Princetown • Dr Gardner-Thorpe
The Book of St Day • Various
The Book of Sampford Courtenay
with Honeychurch • Stephanie Pouya
The Book of Sculthorpe • Garry Windeler
The Book of Sherborne • Rodney Legg
The Book of Southbourne • Rodney Legg
The Book of Tavistock • Gerry Woodcock
The Book of Thorley • Various
The Book of Tiverton • Mike Sampson
The Book of West Lavington • Various
The Book of Witheridge • Various
The Book of Withycombe • Chris Boyles

For details of any of the above titles or if you are
interested in writing your own history, please contact:
Commissioning Editor Community Histories, Halsgrove
House, Lower Moor Way, Tiverton Business Park,
Tiverton, Devon EX16 6SS, England;
email: naomic@halsgrove.com

In order to include as many historic photographs as
possible in this volume, a printed index is not included.
However, the Community History Series is indexed by
Genuki. For further information and indexes to
volumes in the series, please visit:
http://www.cs.ncl.uk/genuki/DEV/indexingproject.html